Britain's Persuaders

Sofia,

Thanks for the thoughtful question...

Helen Ramscar

March 2024

Britain's Persuaders

Soft Power in a Hard World

Michael Clarke and Helen Ramscar

I.B. TAURIS

LONDON • NEW YORK • OXFORD • NEW DELHI • SYDNEY

I.B. TAURIS
Bloomsbury Publishing Plc
50 Bedford Square, London, WC1B 3DP, UK
1385 Broadway, New York, NY 10018, USA
29 Earlsfort Terrace, Dublin 2, Ireland

BLOOMSBURY, I.B. TAURIS and the I.B. Tauris logo are trademarks of
Bloomsbury Publishing Plc

First published in Great Britain 2022

Cover design by Adriana Brioso
Cover image © freevectormaps.com

A catalogue record for this book is available from the British Library.

Library of Congress Control Number: 2021940787

ISBN: HB: 978-0-7556-3427-9
PB: 978-0-7556-3426-2
ePDF: 978-0-7556-3429-3
eBook: 978-0-7556-3428-6

Typeset by Deanta Global Publishing Services, Chennai, India
Printed and bound in Great Britain

Authors

Professor Michael Clarke and Helen Ramscar are the co-authors of *Tipping Point: Britain, Brexit and Security in the 2020s*, I.B. Tauris/Bloomsbury, 2019.

Professor Michael Clarke was Director General of the Royal United Services Institute (RUSI) from 2007 to 2015, where he remains a Distinguished Fellow of RUSI. He is also Fellow of King's College London and Visiting Professor of Defence Studies. He is Visiting Professor at the University of Exeter and Associate Director of its Strategy and Security Institute, and a Fellow of the University of Aberystwyth. He is currently a specialist adviser to the Joint Committee on National Security Strategy in Parliament and in 2020 was made a Fellow of the Royal College of Defence Studies.

Helen Ramscar is an Associate Fellow of RUSI, where previously she was Director of Development. She has worked in China and Kenya, as well as in the House of Commons, the Royal Household and the US Embassy in London. She is a graduate of Durham University, the Centre for International Studies and Diplomacy at SOAS and Cass Business School. Currently she lives in Switzerland and is a board member of the Basel Chapter of the British-Swiss Chamber of Commerce.

Contents

Preface   viii
List of abbreviations and terms   ix

1   Introduction   1

Part One Thinking about power   9
2   Power in world politics   11
3   Persuasive power: Hard, soft and smart   23

Part Two Britain's persuaders   39
4   The convenors: Bringing interests together   41
5   The officials: Speaking softly   56
6   Researchers and innovators: Shaping the global stage   69
7   Leaders and regulators: Setting the standards   86
8   Cosmopolitans and diasporas: Reflecting global cultures   101
9   Educators: Pursuing truthful minds – and truth   113
10   Creatives: Opening new ideas   126
11   Entertainers: Feeding a human need   138
12   Stars and bloggers: Embracing the anarchic   152

Part Three Soft power in practice   161
13   Britain's soft power realities   163
14   Conditions for soft power success   179

Appendix 1: Twinned cities   197
Appendix 2: Statistics   198
Notes   204
Select Bibliography   230
Index   237

Preface

In our previous co-authored book, *Tipping Point: Britain, Brexit and Security in the 2020s*, our attention was focused on the major security challenges of the last decade and how constrained Britain is likely to be during the course of the next one. Britain's prospects are troubling in this respect and it's easy to feel downcast – even though all European powers face a similar outlook.

Our analysis in *Britain's Persuaders*, however, is on a different plane. This book has greatly renewed our faith in Britain and British society. Soft power is generally neutral in terms of party politics and to a large extent detached from the political imbroglios Britain endured in the 2010s. We have found our research into British soft power assets inspires enormous hope. Britain does indeed have many admired strengths, coveted institutions, attractive and enduring qualities, and if protected and played effectively these can be high-value cards for a reinvigorated global Britain to play. By identifying the leading soft power assets, in light of its strategic goals, believing in ourselves as a society and investing in the soft power environment, there is a great deal of low-hanging fruit for global Britain and much to be protected for the long game.

As authors we have enjoyed selecting examples throughout the following chapters to illustrate their points. Readers will doubtless have examples of their own, and we hope we have offered here a way they might think about the contributions their examples do, or don't, make to British soft power. We hope, too, that they will see them in the context of how we think about power as a construct, which we outline in the early chapters.

British history and contemporary Britain is brimming with potential soft power assets. The more we understand just what we have, and the further this understanding is shared across society, the greater the likelihood that Britain as a whole will really believe in its soft power capacity. When seeing them for what they are and what more they could be, Britain's soft power assets have instilled in us a great deal of optimism.

Michael Clarke and Helen Ramscar

List of abbreviations and terms

AI	Artificial Intelligence
AMRC	Association of Medical Research Charities
APPG	All Party Parliamentary Group
ARIA	Advanced Research and Invention Agency
ASOS	As Seen On Screen
BAME	Black, Asian and Minority Ethnic
BBC	British Broadcasting Corporation
BEIS	Department for Business, Energy & Industrial Strategy
Britain	Term that we use synonymously with UK
BSI	British Standards Institute
CAF	Charities Aid Foundation
CBI	Confederation of British Industry
CD	Compact Disc
CEN	European Committee for Standardization
CEPI	Coalition for Epidemic Preparedness Innovations
CERN	European Organization for Nuclear Research
CHOGM	Commonwealth Heads of Government Meeting
CND	Campaign for Nuclear Disarmament
Commonwealth	Commonwealth of Nations
DARPA	Defence Advanced Research Project Agency (US)
DCMS	Department for Digital, Culture, Media & Sport
DESA	Department of Economic and Social Affairs (UN)

DNA	Deoxyribonucleic acid
DTI	Department of Trade and Industry
EEC	European Economic Community
EMA	European Medicines Agency
ESMA	European Securities and Markets Authority
EU	European Union
F1	Formula 1
FCA	Financial Conduct Authority
FCDO	Foreign, Commonwealth & Development Office
FCO/Foreign Office	Foreign & Commonwealth Office, October 1968 to September 2000
G20	Group of Twenty
GDP	Gross Domestic Product
GVA	Gross Value Added
HMG	Her Majesty's Government
HMRC	Her Majesty's Revenue and Customs
ICANN	Internet Corporation for Assigned Names and Numbers
IMO	International Maritime Organization
Integrated Review	Integrated Review of Security, Defence, Development and Foreign Policy
ISO	International Organization for Standardization
LBC	London Broadcasting Company
LIBOR	London Inter-Bank Offered Rate
LSE	London School of Economics
MHRA	Medicines and Healthcare Products Regulatory Agency
MinTech	Ministry of Technology, October 1964 to October 1970

MoD	Ministry of Defence
MoJ	Ministry of Justice
MOOCS	Massive Open Online Courses
NATO	North Atlantic Treaty Organization
OECD	Organisation for Economic Co-operation and Development
ONS	Office of National Statistics
OSINT	Open-Source Intelligence
OU	Open University
PA	Publishers Association
PACES	Practical Assessment of Clinical Examination Skills
POW	Prisoner of War
PRA	Prudential Regulation Authority
R&D	Research and Development
RICS	Royal Institute of Chartered Surveyors
SME	Small- and Medium-Sized Enterprises
SSE	Single Synthetic Environment
UK	United Kingdom
UKRI	UK Research and Innovation
UN	United Nations
USA	United States of America
WEF	World Economic Forum
WHO	World Health Organization
WTO	World Trade Organization
XR	Extinction Rebellion

1

Introduction

At 15 billion miles away, the most distant human object from earth is the Voyager 1 spacecraft, which was launched in 1977. In its long life it has flown past Jupiter and Saturn, and it crossed the boundary into interstellar space in 2012. Voyager 1 is expected to last until 2025 when, after almost fifty years, its power source will finally disappear. It then hurtles further away from our solar system, perhaps to be intercepted by aliens from another world. If and when that happens, it will carry a message of peace to them from the United Nations – in English. Astonishing in one sense, but not in another. In 1977 the UN secretary general who recorded the message was an Austrian. But as Andrew Roberts puts it, during the twentieth century, English had become 'the primary language of stock exchanges, business, air-traffic control and economic development . . . it overhauled German as the language of science and French as the language of diplomacy'.[1] It was natural in 1977 that English should be the language in which to greet any curious space alien. And it was a symptom, a deep symptom for deep space, of political power here on earth. It was an expression of soft power so profound that it seemed entirely natural and sensible at the time.[2] If similar missions occur before 2077, which seems almost certain, will this world still reach out to our alien friends in English?

Why should sending messages in English, instead of French, German or Mandarin, tell us anything about the nature of political power and the ways in which it is expressed in our more immediate and tangible world? In this study we want to dig deeper into the symbolism of Voyager 1's recorded message. We want to consider how soft power seems to work across the board – and in particular, how it works for Britain as the country confronts the immediate decade ahead.*

---

* We use 'Britain' throughout this book as a more elegant term than 'United Kingdom' or 'UK', neither of which is easy on the reader's eye. United Kingdom is the legally correct term, as it includes England, Wales, Scotland and Northern Ireland, and it is the term used by the government and in official publications. 'Great Britain' is a geographical term, referring to the greater part of the British Isles and excludes the island of Ireland and therefore Northern Ireland. Nevertheless, we prefer to use 'Britain' as elegantly synonymous with 'UK'.

We do this because the early 2020s are a very appropriate moment to examine the question of Britain's 'soft power' in the world. The very concept of 'power' and the way in which it operates in the globalized environment is evidently changing. 'Power' was never a simple concept, but in the 2020s we see it manifested in some mysterious and apparently contradictory ways. The big states certainly try to exert their political power through some very traditional, assertive and militarized modes, even as the general exercise of international power, in most other respects, inclines towards more subtle expressions of attraction and persuasion. The exercise, both of 'hard' and 'soft' power, is constantly in evidence, though most governments would prefer to dwell on their own efficient uses of soft power as ways of achieving cooperative and desirable ends. This seems natural in such a complex world where all countries are part of a globalized society, and in these circumstances the unsubtle use of 'hard power', 'raw power', 'naked power' or whatever suggests something either brutal or simply inefficient.

The notions of 'hard' and 'soft' power carry strong intuitive meanings for most people who use the terms, and obvious examples can be cited easily enough to demonstrate them both in action. If Britain deploys aircraft or warships to the Eastern Mediterranean to defend its military base in Cyprus, it is exercising hard power. If it hosts an international conference to discuss the future of foreign military bases throughout the region, it is exercising soft power. In a deeper analysis, of course, these terms have to be unpacked a good deal further and set in their political context. Understanding more carefully some of the ways in which the exercise of international power is rapidly evolving is an important, and urgent, analytical question.

A new examination of soft power is also particularly appropriate to Britain's own situation in the 2020s. The next decade will be internationally challenging for all the European states, no less for 'Brexit Britain' that seeks to chart a new course outside the European Union and pursue a more independent economic and political role in world politics. What are traditionally regarded as a state's 'hard power' resources – military capabilities, economic instruments or those levers of government like policing and regulation that can be used to pressure foreign states or actors – will be more difficult to exercise for all European and middle-range powers. Their military and economic capabilities are all in relative decline in comparison to the big countries like the United States and China and the rising powers of Asia (and also of Russia, at least in military terms). As they pursue their international objectives, European middle-rank powers will naturally lean more heavily on their soft power resources, in which they still have significant relative strength.

This will be particularly true for Britain, where the 'global Britain' orientation created in response to Brexit relies heavily on employing the full spectrum of the country's resources: social, cultural, historical and political, as well as its more hard-edged strengths in economic size, military expertise, intelligence, diplomatic weight and so on. As Boris Johnson put it in 2016 to the Conservative Conference when he was foreign secretary, Britain's hard power, he said,

> is dwarfed by a phenomenon that the pessimists never predicted when we unbundled the British Empire. And that is . . . our irresistible . . . soft power – the vast and subtle and pervasive extension of British influence around the world that goes with having the language that was invented and perfected in this country and now has more speakers than any other language on earth.[3]

Such comments played to one of the political undercurrents behind the urge to leave the European Union, namely some sense of innate British exceptionalism – an assumption that British society and culture were somehow generically different from those of its European Union partners, and that after almost fifty years inside the EU it had become apparent that British society simply did not share the same political and social make-up that propelled its continental neighbours towards close common European goals.[4] Brexit Britain would promote its distinctive social and political culture, its business acumen and its free-trading history, as international strengths – sources of power – in themselves. Among other things, therefore, the Brexit decision represented a confident bet on Britain's ability to use its soft power assets to full advantage.

Subsequent arguments around the Brexit decision also highlighted the historic diversity of British society – diverse in the different kingdoms that now constitute the United Kingdom and diverse in the regions within and between them. We will return to this in the final chapter, but here we merely note that soft power does not flow primarily from a government but from the wider society. And British society is inherently and historically diverse, geographically and socially. That can be a source either of soft power strength or of weakness, and we offer examples in Part Two of both.

In short, many analysts seem to regard soft power as a subject of great intrinsic interest and also of growing contemporary relevance to the external relations of all the mid-ranking countries. This study is an attempt to dig below the surface of traditional soft power thinking, looking at the soft power cards that Britain has to play in its hand and trying to evaluate their worth as the international competition in soft power resources becomes ever more fierce. But to understand such a vague concept properly, soft power has to be situated within an understanding of international power more generally. 'Hard' and 'soft' power are very shorthand terms for resources and relationships that are far more complicated and are always changing. The card game of international power has to be understood more clearly. So too does the nature of the cards themselves and what they are each worth.

In addition to the British institutions that are normally regarded as self-evidently useful cards in Britain's soft power hand, for instance, there are many other institutions and organizations that play roles that are at least as important, even if they may not know it themselves.

Some publicly funded British institutions, like the BBC World Service or the British Council, are explicitly intended to generate soft power in accordance with governmental intentions. But more institutions, like the rest of the BBC, the wider entertainment industries, sport, professional regulatory bodies, hospitality industries or education sectors, have more penetrating soft power effects even as they pursue their own independent or commercial rationales. Around one-third of the world's population have regular access to watch the highly internationalized English Premier League, which is far and away the most powerful football league in the world. Formula 1 racing could hardly be more international, but it was created and initially owned by British sports entrepreneurs, and six of its ten teams are based in Britain.[5] London's Metropolitan Police is regarded as one of the leading international models of urban policing. British expertise is consistently influential in regulating world shipping, air transport or global transit security, and British specialists in finance or in professions such as law, engineering, architecture, publishing or communications are very well represented among global management bodies. Not least, the British Royal Family remains unique and in terms of commercial asset value was measured in 2017 as the third biggest brand in the world.[6] For a country that represents 0.8 per cent of the global population, these are all significant potential strengths, and most of them are not controlled, or even much influenced, by the British government.

A certain amount of attention has been paid in the past to the soft power potential of Britain's 'explicit' persuaders, like the BBC or the Commonwealth, but very little attention has been paid to the far greater number of 'implicit' persuaders, many of whom may not be fully aware of their own international attraction and whose influence has never been surveyed comprehensively within a single framework. Freddie Laker, for example, was a lifelong airline entrepreneur who launched the budget airline 'Skytrain' in 1977. It went bust in 1982, partly because all the big airlines imitated it, but it changed the face of the global airline industry. Or Jim Davis, who had a massive impact on harmonizing different interests in world shipping; or Hamish de Bretton-Gordon, who served twenty-three years in the Army, became a leading international expert on chemical warfare and was training doctors in Aleppo even as barrel bombs were being dropped by Syrian aircraft. Or Trevor Nunn, a noted Shakespearean director who nevertheless launched some of the world's most successful popular musicals, including *Cats* and *Les Misérables*. In the case of internationally famous English football star Marcus Rashford, whose own campaigning drove a British policy U-turn on child food poverty, his personal domestic success had its own international impact.[7] Britain's persuaders can be seen in many different guises across all social spheres.

Compared with the wealth of scholarship devoted to understanding the concept of 'power' itself and the different ways it tends to work in the international system, there have been relatively few studies on soft power since the concept was popularized less than thirty years ago, still fewer on British soft power. In recent years, and under the political pressures of the last decade, however, there has been a growth in the interest around soft power, not so much for its own sake but rather as a component to understanding better what seemed to be happening in world politics as power was visibly shifting – to new international actors and new ways of conducting international politics.[8] A few studies have looked more specifically at British soft power resources and tried to analyse some of the ways they are handled.[9] And there have been some notable reports that have tried, over the years, to list and compare Britain's soft power resources as a means to have them recognized and more consciously supported by government.[10] Not least, there are the 'international rankings' that the media so enjoy, which score different countries according to their apparent soft power acumen and influence.[11]

This book is intended to draw from, and build on, all of these studies. It offers a different framework to analyse British soft power as a contribution to the creation of a *net assessment* approach to the nation's soft power assets. A net assessment of soft power would work in roughly the same way as military net assessments. In the soft power sphere it would involve a deeper dive into the evidence to try to establish the net lead or net loss of international influence British institutions have in relation to close competitors and their natural peer countries. Too many institutions are judged and measured by their outputs – how many visits, programmes, exhibitions, exchange arrangements and so on – as opposed to their impact – who notices and what difference does it make? Difficult as it is to measure 'impact', evidence-based assessments, alongside qualitative judgements, should be set against similar impact assessments that competitors are seen to create. The British government does not undertake such an exercise – certainly not for those institutions outside its own control – though it moved a little in this direction in 2019 when it set out its intention to conduct 'a fundamental' Integrated Review of all external policy.[12]

In this study, we are not in a position to produce a net assessment, which would require much more information about public and elite opinion and also about social trends within other societies, as well as more information than normally exists in the public domain about our own. So we make no attempt to offer a proper net assessment here. But we do believe that it can be done. And we structure Part Two of this study around some different behavioural categories for soft power assessment that are not normally considered and which we believe can capture a greater range of the relevant interactions that could be part of the approach. If it were to be done, a net assessment would doubtless be a big analytical undertaking; and it would require more precise specification than we have attempted in this short book. At least this might be a start. And we hope it will galvanize interest in wider thinking about British soft power.

Britain's prominence in this respect was generally established during the twentieth century when the cultural dominance of Western societies was taken for granted. That era is changing rapidly and international soft power competition has become far more intense in the last two decades. Britain's natural friends, like Germany, Australia or Japan, are putting much more into promoting their soft power. So are its emerging adversaries, like Russia and particularly China. And all the significant powers, like India, Brazil or Indonesia; and in their own ways, smaller countries like Ireland, Denmark or the United Arab Emirates are keen to leverage as much political influence from their international image as possible.[13]

If soft power assumes greater prominence as an arm of national policy in the future, then Britain has some important comparative advantages. The British Council records the belief that 'The UK is a "soft power superpower"', and the country scores consistently high (certainly within the top ten and on many within the top three or four) on all independent rankings of soft power status.[14] But there is a growing danger of national complacency based on the easier soft power environment of the past. Survey material and anecdotal evidence suggest that even those organizations most complimented on their contribution to British soft power have acknowledged that in recent years their position in relation to international competition has become 'precarious'.[15] A more proactive governmental approach, which we discuss at the end of this study, will be required if those comparative advantages are not to be lost to close competitors.

In the opaque world of international power relations, the existence or the sizes and shapes of the institutions under study is less important than the sort of behaviour they represent and the effectiveness of that behaviour in influencing others. To take the analysis on further, this book looks at the institutions associated with the wider view of soft power but analyses them according to the type of behaviours that the authors judge will be particularly relevant for the more complex international environment in which Britain now exists, consisting as it does of integrated manufacturing and services, finance and cyber security, innovation and entertainment, alongside all the more traditional foreign and security policy demands made on the modern state. We assess that nine particular patterns of behaviour are particularly relevant. They may be expressed as the ways in which British institutions and individuals contribute to:

Convening: a reputation for being able to bring a wide range of interests together as in the case of the British Council, the Commonwealth, the Royal Family, the Anglican Church, trade bodies, city-twinning exercises and so on.

Indirect diplomacy: the ability of government officials to sustain deep knowledge of their postings, to promote 'track 2' diplomacy, aid diplomacy and the proactive promotion of liberal free trade values and internationalism of all types.

Research and innovation: having influence to help shape the global technology stage through science and technology, high-end manufacturing, spin-outs and start-ups, and the applied research from higher education.

International standard-setting: through sectoral leaders and regulators, setting or contributing to international standards in fields such as architecture, finance, medicine, communications, publishing and so on.

Cultural recognition and cosmopolitanism: the role of diaspora communities, cultural and cosmopolitan organizations reflecting modern multiculturalism, communities, tourism, leisure and hospitality, and international social linkages.

Education and learning: promoting truthful and self-aware values across the education and higher education sectors, in private schools, galleries, museums, heritage organizations and through online education.

International entertainment: through film and TV, theatre, mixed media, sport, music, performing arts and many others.

Frontier creativity: in exploring the boundaries of established economic and social sectors, such as through advertising, marketing, consultancy, new computing and applied gaming.

Exploring the anarchic: allowing scope for the bloggers and influencers, the eccentric and the socially anarchic to express themselves at the frontiers of social conventions.

In this book, therefore, we try, in Part One, to situate the idea of soft power within some of the fundamental concepts of political power. Soft and hard power are both endpoints on a more complex spectrum. It is important to move forward from the intuitive view that any nation has particular capabilities and institutions that are only meant to be used in a 'hard' or in a 'soft' way. Soft power is part of a spectrum of power and cannot be viewed in isolation, as if it were somehow a capacity we have only recently discovered and are learning to use – though it may be true that it lies towards the end of a spectrum that has been given less attention than it now deserves. In Part Two we review 'Britain's persuaders' in light of the nine types of behaviour mentioned earlier, to try to assess some of the impacts they have on the spheres in which they operate. And in Part Three, we address directly the question of how Britain's persuaders are representing British society and politics. We offer our assessment of their effectiveness and of what successive governments might do to increase their impact in ways that benefit Britain in the world.

Part One

Thinking about power

Power in world politics

In the previous chapter we acknowledged that 'soft power' is an attractive but imprecise term. Most people have an instinctive sense of what it implies but, still, it is difficult to define closely as a political concept. It is obviously an 'aspect' or a 'type' of power and what applies to understanding that grand concept must also apply in its own way to what is meant by the 'softer' version of power. It is important to take a few steps back, therefore, and consider briefly what we think 'power' should mean and thereby have a better idea of how it works in world politics. Soft power may be a relatively exotic concept, but if it represents one way of looking at political power, we might also expect it to follow similar patterns.

Power and politics

The concept of power is one of the most instinctive notions in the human condition. Power makes things happen. Motive power is needed to make engines run, generate heat or be transformed into other key sorts of power like electricity. In the same way, power makes things happen in human affairs. There is a power dimension in all human relationships: between stronger and weaker, more intellectually dominant or less so, between parent and child. Power constantly changes and adapts its expression. It takes different forms over time. It may be more or less evident in any relationship, but it is always, always there somewhere.

Since politics is fundamentally concerned with human affairs, the same applies even more evidently in the political realm. Power relationships are part of the intrinsic nature of all politics, because politics is fundamentally about how power should be handled.

Some have described the essence of politics as the process of regulating the necessarily different abilities and desires of one person as against another in an acceptable framework, to somehow manage the natural differences in their intrinsic power since they have no choice but to inhabit the same temporal world. For the political philosopher Thomas Hobbes, it lay in the concept of the 'Leviathan' state to which all people must be subject – as the only device that prevents a descent into a natural condition of anarchy and misery.[1] Other thinkers, like John Locke, were less convinced that the human condition is inherently anarchic and theorized that a 'social contract' is naturally made between free people to devise ways to pursue common goals through cooperation. It may be made implicitly or – in the 'Age of Reason' – explicitly in devising political constitutions and in the standardization of common laws.[2]

More modern political philosophers proposed that politics is really the process of deciding on distribution. It is about 'who gets what, when and how'; and this can be achieved in many different ways, not all of them pleasant or naturally just.[3] In the mid-twentieth century, politics was increasingly viewed not so much as a normative quest to find methods of achieving common goals but more as an analytical description of a paradise lost to the original sin of the human condition. 'Power', 'violence' and 'decision', it was posited, all exist in an inseparable triumvirate that constantly interact.[4] In this case 'violence' is equated with change – something that disrupts, whether welcome or not. Each of these three forces constantly affects the other two. Wherever we break into it, this endless triangular process is somehow immutable, and politics is regarded as neither inherently good nor bad. It is simply a predicament: a way of understanding how we try to cope with the nature of human existence and its evolution by constantly trying to balance the exercise of power, the violence of change and the need always to be making decisions.[5]

A hard world

The sense that political power is all part of a 'predicament' appears even more relevant in the world of international politics among 200 sovereign nations, where no single, Hobbesian 'Leviathan state' can ever exist nor any Lockean global constitution. International politics generally display a state of natural anarchy, albeit tempered by the needs of coexistence and mutual prosperity, where, as Martin Wight famously put it, 'No state can escape out of the pattern of power'.[6] However calm and peaceful the international world might sometimes appear to be, or however good its future prospects might look, it remains what was accurately termed in 1977 as the 'anarchical society' – a society with many settled political and economic arrangements but one that also contains very disordered and dangerous elements. There is no ultimate authority in this society.[7] And states cannot survive and prosper in the anarchical society, still less manage it, unless the ever-elusive patterns of power in world politics are more or less understood and more or less carefully handled.

That is why, in the title of this book, we are condemned to live in a 'hard world'. The international world is hard in an existential sense, because every state must look after itself. A state can appeal to international law or to the authority of the United Nations, of course, but there is no way to enforce an international legal judgement unless powerful states and organizations are prepared to put their weight behind it. In 2003 the United States unilaterally changed its interpretation of the legal definition of 'self-defence' so it could attack terrorists potentially anywhere in the world. (Britain opposed this interpretation at the time, but in 2017 admitted it had gone along with it and was using the same interpretation for its own drone attacks on suspected terrorists.)[8] In 2016 China was found in breach of international law on every point regarding its claims to sovereignty over Philippine waters in the South China Sea but simply ignored the ruling and continued to build illegal military bases in the Paracel and Spratly Islands. Big states often assume that they can adjust, or ignore, the normal rules of the system to suit themselves. The fact is that law and rules matter much more to smaller states than larger ones. As Henry Kissinger observed many years ago, 'Empires have no interest in operating within an international system; they aspire to be the international system.'[9] It all depends on the power a state can bring to bear to look after its own people and interests.

We also live in a hard world for more prosaic reasons, because Britain is entering a decade where its physical weaknesses are likely to be more obvious than its physical strengths.[10] As we noted in Chapter 1, the 2020s looks set to be a decade where all the European states will find world politics more dangerous and challenging than in the three – relatively relaxed – decades they all enjoyed after the end of the Cold War. Great power politics have returned to the world stage in a big way since 2010 – the complex three-way relationship between the United States, China and Russia, and the rise of Indian influence in Asia, which has also re-energized a traditionally fraught Chinese–Indian relationship. These countries and the issues between them create the political weather for everyone else. Not least, the competition and tussles between them for regional and economic advantage are being conducted in both old and novel, new ways.[11] Their heavy metal military hardware sails and flies around the world, even as artificial intelligence, cyber-war and social media campaigns integrate with military instruments to create 'total strategies', 'hybrid conflict', 'hyper competition' or 'integrated challenges'. It is, said Bradley Peniston, 'the era of grand strategy' because 'it is the era of everything'.[12] And it is very hard for European countries to compete across the board in the era of everything, even were they able to develop grand strategies for it.

More than ever before in this hard world, traditional military resources are meshed with the very fabric of modern societies: the social media outlets, the digital systems, the artificial intelligence and the deep economic structures. It may appear that power is being exercised in some very confusing, perhaps even self-defeating, ways. But dominant countries naturally try to build the international system around themselves. They try, often only half-consciously, to wield systemic power so that their own societies provide the political and economic nervous systems for the rest of the world or at least for large parts of it.

This issue of systemic power is the third reason why we live in a hard world, not just because these days the big players, rather than the Europeans, are all struggling to shape it themselves but because systemic power is where hard and soft types of power naturally meld together and where it's difficult to tell them apart. It's hard because it's hard to understand. Sometimes power is most accurately conceived not as an attribute possessed by one of the players in a competitive game but rather as structural power, something that is wielded anonymously by the system and appears all the more overwhelming for that reason.

International economic power, for example, is so ubiquitous in the way it has structured the international system in the past, along global capitalist lines, that it appears to many of the individuals within it to be a simple fact of life, rather than the accumulation of myriad political decisions and individual choices. And those choices were made, or decisively influenced, by the biggest economic players of the time, first the Dutch and the British with their mercantilist maritime empires and then the United States in its twentieth century 'rise to globalism'. They successively shaped the international economic structure in their own image – not deliberately or as part of a grand historic strategy but because they could.[13]

The global environmental crisis, as another example, was regarded for many decades as something that grew out of a natural state of affairs – a fact of modern life with its need for mass production – rather than as something created by two centuries of decisions that drove a global production and distribution structure which exacerbated, even created, a modern climate crisis. Climate activists may castigate 'the system' that has brought this about, particularly during the last fossil fuel century. But that does not help much in understanding the great anonymity that created this vast and successful economic system which established power relationships between governments, corporations, financiers, explorers, researchers, retailers and consumers. Trying to redirect this sort of *systemic* power by the exercise of the *specific* powers in the hands of world leaders is a tall order for even the most determined and enlightened of them. As Kenneth Waltz observed in his seminal work on *Man, the State and War*, some important things happen in political systems – including wars – not because anyone intends them but because an infinite number of human decisions build anonymously towards an outcome where there is simply not enough to stop it.[14] As it happens, Leo Tolstoy had written something very similar in 1869 in his wonderful *War and Peace*, albeit in a less fatalistic frame of mind.[15]

As we will discuss further in Chapter 3, the structural or systemic expression of international power is particularly relevant to an understanding of soft power, because it bears greatly on the sort of power that is not so evident, that is hard to assess or measure and that seems only to be indirectly driven by politics.

Some of the most interesting aspects of structural power is that it is either unstated or understated. 'Power is at its most effective when it is least observable', says the radical philosopher Steven Lukes.[16] Power that is unstated because it is structural, or deliberately understated because it is more effective that way, is always difficult to analyse and normally causes great intellectual controversy. Classical Marxists argued that the working classes voted again and again, in elections and with their feet, against their own best interests because they suffered the 'false consciousness' that the capitalist system had woven around them.[17] Some of the most potent choices are described as 'non-decisions' – the lack of challenge to a status quo, the failure to perceive the possibility of change, the continuity of existing ways of doing things or the view that there is simply nothing to challenge.

'Unstated power' is also closely related to what might be described as 'uncontested power' – a system or structure that, for whatever reasons, appears to be beyond the bounds of challenge. The Christian church provided a massive power structure that was uncontested in Europe for over a thousand years. 'Well might the Roman Church have termed itself "catholic": "universal"', says historian Tom Holland, 'There was barely a rhythm of life that it did not define.' It was not that the church was somehow non-political. It was extraordinarily political, from dawn to dusk. But for a combination of specific historical reasons, it was uniquely influential and *so* politically strong that it was uncontested: 'from the hour of their birth to the very last drawing of their breath, the men and women of medieval Europe absorbed its assumptions into their bones', he says.[18] It was perhaps the best example in history of structural soft power at its most effective – and with quite a lot of economic and military force not too far away, as and when required.

Most societies have large elements of uncontested structural power, not as great as the medieval church, but still deriving from the deepest social mores in their community. A degree of censorship is an explicit power used by governments, even in a free society. But self-censorship in a free society is much more powerful as people exercise a personal judgement about what is fair, decent or socially acceptable. Nor is it only about government policy.

The 'culture wars' of the last decade in Western societies, and a growth of what has been termed 'cancel culture', are often cited as sources of extensive self-censorship, where individuals, companies and institutions steer clear of certain subjects or opinions for fear of the reaction. The culture warriors seek to affect the underlying social mores of society so that the power to uphold certain values, say of racial equality or gender rights, become so baked into prevailing social mores that governments no longer need to legislate for them. Movements like #MeToo and Black Lives Matter represent both opportunities and challenges to soft power institutions. The opportunity is for organizations to reflect more accurately what is, and to reject what is not, acceptable to growing sections of society – social progress that people in other countries look to, admire and covet. In this respect, they can be considered benign influences and the next iteration of the ever-swinging pendulum of societal trends. Yet, they are also challenges when their momentum leads to attacks on freedoms or where every decision becomes fraught for institutions. There is a balance to be found between self-awareness and self-confidence. Self-awareness, in that within an institution's history there may be aspects or episodes of which contemporary leadership cannot be proud. And self-confidence in that they are not derailed by this awareness. The potential threat to soft power institutions is that self-censorship forces organizations onto the back foot, and they act tentatively and self-consciously. The challenge for all institutions is to navigate a social sea change and emerge stronger and more confident because of it.

And since power relationships are ever changing, 'uncontested' power in any system can eventually slide towards power, which is simply 'untested'. Uncontested power is an interesting phenomenon. But untested power is a dangerous one. All power adjusts and adapts and is constantly being tested, even if it is not consciously being questioned. That is the political predicament of the eternal triangle of power, violence and decision; and in human affairs it is never static. When political systems collapse quickly, like the Russian Tsarist empire in 1917, or then the whole edifice of Soviet communism itself in the late 1980s, or the extant military regimes in the Iberian Peninsula in the 1970s, or the different apartheid governments in Southern Africa in the early 1990s, or the autocratic governments across the Middle East in the 'Arab Uprising' after 2012, it always emerges that the status quo governments had failed to account for important shifts in the balance of forces around them, and their untested power simply collapsed, often with a single push.

Relationship and perception

Even such cursory descriptions of the central importance of power and its elusiveness highlight two central points that are of particular importance to the understanding of soft power. First, power is not a commodity but a relationship. In itself, money is not power; it is merely currency, even if the currency were gold bars. Wealth is power – which is the use of currency to obtain desirable commodities in relationship to a market. Physical strength in itself is not power, unless it is applied to some relationship where it matters to be strong. And armies and military hardware are not, in themselves, power unless they can be applied to some meaningful objective in a relationship with other elements in a domestic or international environment. This last example has seen some particularly dramatic expressions in recent times. The United States applied massive amounts of military capacity in Vietnam in the 1960s, in Iraq after 2003 and in Afghanistan after 2006. The discrepancy between the enormous physical resources available to the US military in all these cases, as opposed to the Viet Cong guerrillas, Iraqi private militias or to Taliban forces in Afghanistan, made it clear that Washington was unable to apply those capacities satisfactorily to the relationships that really mattered. If military assets in themselves created military power, then the United States would have achieved all its objectives in the last fifty years. But like many countries with impressive military establishments, including Britain, the conditions of modern world politics have highlighted the very complex relationships in which armed forces have to be engaged if their physical presence is to deliver *political power* in a useful way.[19]

And second, because political power is only meaningful as some sort of relationship, it is therefore dependent on how it is perceived. The way power is perceived by those who wield it and those who are subjected to it is the only way power actually exists. Human perception acts as the infrared light that outlines shapes in what is otherwise a mysterious darkness surrounding all the various capacities that governments or others throw into an equation to achieve their objectives. When leaders, people, even algorithms, perceive – or think they perceive – a capacity, a force, an attractive opportunity coming their way they will begin to react to it. If they don't perceive it, they won't. And, of course, the relative perceptions between one group of people and another may be quite different. In analysing crisis management, behaviouralists have long observed that political leaders ascribe greater hostility underpinning the actions of their adversaries than those adversaries themselves normally intend.[20] Their perceptions are simply different, and a sense of crisis normally sharpens their prejudices about each other. Dissident groups would never stand up to brutal dictators if they interpreted political power in the same way as their oppressors, if they assumed that the physical capacities of the dictator's police and security forces would always prevail. Independence movements around the world would never have taken on the British Empire so readily if they didn't think they had a better grasp than London of the way power was really working in their own country. It is in the nature of the human condition that the parties to any relationship will tend towards their own interpretations of its actual workings, and this applies in the case of power relationships between countries and organizations as much as between people.

This does not mean that power is somehow purely ephemeral. Perceptions, and misperceptions, frequently bump up against the real impacts of forces at work in the world and have to reassess how they evaluate what they are perceiving. Russian leaders before 2010, for example, did not think that economic sanctions were a very effective coercive exercise against a state, since sanctions had an inconclusive record where they had previously been applied. Russia, they felt, was a big and rich enough economy to be largely immune to any Western sanctions. But when, following the Ukraine crisis, the United States and its European allies developed 'smart sanctions' which restricted the scope of particular Russian oligarchs to operate around the world and cut the Russian state off from international credit, and when oil and gas prices collapsed in the wake of the world economic crisis, it turned out that sanctions were really rather painful for Russia.[21] President Putin spent much effort afterwards trying to get them lifted. Or again, quite famously during the Vietnam War, North Vietnamese and Viet Cong forces launched their massive Tet Offensive in 1968. And they lost – heavily – on the battlefield, but through it, won the war. Because the Tet Offensive changed the perception inside the United States of what was really happening in South Vietnam and convinced the United States that the war was unwinnable.[22] The American public, and Congress, was suddenly confronted by a reality they had misperceived and the incoming Nixon Administration in 1969 committed itself to withdrawal rather than the sort of victory its predecessors had envisaged. And whether the vainglorious boasting of classic dictators before they ignominiously collapsed, like Nicolae Ceausescu in 1989, Saddam Hussein in 2003 or Colonel Gaddafi in 2011, was a misperception of power, or just simple stupidity, hardly matters. Their individual stories, and many to come in the future, repeatedly demonstrate that autocratic political systems are generally bad at making mid-course policy adjustments as their expectations bump up against hard facts. Good government involves constantly learning and adjusting as leaders feel their way forward in the ever-shifting relationships of political power.

It is for these reasons that democrats around the world have become so concerned about the influence of social media on global politics. The creation of social media 'echo chambers', the formulation of massive and absurd conspiracy theories and the proliferation of untruths that dilute real truth and hard facts all suggest that it is somehow possible to *manufacture* a political reality that accords with a perception, rather than the other way round.[23] The manipulation of social media is, in itself, a capacity – an instrument that can be used – and can be translated into political power if it can somehow change the 'facts on the ground'. Some have called this the explicit attempt to 'weaponize soft power'.[24] Clearly, in some spheres this may be possible, as in affecting public attitudes towards elections or important issues in foreign countries, or trying to create or change a prevailing public image of something. Conversely, social media's capacity to create its own reality is far more limited in other cases, such as basic economic facts, demographic trends, meteorological events created by climate change or even – perhaps especially – the impact of a global pandemic![25] Social media can try to spin many things, but some hard facts remain facts – however many conspiracy theories surround them. Nevertheless, for a phenomenon that is less than twenty-five years old there is some real concern over the potential of social media to make some things that are manifestly unreal become somehow *politically* real and therefore genuinely powerful.[26] Social media, in other words, may not just be another potential instrument to be wielded in the endless competition of political power but a medium of power in itself that determines its own rules for the relationships between perception and reality.

Soft power and its diffusion in a hard world

The idea that power always exists in some sort of relationship and that human perception is the only way it can politically manifest itself are observations that apply with particular force to any discussion of soft power in the contemporary world. We will define soft power more carefully in Chapter 3, but even the most intuitive use of the term implies that the softer end of the power spectrum depends very much on the way people and organizations see each other, what they assume to be their respective characteristics and how much they admire or are prepared to be persuaded by them.

This applies all the more so in a highly globalized world, where the depth of human interaction, both individually and collectively, is greater than at any other time in history. People, organizations, companies, families, traders, entertainers from every part of the world all interact with each other more frequently and, if they choose, more deeply than anyone born before the 1970s could possibly have imagined. Globalization is not just a slogan or an easy shorthand term. It has been a genuine political game-changer, and it has arrived within the span of a generation.

What is often described as 'globalization 1.0' is less than forty years old. It began in the late 1980s and developed fast and dramatically. But following the global economic crisis that started in 2008 and the many social concerns driven by the impact of climate change and the effects of the Covid-19 pandemic, its momentum stuttered. A different sort of 'globalization 2.0' appears to be emerging for the 2020s.[27] Globalization 2.0 will be driven less by the economic motor of the Western economies and may take a less free-flowing form than in its first flush. Governments around the world are catching up with the implications of globalization and bending it more towards their own wills.

But the underlying forces that created the globalization revolution are still very much in evidence and they will continue to offer the massive, and expanding, human arena in which soft power will play out in the coming era. In brief, they include the growth in world population and the relative *and* absolute increase in wealth among that enlarged population. Between 1980 and 2015 the proportion of the world living in what was defined by the United Nations as 'absolute poverty' fell from 42 per cent to 10 per cent (in China it fell from 67 per cent to 1 per cent), and 60 million people were annually crossing the economic threshold into what is globally defined as 'middle-class' income groups. That stimulated unprecedented levels of economic growth over these years in both world trade and multinational manufacturing to meet increasing demand. The international market was king. This was a heyday of neoliberal market thinking and it drove manufacturing towards the greatest cost efficiencies it could find anywhere in the world to meet the challenges of an ever more competitive market. That, in turn, was based on the steadily falling real costs of international travel and transport, which had been consistently diminishing since the 1950s. And, of course, the astonishing series of communications revolutions, from intercontinental satellite links in the 1960s to the creation of the World Wide Web in 1989, alongside another computing revolution in the 1990s, underpinned the whole globalization phenomenon, not least by facilitating essential financial flows.[28]

By the turn of the century it was widely recognized that 'globalization' represented something significantly different from the 'internationalization' or even the 'interdependence' of previous eras. It describes a situation where whole societies (not just states and their governments) effectively overlay each other in very significant respects. The social and economic fabric of all societies in the world – some more intensely than others – have become dependent on each other in ways that political leaders, at best, can influence but no longer control.[29] And it works for both good and bad. When the Covid-19 disease emerged in Wuhan, China, in December 2019, few could have guessed that it would be causing great distress among tribal societies in the remotest Amazon villages by May 2020 – all on the basis of human-to-human transmission. But they might also have failed to imagine that so much practical cooperation between medical professionals would so swiftly create several effective vaccines to combat the disease. Economic and political trends rise and fall, driven by the impact of events like the Covid pandemic. But the underlying conditions of global interaction are not likely to change very much for the foreseeable future.

Political power in world politics, it has been noted many times, is now therefore more dispersed across the world than in any other period of modern history.[30] It is dispersed not just across a greater number of states than have ever existed in history before but also because they can play more distinctive roles in world politics than were open to them forty years ago. As President Biden's first National Security Strategy recognized in early 2021, even the United States has to recognize a world in which political power is dispersed between more types of actors, including the new-tech giants, the major corporations, the finance institutions, international organizations and regulatory authorities, and influential non-governmental organizations of many different sorts.[31] And, yes, groups and single individuals around the world have shown themselves able to harness the communications revolution to exert their own political power on certain issues. Social media was a major driver of the popular mobilization that created the so-called colour revolutions throughout the former Soviet Union in countries such as Georgia, Armenia and Ukraine, and again, in the 'Arab Uprising' across the Middle East a few years later. And even young individuals could be seen to mobilize political power. In 2012 Malala Yousafzai of Pakistan was shot by the Pakistan Taliban. She came to Britain for emergency treatment and her case focussed a wellspring of international support for more secure education for girls in developing countries. And Greta Thunberg, a Swedish teenager, was able to drive an international campaign on the imminence of the climate emergency in a series of big campaigns across many Western countries.

Domestic politics in many Western states, and certainly in Europe and the United States, have all been subject to social upheaval of different sorts. In 2020 the unlawful killing of George Floyd by a US policeman in Minneapolis sparked a new wave of 'Black Lives Matter' protests across a number of Western countries. Meanwhile, strong populist and nationalist forces changed the conventional shape of domestic politics in societies as different as those in India, Southeast Asia, Eastern Europe and Latin America. The precise reasons for political upheaval are somewhat different in each country; the issues that upended British politics from 2014 to 2020 were not the same as those in France, the Netherlands, some of the Scandinavian countries or in Germany. But the volatility of public attitudes to their leaders and many established symbols of their societies has been well noted.[32]

In short, over the last couple of decades it has become apparent that populations around the world have a more tenuous connection to their traditional national institutions than was the case for their parents or grandparents. And though it may be expressed differently from place to place, this seems to apply from all but the strictest autocracies to the most liberal of democracies.[33] This is not necessarily a bad thing. It may be the precursor to an era of social change that will help drive more progressive and peaceful trends in world politics as a whole. The essential point for our purposes is to note that in this diffusion of political power, in this era of political volatility, in the globally shared intellectual space that the cyber revolution has created, the phenomenon characterized less than thirty years ago as 'soft power' may be set to emerge as the most important trend in the world politics of this century.

Persuasive power

Hard, soft and smart

Power, as we observed in the last chapter, is a fact of political life. All politics are largely concerned with managing power – who controls it and under what conditions. Power is persuasive, whether by noisy, overwhelming force or by quiet, reasoned argument. We also observed that power can only be expressed in relationships, between people or organizations – whether between two actors in a single relationship or else multiple different actors in a complex system.

Power relationships in politics are driven overwhelmingly by human perceptions between one and another or one organization and another. And there is huge scope for human perceptions to see things differently, as between individual people and the social conditions in which they live, not to mention the different cultures that have shaped them. Human perceptions do not only differ as between people and organizations, however. There is also a slippery relationship between human perceptions and objective reality.

It is possible that widespread human perceptions can diverge from hard underlying realities for a long time before they are eventually brought to book by them. A dramatic example would be the case of climate change. The underlying realities of climate change emerge ever more strongly in the current era, and regardless of how far some strands of global opinion may want to deny its existence or importance, there will eventually be a reckoning between the human perceptions of climate change and the scientific realities of it.[1] Credible studies of climate change are now unambiguously of the view that it will not disappear within any humanly foreseeable future; it will not, like some objectionable political ideology, just decline of its own accord or become unfashionable. It will continue to shape our physical world unless or until human perceptions of its impact create the political impetus to address it adequately at a global level.

But conversely – and just as importantly – in some other spheres it is evident that people can create their own political realities, where to believe something for long enough is to make it true. Common perceptions can become self-fulfilling prophecies. The view, for example, that liberal democracies, or the economic systems that back them up, are incapable of rising to current challenges, or are simply failing, can create the very failures they fear. When democracies die, it has been observed many times, they fundamentally die from within, rather than because of any opposition from outside.[2] The perception of widespread failure, whether accurate or not, can eventually become the objective reality for systems like government or economic organizations which rely on public credibility to function.

Nevertheless, no matter how slippery the concept of human perception may be, understanding its importance to the way all power operates is critical to defining more carefully what we mean by 'hard' and 'soft' power, and all forms in between. As we discussed in the previous chapter, it seems that the contemporary world emphasizes the prevalence of both hard power assets, as the great powers again square up to each other in assertive ways, and the prevalence of soft power relationships, as globalization creates so much human interaction between quite different societies. So, it is important to understand more carefully how we define the ways in which soft power might be working.

The power spectrum

One of the virtues of the term 'soft power' is that it seems to have an intuitive meaning. Most people show an instinctive understanding of it, mainly as a counterpoint to what they assume the opposite idea of 'hard power' must mean. 'Soft power' is a valuable term, partly for this reason. It was coined as a phrase and then developed as an organizing idea for political analysis around thirty years ago.[3] But it is also a difficult concept.

It is often assumed that 'hard power' describes military activity or some sort of physical pressure, and 'soft power' is, therefore, everything else. But the spectrum of hard and soft power does not lie between explicit violence at one end and pure persuasion at the other. The difference between a state using its hard, as opposed to its soft, power capabilities is better understood as the distinction between a state deliberately applying its strength – whether military, economic, social or political – to achieve a particular outcome, as opposed to a state having some sort of natural magnetism and attraction for other reasons, whether or not it applies such influence directly to the objectives it desires. So, for example, any levers of governmental power, say in the economic or cultural spheres, can be used in a 'hard' way if they are specifically applied to pressurize another actor. As a result of your outrageous policy, one government might say to another, we intend to cancel the cultural exchanges we had planned to hold with your country, we will boycott the Olympic Games or the football World Cup due to be held in your country next year, we will delete your products and fashions from our annual trade fares, drop your television series from our national broadcasters and so on and so on. This happened in Chinese-Australian relations in 2020 when Canberra criticized Beijing's stance on a number of issues. And following heightened criticisms of repression and forced labour in Xinjiang, a number of Western retail brands found themselves being denounced on social media throughout their Chinese markets.[4] Arts, culture, sport, marketing or any other aspects of social life not normally associated with politics can be examples of 'hard power' at work if a government tries to use them explicitly to achieve a particular objective – and if those particular spheres of activity have some leverage against the leadership of the target country.

And conversely, governmental capabilities as forceful as military establishments, policing, border protection, taxation structures or other economic management tools can be soft power assets if they are used indirectly to promote good relations with another country. To take the most obvious example, a great deal of the normal day-to-day work of the British military establishment around the world is subtly diplomatic. Its explicit purpose might be to provide technical training for the forces of a partner country or in joint endeavours with another military establishment. But the implicit purpose of British military forces undertaking such work is for those forces to be admired for their professionalism, to create political magnetism and the desire on the part of others to imitate them. These were the very objectives expressed in the government's defence review of 2021 when it described its intention to pursue a 'persistent engagement' across the world for British armed forces.[5]

In other words, the type of assets being employed is not what distinguishes soft from hard power. It is the purpose they serve that makes the key difference; inherently persuasive assets like art and culture may be used in a coercive way, and inherently coercive assets like military force or economic regulation may be used in persuasive ways. It depends on the context of the relationship of which they are a part and how the use of those capabilities is perceived by the recipient.

In fact, the trend towards imitation in the behaviour of others is the element that most distinguishes the exercise of soft from hard power. A country that is admired for some virtue or another is likely to create the desire in other countries to imitate it. The power of imitation is a very potent source of political influence.

When different countries and their societies wish to imitate what they see in another society, the admired society has the potential to shape its international environment to be more like an image of itself. It could be argued that the soft power of imitation was critical in ending the rule of the Soviet Union across its internal and external empires at the end of the last century. Eventually, Soviet and other Communist Party leaders simply could not meet the aspirations of their populations to have societies more like those they saw in the West. Communist authorities in East Germany, for example, were unable to prevent their population tuning in to West German television, and they claimed to be relaxed about its staple diet of American series that showed the decadent West in all its fascination.[6] But they were furious about the ad breaks, because they showed shops brimming with food and everything else money could buy. They conducted long campaigns claiming that the TV advertisements were a tissue of Western lies, nothing but propaganda. But their protestations were all in vain.

If this was a spectacular example of the soft power of imitation, however, it also demonstrated the dangers of cultural hubris in what subsequently happened. For when the Cold War ended in 1991 many Western writers assumed that the long victory of liberal democracy over communism showed just how much the rest of the world wanted to imitate the life of Western capitalist countries. The soft power of the West, it was argued, had underpinned all the hard military and economic competition of the Cold War to create a moment in history where the international order could now be shaped around an imitation of Western liberal society.[7] Perhaps for a while that was true. But the moment did not last or maybe Western influence was carelessly thrown away when it could have achieved so much more. Instead, autocracy and dictatorship were on the rise throughout the world after the year 2000, Western economic models of development came under sustained pressure as protectionism grew and religious challenges to the West's largely secular society became ever more strident. The last couple of decades have demonstrated repeatedly that the rest of the world is not as keen to imitate the political and economic models of liberal democracy that seemed likely in the early 1990s. For the 2020s, autocratic governments preside over more than a third of the world's population, and according to the Economist Intelligence Unit the number of countries who meet the criteria of being 'full democracies', as opposed to 'flawed' or 'hybrid' democracies, hovers in the low- to mid-twenties most years.[8] The potency of imitative power is not always appreciated, even by those who can most benefit from it. The surreal antics of President Trump's White House before and after it was defeated in the 2020 presidential elections was a gift to the world's autocrats, because it seemed to create enduring images of what US society now *was*, even more than what the outgoing president *did*. At least at the time, it suggested a democracy that few would want to imitate. 'There is no question that our democracy is fragile', said US Secretary of State Anthony Blinken in his very first speech.[9]

Another distinguishing characteristic between soft and hard power may be expressed as the difference between power projection and power magnetism. Hard power, whether it is expressed through military prowess or cultural eminence, is an attempt to affect the behaviour of others by projecting those attributes of power in an implicit or explicit bargain with others. It goes on all the time and the process of endless bargaining occupies diplomats and foreign ministries for most of their existence. Hard power, therefore, is applied; it represents what governments *do*. Soft power, by contrast, simply exists because of what a society *represents*. It is the political magnetism that arises from some natural strength or the special characteristics embodied in a society. As the poet Emerson put it, 'What you are stands over you the while, and thunders so that I cannot hear what you say to the contrary.'

The most general characteristics of strong soft power in this magnetic sense can be stated straightforwardly – the things that create 'what you are' in the image of the world. Quite simply, the most potent parts of a national image that makes a country magnetic (in several ways) are that it is seen as *prosperous*, that there appears to be genuine *opportunity* within that society and that it is governed under *law*. But if such obvious attributes are easy to state, they are all contestable in practice and are not necessarily well represented in the policies or attitudes that countries adopt over particular issues. Nor are the transmission mechanisms clear by which societal activity across so many institutions and activities builds into these three great abstractions – prosperity, opportunity and law. International surveys endlessly confirm the pulling power among people all round the world of these virtues, wherever they see them. We will trace some of the detailed transmission mechanisms by which institutions and individuals contribute to such soft power attributes in Part Two. But it has to be admitted that as descriptions of political magnetism, they are very difficult for governments and leaders to grasp.

Some writers on strategy have effectively dismissed the notion that soft power can become a national asset precisely on these grounds, that it cannot be applied in the same way that military force or economic strength manifestly can. If a national asset cannot be consciously and deliberately applied to a particular political goal, they say, it has no place in 'national strategy' where a country is trying to pursue policies over which it has some control, to navigate its way through the dangers and opportunities of international politics.[10] But this seems to miss the point. Soft power, by definition, is not applied directly and it arises precisely through the perception of others; it comes from the reaction of the external world to what it sees in a country. The fact that these largely perceptual advantages defy easy aggregation into some sort of political campaign in the international balance of power does not mean that its effects are absent or somehow non-strategic. Just ask the old Cold War leadership elites in East Germany, Poland, Czechoslovakia and most other Warsaw Bloc countries who had to live on the doorstep of societies that demonstrated their superior success on a daily basis.[11] Finding ways to nurture and make the most of one's own societal strengths in things the rest of the world recognizes is a good long-term bet on a better strategic future for any country.

Clearly, then, the exercise of political power can be viewed along a spectrum, from attempts at outright coercion at one end – where explicit threats, retaliations or sanctions might be involved in a test of political will and nerve – through the more normal, ongoing bargaining processes of diplomacy and inter-societal contact, to the existential magnetism of an admired and imitated society at the other end of the spectrum. Political power exists along the whole spectrum. Most, but certainly not all of it, can be mobilized one way or another by government. Understanding better how governments can use the whole spectrum of hard and soft power, and especially how to benefit from those elements towards the softer end that they cannot directly control, has been referred to as the essence of using power 'smartly'.[12]

The idea of 'smart power' involves the ability to integrate and mobilize the most appropriate elements from across the power spectrum to achieve the best results.[13] In principle, this seems like a statement of the obvious, but experience shows that in practice it is remarkably difficult for governments to achieve. National governments are complex machines, operating simultaneously at national and local levels, typically stove-piped into different functions, and facing a globalized environment that intrudes on domestic society in very significant ways. Indeed, making a reality of 'smart power' has become something of a philosopher's stone for modern complex government. In Britain it has gone through at least four Whitehall campaigns in the last quarter century. In 1997 the incoming government of Tony Blair spoke brightly about the push for 'joined-up government' across the board. That was replaced within five years by a more focused 'combined approach', and when that was found to be too difficult, by a more modest 'coordinated approach'. By 2015 the whole 'joined-up' lexicon was back in fashion in a fearsomely titled 'fusion doctrine' which is projected to meet the governmental challenges of the 2020s. And yet, in the Brexit hiatus after 2016 and then the Covid crisis, most observers could not recall a time when the government seemed less internally coherent or doctrinally 'fused' about anything. In truth, Whitehall is normally better than most of its competitor governments in being coordinated. A great deal of energy goes into intra-governmental liaison in Whitehall.

But a period of fragmented politics and a national leadership team that became defined by its personal Brexit credentials undermined, for a time, the normal flow of coordination and left the government struggling to pursue its stated policy goals with genuinely collective and properly focused efforts.

The plain fact is that it is a challenge for any national policy-makers to grasp the breadth of the real power spectrum and even *conceive* of wielding power that is genuinely 'smart', let alone go on to apply it effectively and consistently. Most policy-makers are certainly aware of the softer end of the spectrum but spend their lives nearer to the middle and the hard end of it – looking for 'levers' to pull that will deliver the results they desire and within a time frame that will have some tangible political benefit. For them, the softer end of the power spectrum may seem very favourable to their political aims but does not offer the obvious levers that can easily be manipulated from the top of government.

In a society as complex as Britain's, therefore, the soft power end of the spectrum resides in very many institutions.[14] Some of them, like the Royal Family, are part of the state machinery. Others, like the British Council, the BBC, or the Arts Council, are agencies of it or else public institutions. Most, however, are institutions over which the government has little direct influence. In 2017 Jonathan McClory, the leading analyst of comparative studies of soft power between one country and another, defined the 'objective categories' of soft power as 'enterprise, culture, digital presence, government, engagement and education'.[15] Even the naming of these categories suggests the problem for governments. They can do what they will to affect the ways institutions and citizens react to the outside world in these various ways but, in reality, their influence is peripheral at best.

For governments to employ power 'smartly', therefore, they must be capable of thinking and acting strategically: creating clear objectives that are attainable and which can be pursued reasonably consistently across the parts of the power spectrum they can control, and which are also in general harmony with the characteristics of the softer, societal end of the spectrum they cannot control. Governments that adopt policies, which are inconsistent or antithetical to the nature of their own societies, tend, over the long term, to fail. Using power smartly also requires that governments are able to take an 'effects-based' approach to their policies. It is much easier to see and measure the output of policies rather than their effects. Policy outputs can be expressed relatively straightforwardly in money spent on something, people deployed to it, statements made, allies recruited for it and so on. Governments feel on safe ground when they measure policy against such metrics. It is normally much more difficult, however, to judge policy according to the effects it is designed to have and then subsequently may, or may not, actually be having. But smart power is intended to be targeted carefully, whether to achieve a very specific, or a more generalized, effect in the outside world. So the 'effects-based' approach is intrinsically important to thinking about the employment of political power if it is to be used 'smartly'.

The soft power end of the spectrum

To get to grips with the characteristic elements that are evident towards the softer end of the power spectrum, governments have to try to integrate into their strategic and effects-based approaches an understanding of the things that make soft power elements somewhat special – not always easily grasped, still less manipulated, but magnetically influential nevertheless. Four general characteristics are particularly relevant to understanding how soft power tends to work at its own end of the smart power spectrum.

First, soft power is conceptually different to what we might call formal governmental power. If it is based, in Emerson's phrase, on 'what you are', then it hinges on what societies are perceived to *be*, rather than what their governments *do*. Soft power assets, therefore, tend to provide a country's more sustainable reputation, for either good or bad. Political leaders frequently undermine their own credibility and that of their country when they drive through the morass of immediate policy problems confronting them and break their promises, misstep and make mistakes or turn their previous policies inside out. All governments zigzag under the pressure of events, but they hope that the rest of the world, and their own citizens, will believe in an underlying trend – a deeper consistency – that expresses more powerfully the national values they would prefer to project; what you are thunders more loudly than what you say. Governments rely on the deep-seated and longer-lasting images created by their society and its institutions. They fall back on the ingrained trends in societal behaviour to get them off some of the contradictory hooks on which they impale themselves.

The international image of a country certainly provides a general background for effective diplomacy, but it may also constitute an important diplomatic asset at key moments – where it affects issues in those small margins of others' decisions that determine success or failure. An international reputation for business-like honesty, tolerant pragmatism or for fashionable innovation, for example, can be a real diplomatic advantage at critical points in the decision cycles of other groups and governments. Of course, it can work the other way as well. Governments may try to enhance a policy of friendship and cooperation by very extensive acts of international generosity but find that the general image of their societies in the rest of the world remains stubbornly negative, diminishing any effects of what the government is trying to do. An interesting juxtaposition of perspective occurred in the five years between 2016 and 2021. The United States undoubtedly damaged its international standing across the world during the Trump Administration, as did Britain in its handling of the process for leaving the European Union. Both of these events, unsurprisingly, were reflected in the United States and Britain losing some of their leading status in the international soft power rankings of 2017 and 2020.[16] Meanwhile, China and Russia undertook extensive policy initiatives during the Covid-19 crisis to improve their international image, providing lots of bilateral medical aid to other countries and moving fast to distribute their domestic vaccines worldwide with each vial intended to convey a favourable impression of the country's biotechnical prowess and effectiveness as a global health leader. But the net result in soft power terms of what these four governments were doing was that the United States and Britain both fell a couple of places among the top four or five in the soft power rankings, while China and Russia enjoyed the appearance of bounces that may prove relatively short-lived and didn't noticeably improve their overall long-term images in soft power terms.

Second, therefore, there is a clear difference in the timescale over which soft power should be perceived and assessed. Soft power assets are long-term bets. The international image of a society – whether it and its people are liked in the world – persists for a good deal longer than the virtuous, mistaken or downright foolish policies any particular government may pursue. It takes quite a lot to change, or undermine, a societal image in the eyes of the rest of the world – and correspondingly longer to recover a reputation that may have been diminished or lost.

Third, public images of any given society are naturally translated in the minds of those outside as societal attributes or even more vaguely as some expression of 'national character'. Tiny and partial glimpses of naturally complex societies are enough to create firm images for outsiders to decide on another society's essential attributes. Societal attributes – and the perceived image of their strengths and weaknesses – are very slippery concepts, much given to cartoon caricatures and polemical journalism. The 'national character' of a nation is a concept that analytically never stands up, but politically it never quite lies down either. It is what people around the world think they see when they look at another society, however impossible it may be to sustain with hard evidence. It is, therefore, politically important. British national character is often presented simultaneously as both inoffensively polite and deeply cynical, depending on whether the commentary is favourable or hostile. Favourable images stress British charm and unflappability or some version of the 'English idyll'. Negative images, particularly in Europe, fall back on 'Perfidious Albion', or in the wider world, on an image of post-imperial arrogance. Britain had an empire 'on which the sun never set', it is still pointed out, 'because God wouldn't trust an Englishman in the dark'. Such images – good, bad and absurd – are never far below the surface of foreign journalism whether reporting on politics, sport, tourism, arts – everything. And British journalism, it hardly needs to be said, is replete with time-worn stereotypes of other nationalities, most of them trumpeted without any apparent sense of irony.

Recent work on soft power has tried to pin the concept of national image down a bit more seriously and precisely.[17] 'National character', as reputation in the world, translates best in terms of trust in the authenticity of a society's fundamental values. This recognizes any society's unique culture and its religion or core beliefs. A society may be admired by many people around the world for its values of austere religiosity, if they are authentically presented – just as most others will admire determinedly secular societies, if they represent those values consistently. Four particular elements emerge from the analysis as important components of the trusted values others might perceive and hence ascribe to the 'national character' of a society. One is the degree of 'openness', or else the different 'ways' in which a society is open. This comes down to its political culture. As we have observed, Western writers in the past have tended to assume that 'openness' was an absolute value – that everyone wanted the sort of openness practised in the liberal West. But it has become clear that Western versions of what it is to be open vary from one political culture to another. Similarly with the second element: the practice of justice and the rule of law. Legal codes and judicial systems vary greatly around the world. Their importance in the perception of national character is that a rule of law is seen genuinely to exist and is pursued consistently and equitably within a society. Those observations are at least as important as the principles on which a nation's law may be based, a perception that there is a meaningful rule of law is the important ingredient. A third element is the arts and high culture of a society. For many outsiders, these are the most obvious windows on another community and go a long way to create the images that others hold of a country's character. There are good reasons why, for the last hundred years, dictators and autocrats around the world have been frightened of progressive art in all forms and why open societies in the West have promoted progressive art, even including its questionable or unpleasant excesses. The windows that art and high culture offer on another society may not be particularly accurate, but they speak to the freedom of artists to express themselves as they choose, and that has a big effect on the perceptions of foreign observers. Finally, the perceived 'role' of a country in the world is also an important ingredient in the way others assess a society's 'national character'. If a country is regarded as a natural international leader in some respect, a reliable partner or a successful mediator or problem-solver, this will affect the image the rest of the world has of its people. So too if a country is regarded as behaving in over-assertive or aggressive ways, if it is seen as a spoiler or a troublemaker in world politics. Even simplistic characterizations of an international role have proved to be potent in shaping perceptions of national character – and they create remarkably persistent images.

Such depictions of national character also appear to make a difference in the less soft realms of international economic bargaining and relationships. A national image that a society is open, fair and above all that it operates a meaningful rule of law underpins economic confidence in dealing with companies and economic institutions based in that society or operating within its norms and boundaries. Evidence from the international business community underlines the fact that even in the hard-nosed calculations of business, essentially soft perceptions of national character influence the confidence with which commerce is conducted.[18]

Finally, the most recent evidence on effective soft power indicates that certain things matter when soft power is being assessed, not all of them naturally obvious.[19] National societal institutions matter rather more than government policy – since institutions express continuity and wider and deeper values than a government of any political persuasion can ever express. Direct, lived experience matters when others are making judgements on the attractions, or otherwise, of another society. Living, visiting, touring or meeting citizens of another country are, by far, the most persuasive processes that lead people to draw conclusions about another society. Then, too, size matters. Bigger countries with bigger societies are taken more seriously precisely because of their size, compared to smaller countries that may be liked more but are perceived as less relevant. Scandinavian countries, for example, are almost universally liked by the rest of the world. Ireland, and Irish society, is one of the most fashionable national brands in the world; New Zealand and Australia are widely popular, not just around the Western world. But smaller countries find it difficult to translate liking of this sort into a more positive perception of their soft power capacity.[20] Bigger countries may be respected more than they are liked, but that carries its own soft power benefits. Similarly, prosperity matters. Societies that are self-evidently prosperous are more influential in soft power terms, and they certainly encourage some imitation. In this respect, 'prosperity' should be regarded as per capita, not total, GDP, since this determines how prosperous the citizens of a country are seen to be. In GDP terms, Russia's total economy is almost nine times bigger than that of the tiny Gulf state of Qatar. But Qatari citizens are six times wealthier than their Russian counterparts (and 38 per cent richer, on average, than British citizens). Personal prosperity matters. And so, it turns out, does history and the view the rest of the world chooses to take of a society's 'heritage'. The image of a long heritage is more influential than that of a short one, but it works both for and against a national image. A long heritage can be dominated by images of imperialism or by the struggles against imperialism; by grandeur or humiliation; or by historical trajectories that seem to emphasize national decline just as much as an image that speaks of a new rise to global influence.

Britain and soft power

A good deal of recent research has gone into understanding better the phenomenon of soft power, and it is being applied more carefully to individual countries, using some of the four insights outlined earlier. It is difficult for governments to instrumentalize soft power to any great extent – to 'dragoon' the institutions and components of it and direct it to some particular policy purpose. This is partly because some of the attributes that matter, such as 'prosperity', 'size', 'lived experience' or 'heritage', don't exist neatly in any institutions or in tangible form. And most of the institutions in which certain soft power capabilities do take a tangible form, such as arts and cultural institutions, sports bodies, private companies or business communities, are naturally resistant to being organized by the government or somehow brigaded to a political purpose.

Autocratic governments have frequently been tempted to try to control their own soft power assets in just such a way, and totalitarian thinking, making a strong comeback in present-day China, is based on the idea that the state has a right to demand from the population not just lawful behaviour but conformity of thinking. This has not proved to be viable or successful anywhere in the past, though modern technology might now be opening possibilities for China to practice totalitarianism more successfully.[21] But Britain has a long heritage of abhorring any drift towards such social control on the part of any government; it celebrates its own laissez-faire society. British governments must therefore embrace the conceptual challenges of building smart power approaches to external policy that use the whole spectrum of power, from hard to soft, in a strategically coherent way. That means understanding the limits on governmental power and influence over the soft power attributes that British society embodies: working carefully with those few relevant institutions it can directly control and cooperatively with the broader swathe of institutions that it can influence but not control. And in relation to those institutions, organizations and individuals in British society over whom it has no relevant power at all – wherein the most potent agents of soft power seem to lie – it must work to help create a domestic and an international environment that enables them to play to their strengths and in which they are more able to flourish.

These are all tall orders and potentially expensive. But in 2021 the government produced its long-awaited 'Integrated Review' in which it asserted that Britain was 'a soft power superpower'.[22] The review had been designed to consider 'the totality of global opportunities and challenges the UK faces' and 'how the whole of government can be structured, equipped and mobilized to meet them'.[23] It certainly did not lack for ambition, though the Covid-19 pandemic that followed hard on the announcement of this review process only highlighted how difficult it is to pursue cross-governmental and cross-sectoral approaches to the challenges that emanate from the external world.

The following study of British soft power attempts to draw on a clear understanding of the tricky concept of 'power' in world politics, alongside these various insights from recent research on soft power. In particular it tries to assess the strengths and weaknesses of British soft power and its ability to shape or influence the international environment. Only by understanding how Britain fares at this – softer – end of the political power spectrum is it possible for British governments to exercise power 'smartly' as they attempt to do, and as the Integrated Review indicated that they should, in the future.

In general, it is evident that Britain has scored well on most of the dimensions of soft power – at least those that have been subject to measurement or structured assessment. In a range of ways, British society and its institutions remain attractive to the rest of the world, whatever the government of the time might or might not do. Britain's rule of law, political institutions, prosperity, its heritage, arts and culture, its education and literature, its international language, sporting profiles, its leading international companies and prominent global individuals, the daily projection of its fundamental values have all given it an enviable position as a country with significant soft power assets that are well recognized throughout the world.

But on the other hand, recent research also indicates that most of these desirable characteristics were accidents of history more than deliberate policy, and as the global balance of power inexorably shifts and as other countries compete more vigorously for international attention, it is clear that Britain faces a crossroads. If it is to seize the 'Brexit moment' and deploy smart power more efficiently, it faces three interlinked challenges. First, the emerging trends of the 2020s all point to a diminution of Britain's physical capacity in those assets that tended to be used at the harder end of the spectrum – a lower absolute capacity in those military, security and economic instruments that are under the government's direct control. This will be the case for all European countries, and Britain will feel the strain in much the same way as them, regardless of the fact that it is outside the EU. Second, the current evidence on soft power also suggests that Britain's status in the rankings is not as robust as its natural and historical soft power advantages might imply. Other countries are making vigorous efforts, and spending a good deal of money, to catch up. Given that soft power is such a long-term and essentially laissez-faire phenomenon, it is not clear that the competitors will be so quickly rewarded for their efforts and expenditure. But they are clearly targeting Britain and the other mid-range powers who are leaders in soft power as their immediate competitors. As one official source expressed it, Britain's status as a leading soft power player in world politics, generally described as 'enviable', was now 'vulnerable', even 'precarious', and Britain was perceived in the world as falling behind in some key sectors such as science and innovation – on which so much of its previous reputation, and hopes for the future, rested.[24] Third, the Covid-19 crisis and the attendant economic disruption made it very difficult for the British government to focus on the fundamental reform it wanted to initiate in its approaches to the external world and its desire to translate its determination to use power 'smartly' into a series of concrete policy ideas with the machinery and resources to back them up. Indeed, just as the government was announcing its integrated approach to soft power, it was also controversially cutting its overseas aid budget under the strain of Covid-19 economic pressure. The strategic logic of this was very hard to discern and ministers squirmed under the sustained criticism that followed.

For this reason, we present in the following section a brief audit of Britain's soft power capabilities – audited in terms of the relationships of which they are a part and understood in the way they are perceived by others. And to investigate soft power more carefully in these terms, we have chosen not to focus on institutions per se, since there are so many of them that have a potential soft power role to play within a modern digitalized society like Britain, operating in a highly globalized world. Instead, we try to define some broad categories of behaviour, most of which cross several institutional boundaries, as a way of understanding what Britain brings to power relationships at the softer end of the spectrum – what it already does, and what it might do more and better if it is properly understood and nurtured with rather more care than hitherto.

The government will have some immediate opportunities to test its ambitious approach to the country's soft power for the 2020s. In 2022 the XXII Commonwealth Games will be staged in Birmingham. The year will mark Queen Elizabeth's Platinum Jubilee. The Church of England's periodical (and delayed) Lambeth Conference is due to take place. The BBC will mark its centenary year. Not least, the 'Festival of the UK', announced after the Brexit vote to 'bring people together', will champion British innovation in 2022. Subsequently, 2023 and 2024 will include the twenty-fifth anniversaries of the Good Friday Agreement in Northern Ireland, the Welsh Assembly being opened and the Scottish executive receiving devolved powers. The notion of 'British soft power' will be on many minds during these events. Our hope is that it will also be better understood in the context of the British society that events like these have the power to reflect.

Part Two

Britain's persuaders

4

The convenors

Bringing interests together

In November 2021 Britain convened the 'COP26' UN Climate Change Conference in Glasgow and made much of the diplomatic opportunities it offered to show Britain taking a lead, on behalf of the United Nations, on the need to deal more internationally and effectively with environmental stress. It was a good example of high-profile 'convening'. But a really spectacular example had been set in virtual convening in April 2021 by US president Joe Biden who created a Leaders' Summit on Climate. President Trump had taken the United States out of the UN forum to tackle climate change and set his face against any recognition that climate change was a genuine global problem. On his first day in office, however, President Biden reversed this policy and then announced that he would convene a 'summit' as soon as possible to encourage the major powers to make hard commitments on carbon emission reductions for the future. Only three months later, no fewer than forty leaders from around the world, including China's Xi Jinping, Russia's President Putin, Indian Prime Minister Modi and Brazil's President Bolsonaro, all lined up on giant screens to announce the percentage reductions and the target dates by which their states would now reduce their carbon emissions.

The stark lesson was that when the United States decides to take a lead on something and really commits itself to a significant policy initiative, no one else can afford to ignore it. When the United States 'convenes' *and* takes a policy lead, everyone pays attention. So far, this can only truly be said of the United States. It represents an enviable diplomatic asset that other countries would imitate if they could, and they look for opportunities – as Britain did in COP26 – to exercise their own sort of convening diplomacy where they can.

'Diplomacy', however, is a big concept and is not just the business of diplomats. It is the collective term we give to the way states, organizations and individuals relate to each other. Diplomacy can be good or bad, successful or unsuccessful, aggressive or gently persuasive. Of course, there is a certain profession of diplomacy among those who are professionally trained to be diplomats which regards it as a special skill: a way of looking at events that facilitate the best mutual outcomes in the circumstances. Britain's own Diplomatic Service, as run by the Foreign, Commonwealth and Development Office (FCDO), is a small cadre of professionally trained people with very specific roles to perform on behalf of British national interests, as the government specifies them. In 2015 Britain opened a Diplomatic Academy (now International Academy), specifically to help train FCDO staff and other officials working internationally in the skills and background needed to deliver foreign policy.[1] Professional diplomats, like lawyers, see it as their job to represent the interests of their client without much personal bias or individual emotion but with a hard-headed realism over what can be achieved.

Nevertheless, 'national diplomacy' is practised by a much wider group of people than the professional diplomats in any nation's foreign ministry. Politicians, leaders of national organizations, the business community, civic and religious leaders or various trade associations all contribute to what might be regarded as a country's national diplomacy, even if some of them are not fully aware of it. The various 'diplomatic messages' they send, or the way they present the country's interests, or their ability to arrive dispassionately at the best possible outcomes may be only partly consistent, or frankly contradictory, with the British government's own conception of the national interest. Most of these people are not, after all, trained diplomats with terms of reference set by central government. But for good or ill, they all contribute in their own ways to Britain's diplomatic presence in the world.

Whatever they represent, one of the greatest advantages that both professional diplomats and the wider diplomatic community can confer on British diplomacy is the power to convene. The ability to bring different foreign interests together to discuss, debate, decide – even just to carouse together between times – is a considerable diplomatic advantage. The convenors tend to set the international agenda of whatever is under discussion, or if not, at least to influence it. The convenors tend to 'own the outcomes' of international meetings and engagement. Convenors can make things happen in the globalized world, especially where they have the confidence to step back and let others take due credit for any progress. The power to convene is one of the more subtle, often unobtrusive, exercises of soft power in global politics. Convenors come in all shapes and sizes, some explicitly governmental, others deep within the non-governmental and private sectors.

Not everyone can be an effective international convenor. Certain hard-won attributes are normally required. Successful convenors need some international credibility in the field under discussion; or they need to be one of the leading players in it themselves. They may have convening power because they are so intrinsic to the issue that they cannot be ignored. Or they may have convening power because they are regarded as effective mediators or honest brokers between different interests in that field. They may have convening power because they just have a good reputation for efficient diplomacy and implementation or because they have the power to follow up discussions with effective action. They may be acceptable convenors because they have active links to different, perhaps antagonistic, interests that are not otherwise connected. Not least, successful convenors are usually able to play a long game, exploiting some erstwhile respect or regard that makes others listen when they have something to say.

For example, a convening government might want to act as an international mediator in a long-running international conflict. The United States, as a superpower, has enormous convening power when it tries to mediate, as it has over many years in Arab-Israeli disputes and as it did in late 2020 regarding intra-Arab disputes in the Gulf – though 'convening' is no guarantee of success, even for a superpower. On the other hand, the United States stepped into the Balkan crisis in the mid-1990s, convening all the parties together at Dayton Ohio – effectively locking them in until they came to an agreement – and then Washington 'owned' the outcome, effectively dictating how it would all be implemented. By contrast, Russia tried to act as a convenor in order to mediate a peace settlement in the Syrian civil war in 2012 and again in 2013. But unlike the Balkan case, Russia was regarded an active participant on the side of the Assad regime and its mediation was widely interpreted as a largely cosmetic exercise to cover its drive to give a ruthless victory to its client government in Damascus. Very small governments might have effective convening powers for other reasons. Norway, Switzerland and Sweden have long-held reputations as effective and patient mediators in conflicts in which they themselves have no direct interests. The tiny, gas-rich state of Qatar has acted as a surprisingly effective convenor in a few cases where it used its own personal links to governments and leaders who otherwise would not sit down together.

Non-governmental organizations may be effective international convenors for their own reasons, perhaps because they operate international protocols to regulate some global activity or want to improve functional international arrangements in some way. ICANN, for instance, is one of the least known and most significant convening organizations in modern history. ICANN regulates the domain names and numerical spaces available to everyone on the internet. It is a non-profit organization that describes itself as a 'multi-stakeholder group' acting on behalf of the global commons. Its regular work goes unreported and is largely taken for granted, but if it did not operate as a single coordinating body, global connectivity would simply not exist in the way it does.[2] Equally, a private organization may be an international convenor because a significant international community might be part of its essential nature. Religious leaders and centres are natural convenors in this sense, having adherents in different parts of the world. Thus, the Pope, or the Dalai Lama, has the natural power to convene a public conversation within their international religious communities, even if no actual meetings take place. The Anglican Communion, led from Lambeth Palace in London, is both a natural and an actual convening organization among the 85 million Anglican adherents, speaking over 2,000 languages in no fewer than 165 countries in the world.*

It is often observed that Britain has an enviable reputation as a country that has the power 'to convene'.[3] That implies it is taken seriously if it tries, on its own authority, to create international momentum on a particular subject or create the basis for some sort of multinational engagement. It must choose its issues carefully. In the immediate aftermath of the economic crisis of 2008, Britain tried very hard, and was largely successful, in convening the global powers and financial organizations within the G20 framework to ward off the worst effects of the crisis and avoid a complete meltdown. Britain didn't engineer the outcome – bigger forces were needed to do that – but it had the attributes to be a principal convenor of those forces at the right moment in the cycle of the event.[4]

In the troubled and distracted decade that followed, however, Britain did not show itself keen to act as a convenor on some of the bigger political issues that mattered to it, such as the Ukraine crisis and the Russian annexation of Crimea, the civil war in Syria, the European migration crisis, the effective collapse of arms control in Europe or the security meltdown in Libya and across the Sahel region. It had policies on all these issues but made no serious attempts to shape the international agenda by convening the effective players, either formally or informally. It was essentially reactive in all cases.[5] On the other hand, these years saw Britain turn to its convening powers on a different order of issues – preventing sexual violence in conflict, tackling modern slavery and people trafficking, media freedom and social media truthfulness, recognizing the

---

*   There are officially 7,111 different languages spoken in the world today, not counting dialects. The Anglican Communion therefore operates in 28 per cent of them. See www.archbishopofcanterbury .org/about/anglican-communion.

importance of disability within domestic societies and addressing some of the uncomfortable truths about corruption and misconduct in the international aid agencies, including in British agencies. In 2018 the government suspended all new funding for Oxfam following allegations of personal misconduct by the charity's field workers arising from 2011, and in 2021 it repeated Oxfam's exclusion after more allegations arising from long-standing operations in the Democratic Republic of Congo.[6] In 2021 Britain put a great deal of diplomatic capital into its convening role for the COP26 climate change conference in Glasgow. If there had been a lack of confidence and commitment at the grand strategic level, there was nevertheless a willingness to engage as an international convenor on some of the human dimensions of world politics where the governments felt they could offer effective chairing.

How, then, should we describe the size and shape of Britain's convening powers, and by what standards should we judge their impact and effectiveness abroad?

Britain's natural convenors

The power to convene naturally overlaps with professional diplomacy. Individual ambassadors, as much as foreign ministries as a whole, spend much of their time convening a range of foreign and domestic interests as they go about their work. Any ambassador might find themselves convening business representatives or civic groups in the countries where they work to meet with individual companies or prominent organizations and individuals from their home country, promoting city linkages, art exchanges or running national exhibitions to commemorate some significant date in the bilateral relations between countries. They are 'convening' all the time. The role of government personnel and organizations – ministries, political leaders and diplomats – will be discussed in the next chapter. We are interested here in the organizations and groups that may be the less obvious convenors. Some are closer to central government than others and more naturally part of the official British approach to the world. And some are semi-detached, or completely separate, exercising their convening powers according to their own interests.

The two most effective convening institutions that Britain officially deploys are undoubtedly the Royal Family and – closely related to it – the Commonwealth. At least in formal terms, both have an astonishing reach and few other states have anything comparable to them with similar convening power. Very few international leaders are too busy to respond to an invitation from the British monarch or the institution of the Royal Family. For reasons of curiosity and mystique as much as grandeur and tradition, it has repeatedly demonstrated its powers to bring people and organizations together around the world, whether at a royal residence, corporate headquarters or even at a local community hall. The collaborative results can be quietly effective.

As a constitutional monarchy in a parliamentary democracy, the British Royal Family cannot have a political or executive role, but it convenes a very wide array of people and organizations, playing as it does so a uniquely subtle role that backs up the work of the government. Downing Street certainly does not set the royal agenda – not least because that agenda is established up to two years, or more, ahead. But then, the personal staffs serving the Royal Family will make sure that their principals undertake work that is generically useful to Britain in the world, particularly engagements selected for Royal Tours that are organized by the FCDO.

Though there have been some well-publicized personal embarrassments among some of the royal principals themselves – around the estrangement and death of Princess Diana, around the withdrawal from public life of Prince Andrew or the move of Prince Harry and his wife to live in the United States – the synergizing system that exists between the royals and the government actually works well. And none of these embarrassments have dimmed the convening power of British royalty or the representational work that the whole family does. During 2019–20, members of the Royal Family undertook almost 3,200 official engagements between them, 296 involving HM The Queen. Over 139,000 guests responded to the magnetism of an invitation to one of the royal residences, particularly for garden parties and various investitures.[7] During 2021, despite Covid-19 restrictions, the monarchy was more visible than ever. The 'Oprah interview' on 7 March was viewed by 17.1 million in the United States and over 49 million worldwide.[8] It shone a spotlight, and cast a shadow, over the British royal household – presenting accusations of racism and neglect of mental health issues. The following month, the funeral of HRH The Duke of Edinburgh was watched by some 13 million in the UK,[9] and the surrounding coverage told the story of Prince Philip as a young outsider who had been instrumental in modernizing the monarchy during the reign of Elizabeth II. The juxtaposition inside two months was jarring. Some of the most touching photographs released at the time of Prince Philip's funeral were taken by the Countess of Wessex and the Duchess of Cornwall; women from within the Royal Family captured images that helped marry the necessary formality of a state occasion with a deeply personal one.[10]

The essence of royal convening has not traditionally been to negotiate or mediate; that would be inappropriate and politically charged. But these activities generally aim to connect problems with solutions, or at least to sources of support, and to reinforce the identification of common goals. The work of the Prince of Wales and his office has been particularly focussed on just these sorts of outputs in relation to environmental stress, climate change, the built environment and to the engagement of younger members of society with these sorts of challenges. The Prince's Trust, for example, since it was established in 1976, has reached more than 825,000 young people through its education, employment and training programmes.

For historical reasons the modern Commonwealth is intrinsically linked to the Royal Family and provides a very extensive convening forum that tries to achieve largely the same objectives: linking problems with solutions, potential sources of support, and articulating common goals. Indeed, the modern Commonwealth evolved largely as an organization whose *primary* purpose was to convene its own members. No one designed the Commonwealth or wrote a constitution for it that enshrined its future objectives. It evolved as a pragmatic British response, first to an Empire that included major Dominions that were all very different, then as a way of smoothing the path to British decolonization, creating the so-called modern Commonwealth, and thence to an organization that has taken on useful and positive post hoc rationales and has now admitted new members who were never British colonies at all.[11] The Commonwealth of Nations, as it is now more formally known, performs (but also fails to perform) in many spheres of activity it now designates as priorities for the future. But whether successful or not in its adopted goals, its fifty-four members across all six continents regard the Commonwealth primarily as a unique forum in which to convene. Its particular size and shape are not replicated in any other international forum.

Commonwealth Day in 2019 marked seventy years since the founding eight nations came together to agree the London Declaration, conducted back then 'in an atmosphere of goodwill and mutual understanding . . . united as free and equal members of the Commonwealth of Nations, freely co-operating in the pursuit of peace, liberty and progress'.[12] The fifty-four nations – large and small, rich and poor – that make up the modern Commonwealth are home to one-third of the world's population, 60 per cent of whom are under the age of thirty.[13] The members meet formally through the mechanisms of the quadrennial Commonwealth Games, the biennial Commonwealth heads of government meeting (CHOGM) and many of them, annually, on Commonwealth Day.

As HM The Queen is the symbolic head of the Commonwealth, Britain can still be considered *primus inter paras* when it comes to convening the member states – but, as it has found on many occasions, Britain cannot direct them. Much of the real diplomatic value of the Commonwealth lies in the opportunities to network and connect and – from Britain's perspective – to access the myriad of inter-Commonwealth relationships. The Commonwealth Parliamentary Association, the Association of Commonwealth Universities, the Commonwealth Scholarship Commission, all based from London, are lauded officially as symbols of British commitment to the organization, but they are also institutions of Britain's convening influence within the organization. The emotional bonds of the Commonwealth were particularly audible in the wake of the death of HRH The Duke of Edinburgh. In a statement the following day, the prime minister of Australia offered a very affecting message to Queen Elizabeth: we 'say to you as a Commonwealth, let us also now be your strength and stay, as you continue to endure, as you continue to serve so loyally and so faithfully, as you have done over so many generations. She has been there for us over such a long time. Let us be there now for you'.[14]

Nevertheless, though the sentiment honouring the role of royalty is habitually expressed, there is persistent disappointment that Britain somehow fails to get the best out of all the Commonwealth really offers. It cannot easily be mobilized to a single, high political purpose, but the organization offers unique networks of human linkages between so many peoples. Human networks that cross cultures are more valuable and important than ever, and the Commonwealth seems to be an ideal forum among different peoples that, if it did not already exist, would now be very difficult to create. The organization runs initiatives it calls the 'Commonwealth Network' which includes, for example, a forum of national human rights institutions, and the Commonwealth convenes a 'People's Forum' every two years ahead of its heads of government meetings. But many still argue that, unlike the Royal Family, the British political establishment has been slow, or even frankly reluctant, to embrace the unique human networking opportunities on offer. A re-think is required, say some, and a 'Commonwealth mark two' should be outlined by the organization's premier member.[15]

A British government agency that occupies an interesting grey area between official policy and independent control of its agenda is the British Council. Unlike the Commonwealth, it is an exclusively British organization, but it is intended to operate with a great deal of independence and flexibility. And like the Commonwealth, it is also a natural convenor as it goes about its work. The Council receives government grant-in-aid funding – some £161 million in

2019–20 – but operates as a separate and autonomous agency. Almost ten times more funding for the Council is raised as revenue through earned income, almost £1.2 billion in that year.[16] By any standards, this makes it a commercially successful organization. Part of its business success clearly derives from its pseudo-official status as an agency of the British government. It could hardly be so commercially successful without this cache. Yet its real unique selling point is its credibility as an honest source of information and comment not about government policy but about the nature of Britain *as a society*. For years the establishment of the British Council was somewhat unique among Britain's competitor nations. It was established in 1934 in an enlightened attempt to promote the English language, particularly in Eastern Europe, and so find subtle ways to counter the worrying rise of fascism. Until recently, there were few direct counterparts to it and the Council has shown more genuine independence than the departments of public affairs – usually housed within foreign ministries – of many other countries. As such, the Council's credibility is obviously to the long-term advantage of British government, even if its portrayals may be unflattering to a particular administration. But government figures and MPs regularly decide that the British Council is not reflecting government perspectives closely enough.[17] The greatest fear for its senior staff, reportedly, is 'instrumentalization' – being used directly as a government instrument and thus having its credibility and independence in the wider world fatally undermined.[18]

The Council undertakes a wide range of work, aiming to create personal and inter-societal connections on the basis of arts, culture, education and the English language. In 2020 it claimed to have reached 80 million people directly and over 790 million people around the world overall through its online work, broadcasts and publications.[19] In a sense, almost ninety years of government support and investment in the British Council represents a long-term bet on openness, independence and honesty as an instrument of convening for the sake of soft power.

Closely related to the history of the British Council and often operating in conjunction with it is the FCDO's institution commonly known as Wilton Park – an estate in East Sussex that hosts meetings of all sorts sponsored or at least with the approval of Whitehall. Again, it has a pseudo-independent role from the government even though the FCDO core-funds it and Wilton Park would not survive if that were withdrawn. Wilton Park began in this role immediately after the Second World War, hosting more than 4,000 German prisoners of war (POWs) for re-education classes, where they were visited by such luminaries as Bertrand Russell, William Beveridge and the first female MP, Lady Nancy

Astor. POW classes ended in 1948 and Wilton Park gradually widened its remit to other European countries, then Asia and Africa and then, with US money, to North America. It became the quiet venue for Anglo-French discussions after 1973 concerning the enlargement of the EEC. Highly sensitive discussions were held there with South African representatives. And it played its due role as the iron curtain crumbled across Europe in the late 1980s and everyone wanted to speak, and be accurately translated, off the record. The organization sets its own conference agenda and claims that it is 'building and curating trusted global networks', alongside the services it provides to the FCDO's diplomatic initiatives. Most governments run similar foreign ministry facilities and undertake the same range of work. But among them, Wilton Park has some of the biggest and most long-standing convening networks and the pedigree to be able to use them with some effect.[20]

The Anglican Church is a great natural convenor, with a typically British anomaly at its core that gives it a certain sort of unique power to convene different interests. The Anglican Church is the established church of the country. And though 'established' with a formal role in the constitution and within Parliament, and deeply entrenched within the institution of the monarchy, and as an upholder of evolving British values, the Anglican Church is, in practice, highly independent. There are few 'established' churches in the world with more independence from their state or a more effective working relationship with their secular and multicultural societies than the Anglican Church in Britain.

Lambeth Palace is the London home of the Archbishop of Canterbury and the centre of his ministry and hospitality. Since the arrival of Augustine to Britain in 597, the archbishop's own See has been at Canterbury. The Anglican Communion is the vast worldwide community of worshippers, across over 165 countries, organized into more than forty provinces. Each province has a reciprocal relationship with the See of Canterbury and recognizes the Archbishop of Canterbury as spiritual head. Yet there is no central authority in the Anglican Communion. All of the provinces are autonomous and free to make their own decisions in their own ways, guided by recommendations from the four Instruments of Communion: that is, the Archbishop of Canterbury, the Lambeth Conference, the Primates' Meeting and the Anglican Consultative Council. It is in this respect that the Archbishop of Canterbury and the staff at Lambeth Palace, standing beside the River Thames, has a convening power with more extensive reach than any single FCDO department or official. The magnetism is not felt uniformly; for some provinces the 'Anglican Communion' carries more meaning than for others, who prefer to act independently on matters of doctrine and practice. The Anglican Communion has, for example, found itself deeply divided on the matter of female bishops or gay rights, trying to reconcile some deep cultural differences between communities around the world. Of course, it cannot always reconcile them, but at least it can always convene them to discuss their differences, which is more than many foreign ministries are able to do.

The Lambeth Conference is an important assembly of bishops worldwide, meeting every ten years to discuss one particular issue that matters to them. Lambeth Conferences began in 1896 and have been one of the most high-profile, and regular, international convening forums across any world religion. That does not make them automatically harmonious. The fourteenth Lambeth Conference in 2008 tried to concentrate on 'listening and a prayerful mission', but in the event was preoccupied with loud controversies over gay clergy and same-sex marriage that centred on the stance taken by the Episcopal part of the Anglican Communion in the United States. The fifteenth Lambeth Conference, delayed because of the Covid-19 crisis, was eventually scheduled in 2022.

Even if it wished to, the organs of the British state could not operationalize the Anglican Church to its own ends. But it is fair to consider the church as background music to national life. There is an Anglican church at the heart of almost every community in Britain – often the most historic building in a village or town, architecture originally designed to inspire. There are over 16,000 of them in England, 12,500 officially listed by Historic England.[21] They can offer food, emotional support and a physical place to meet or shelter. And some have English-style bells for 'change ringing', rung on Sundays, christenings, weddings and funerals, and often part of major national occasions. Some churchmen think the social influence of the network of Anglican churches is drastically underrated.[22]

Less than two miles downriver from Lambeth Palace lies the City of London, a city inside a city. Around the north side of London Bridge, and these days with a high-rise appendage at Canary Wharf, 'the City' contains all the economic and financial power which that phrase conjures up. And it is surrounded by all the services and facilities, the churches, the heritage and the new start-ups, of the Corporate City of London itself. Like the layers of an onion, the financial city sits within the Corporate City of London and that in turn sits within what most people take to be London – greater London – that now extends, at least in the imagination, to that large circle of communities enclosed by the M25.

In the 2021 Boston Consulting Group's global survey of 209,000 working professionals, looking at their preferences for 'work relocation', Britain was rated the fifth most desirable country in the world, both in 2018 and again in 2020, in which to relocate. But 'London', however respondents understood the term, was rated in first place and ahead of New York as the most desirable city in which to live and work.[23] All this offers an internationally unique role to the City of London as a soft power asset. Nor is it much affected by Brexit, whatever effect that may eventually have on London's financial status. In 2021 fewer than 8,000 jobs in the financial services industry had moved into the EU, within a sector that employs around a million people.

The Lord Mayor of London, as distinct from the very recent establishment in 2000 of the metropolitan Mayor of London, is head of the City of London Corporation – the governing body for the Square Mile (the 'City'). The Lord Mayor serves as an international ambassador for Britain's financial and professional services sector. The first London mayor in 1189 was a draper named Henry FitzAilwin and, yes, Dick Whittington was a mercer who famously held the post no fewer than four times between 1397 and 1419. 'Nowadays, the Lord Mayor has a major international convening role to perform. There are plenty of good stories to tell and it is the Lord Mayor's job to tell them, at home and abroad.'[24] The role, so historic and rotating every year, cannot be executive and therefore is almost entirely one of convening, in the same way – and often for identical purposes – as that of the Royal Family. She or he who is Lord Mayor for the year hosts at Mansion House visiting heads of state, heads of government and foreign dignitaries on behalf of the monarch and government. It is a hard-eating but great honour that successive Lord Mayors have performed with considerable panache.

Alongside Britain's formal diplomatic and political machinery, these are only some of the most obvious British convenors acting across the international world. There is a plethora of less obvious organizations and linkages that seek to facilitate different types of international convening, either as a way to help achieve their objectives or as a natural expression of what they are there to do.

No fewer than 670 cities and towns across Britain, for example, are twinned with counterpart communities, mostly in France and Germany. In many cases, one British location has multiple twins abroad. Coventry, famously twinned with Dresden in Germany – both of which suffered dreadful civilian bombing in the Second World War – is also paired with twenty other countries worldwide.[25] Birmingham will host the Commonwealth Games in 2022 and leverage that event to create even more city-twinning linkage than the seven it officially operates at presently.

What began as civic friendship mainly between towns, however, has gone some way beyond that as major cities in Western countries have begun to exercise greater autonomy from their own central governments, establishing tangible policy links with counterpart cities elsewhere in the world. The political power of cities is rising dramatically. Around 4.6 billion people – almost 60 per cent of the global population – already live in cities, and that proportion is steadily rising. All Western countries are feeling the decentralizing effects of globalization and the consequent demands for more power to be exercised at local and individual levels.[26] The dictatorships and autocracies resist decentralization, though they pretend that their major cities exercise more autonomous powers than they do. But there are already more than 40 cities with populations in excess of 10 million, and London is not yet quite among their number. Political and economic power is increasingly bound up in any state's great urban centres. Cities can succeed even where the state itself is failing. But the reverse is not true; for the first time in history, no modern state can succeed if its cities fail. All the great capitalist cities of the world, therefore, try more than ever to learn directly from each other, on 'smart city' innovation, green energy, housing, urban regeneration, transport, social policy, policing, community innovation and much besides.

The significant international linkages between major cities in the world constitute a powerful and surprising set of networks, presented in Appendix 1.

Drawing strength from Britain's long-standing international reputation for nurturing mature cities, civic planning and technical innovation, British city leaders have found the political space over recent years to act as international convenors on their own behalf, sometimes initiating, sometimes responding, to collaborative initiatives. They both contribute to and benefit from Britain's natural soft power assets in this way. All major Western cities perform some such role and the results naturally show considerable variations. But British cities generally regard themselves as effective convenors.

And then there are all the business, trade, chambers of commerce and professional associations – more than 400 significant ones in Britain. Where Britain is seen as a significant presence – or at least within the top tier of countries in a particular field – such as aerospace, pharmaceuticals, agriculture, computing, electronics, retailing, finance, law, insurance, in particular, there is a corresponding international influence in their professional bodies. Organizations like ADS in the aerospace and defence business, the Financial Conduct Authority or the Chartered Society of Designers provide typically diverse examples. A British organization, or indeed an international organization that chooses to base itself in Britain, in areas of particular national strength, has more convening power than one from a country that is not regarded as top tier in such fields. Whether or not they can shape the sector around particular interests, their organizational voice has some power. They can convene the attention of other players within their own industry or sector.

Convening in the current global environment

Opportunities and instruments for international convening, of course, are not in themselves any guarantee of success. We live in transformational times in most areas of human existence, not least in the political and social spheres. The traditional hubs of national political power – at the governmental level – are being dispersed outwards into the international arena and downwards towards the non-governmental and individual levels. The considerable number of autocracies and dictatorships in the world try to buck this trend, though even with all their populism and domestic repression, it seems likely that their centralization will not make them into more successful societies, though it may keep their leaders in power for a long time. Even in present-day China – the great outlier and human experiment that tests all other political trends – the repression that supports a one-party state is nevertheless accompanied by economic decentralization that disperses Beijing's power among China's different regions and sectors.

We live, it has been said many times, in 'An Age of Distrust',[27] as well as in a 'New Economic Age' where different economic processes and new arbiters of economic power have quickly appeared on the international scene.[28] In these circumstances having the power to 'convene' is more than a matter of having a legacy, a track record or even the sheer political or economic weight to be taken seriously. Contrary to a previous idea famously articulated by Marshall McLuhan in 1964, and seemingly reinforced by the first phase of the social media revolution half a century later, that 'the medium becomes the message', successful convening has actually been seen to result from something far more substantial than mere communication.[29] The medium is important and has changed and diversified out of all recognition in recent years. Even Marshall McLuhan could have had no idea how revolutionary modern communications would eventually be, when he understood the attractions and ubiquity of the 'medium' in his day. 'Convening' has never been easier or cheaper. But the very ubiquity of the modern medium makes the substance of convening more important still. Mere connection is not enough.

Put simply, it may be said that successful convening must display some basic qualities. Successful convening must be for a purpose – not for its own sake. Successful convenors may be putting their own direct interests in abeyance in favour of promoting a multinational dialogue in their sector or playing it long to reap the eventual benefits of an environment more suited to their interests. But convening must have purpose and objectives – something that all participants agree are worth discussing and perhaps something for which they are prepared to meet many times in open-ended dialogue. Meeting for its own sake does not convey any power or prestige to the convenor of it.

The successful convenor must also be authentic – a genuine and significant player in the particular field, or a sincere mediator to whom the outcome matters, or a chairing agent whose reputation would suffer in the event of outright failure. A successful convenor must have some real skin in the game and not be perceived as merely opportunist or simply playing to an international gallery.

And just as evidently, successful convenors must maintain engagement with all the players. Very few significant international decisions or arrangements are arrived at quickly, even fewer of them implemented and followed through speedily. Successful convening is not for the impatient or the faint-hearted. Taking decisions or agreeing on new norms or procedures often turns out to be the easy part. Putting together a coalition of necessary implementing agencies, and *holding it together* long enough for something to change, or something else to be created, requires constant and persistent engagement by the convenor. The international agreements and understandings that either quickly run out of steam or simply never get past the initial agreement are too numerous to count. The United Nations Organization is littered with them.

Successful convening, it might be said, whether in the governmental sphere or in the private and economic sectors, is a job for professionals. And in the ephemeral 'post-truth world' of the 2020s, the power to convene international others in favour of some free, liberal, democratic, political, human or economic purpose – authentically and with courageous and committed engagement – has never been so important.[30]

The officials

Speaking softly

In January 2021 Sir Brian Urquhart died at the age of 101. He had served as a British civil servant to the United Nations since before its first Security Council meeting at Church House in London in 1945; he was the de facto secretary-general until the official appointment of Trygve Lie to the post, and he continued to serve and advise the next four secretaries-general until his retirement in 1986. His was a most effective diplomatic career, largely in the shadows, that had a remarkable influence on the way the UN navigated its way through the tricky early years of the Cold War. And when the Cold War came to an end in the late 1980s, it was in no small measure because of the demands for human rights across the Soviet bloc that had been stimulated by the Conference on Security and Cooperation in Europe – the CSCE that had been running for years. In the early 1970s the British ambassador to Russia noted that bilateral relations had improved sharply, according to official documents, because of 'Russian recognition of the leading role being played by British diplomats in determining western tactics during the CSCE'.[1] It was the British who pushed the potential for offering Moscow a grand package deal – statements that the West would accept the territorial status quo in Europe in return for Russian commitments to agreed standards of human rights. They were some way ahead of US Secretary of State Henry Kissinger on this one. And Moscow could not have guessed that making human rights commitments would so undermine the political control Russia thought it had wrought from the West in the grand bargain it accepted.[2]

There are any number of examples that might be cited from memoirs and papers covering what now seem to be the halcyon days of Britain's quiet diplomacy, particularly during the second half of the last century when Britain's persuasive diplomatic influence appeared to be disproportionately greater than its physical resources.[3] Some of those skills still evidently persist, but the context in which British diplomats can 'speak softly' and have such effects has just as evidently changed in the present age of globalization.[4]

Everyone's a diplomat

We discussed in the previous chapter how British diplomacy is not the preserve only of professional diplomats. Nevertheless, formal, professionalized diplomacy remains very important in the way Britain pursues its interests in the world. Foreign officials and business communities look to Britain's diplomats and the Foreign, Commonwealth and Development Office as their first point of contact in understanding the British government's position on any matter, and the job of all diplomats is to get out and about and make contacts with as many people as possible who might have some bearing on their area of responsibility.[5]

This sort of formal diplomacy has broadened a great deal in the modern era. Britain's official diplomats now have to handle a wider range of foreign groups and issues than ever before and need to show competence and understanding in technical areas that are a long way from the broadly political relations between one government and another. It is also the case that other British officials from many sectors across Her Majesty's Government have important diplomatic roles to perform as they go about their own jobs.[6]

In other words, in a highly globalized world, everyone in the top echelons of HMG is liable to have some linkage to Britain's external policies and to shaping its reputation in the world. Everyone's a diplomat, though a small cadre of trained personnel are more formally so than others. But 'British officials' – synonymous with 'HMG' to the outside world – come in all shapes and sizes and can represent any part of government as far as other nationalities are concerned.

A basic flowchart depicting those parts of central government that are regularly involved in Britain's external environment would have to list the Foreign, Commonwealth and Development Office, the Ministry of Defence, the Treasury (alongside the independent Bank of England), the Home Office, the Department for International Trade, the Department of Business, Energy and Industrial Strategy, the Ministry of Justice and the Attorney General's Office; as well as the major agencies that work formally within these ministries, such as the intelligence services, the police, Border Force, Her Majesty's Revenue and Customs, the National Crime Agency or the National Cyber Security Centre. There is also the central coordinating machinery – that within the Cabinet Office, plus the key policy and advisory staff at No.10, and the bureaucracy around the National Security Council. Then too, there is an extensive system of parliamentary oversight for all this, which, in itself, draws on relations with other legislatures internationally. The average flowchart would show these different departments and organizations touching the outside world through Britain's overseas posts run by the FCDO, through the foreign outreach of other formal bodies and agencies such as the police, the extensive liaison and training work of the three armed services, and through a host of inter-parliamentary links and comparable arrangements between legislative bodies.[7]

But the modern reality of these international policy nerve-endings is more complicated again. The national economy and civil society in both the domestic and international spheres are far more intimately connected to the central policy-making process. For however well or badly national policy is made, the implementation of it is mediated through many elements of domestic and international civil society even as the official implementers get busy in their agencies and embassies, carrying out instructions to make policy work in the outside world. And those implementers must work back into Britain's own civil society and economy as they carry out their instructions. There is a constant iteration between the implementers of policy and the targets of it. This would not be thought unusual in the case of traditional domestic policy, as in health, local government or education, where there has to be an ongoing process of learning and policy adjustment as the targets of policy so closely interact with the implementers of it. But in many respects, this is now the case for external relations as well. Domestic and foreign policy are increasingly difficult to tell apart. Britain's trade deals with foreign countries, for example, might well be affected by the high politics in their region, say in Africa or Asia, but the practical effects on businesses or individuals of any deal will quickly circle back into Britain's civil society and economy and become part of ongoing policy discussions within ministries and agencies. Britain's foreign relations with China in recent years have been much exercised by Beijing's contempt for the Sino-British Joint Declaration on Hong Kong (which should have remained in force until 2047), by Britain's decision to freeze Huawei out of its 5G telecoms network and by Beijing's reactions to Britain's new naval deployments in East Asia. These are all specifically bilateral issues, outside the Western world's more general criticisms of China's trade policy, or its assertions of sovereignty in the South China Sea. The political fallout just from the bilateral issues, however, impacts directly and with some force on Britain's economy and society since Beijing always retaliates when it gets into particular rows with Western countries and normally does so by manipulating its economic muscle and large investment funds.[8] Adjustments usually have to be made regularly as the practical domestic effects of international policy are felt.

In former times the professional diplomats of the old Foreign Office had a global reputation for speaking softly, pragmatically and effectively, being persuasive by being classically good diplomats. Former ambassador Christopher Meyer records that Japanese diplomats had once made a particular study of several European diplomatic services and decided that they rated the British service the most highly.[9] In fact, a recently de-classified conversation back in February 1973 between US President Nixon and Henry Kissinger, his National Security Adviser at the time, virtually says it all:

> Nixon: And I actually think that our guys – I have the feeling about this being about the British. You may disagree. They're no longer a world power, but the British are bright and they think strategically. And I think the right British guy is better than the right guy in the State Department.
>
> Kissinger: No question.
>
> Nixon: Now, what I want you to do –
>
> Kissinger: They're better trained.
>
> Nixon: – What I want you to do – Take a fellow like [Sir Robert] Thompson. We haven't got anybody in our government that is as good as Thompson on that field. Take a fellow like that guy, that Alastair Buchan. I don't find many people around here in the State Department that think as, you know, in the broad terms . . . I would like you to take the best British brains and the best American brains and put them together.[10]

'Speaking softly' in those days was about exerting quiet influence in the right places. A British ambassador who served in Washington in 2016 knew that all the same principles still applied, if they could be realized fully.[11] None of this implies diplomatic meekness. Tough and resolute messages were all part of the stock in trade. But understanding the most effective and timely way to be tough and resolute is often as important as the message itself. British diplomacy, for instance in relation to the Soviet Union during the Cold War, within NATO or as a Security Council Permanent Member within the grandstanding arena of the United Nations, was traditionally regarded as constructive and generally successful. British diplomats at the UN and in many other international forums had a reputation as the natural drafters and crafters who could formulate compromise texts to which everyone could sign up. The diplomat and writer John Ure described his experience of diplomacy as 'building ladders for other people to climb down'. A later diplomat, Tom Fletcher, describes the task as *selling* such ladders for the same purpose: vigorous diplomacy for a more relaxed eventual outcome.[12]

More than that, British diplomacy frequently showed an ability to influence the general international environment in which more divisive policy questions would arise – sometimes, for example, by softening the interpretations of more ideologically driven US policy towards the European allies or else maintaining practical channels of communication between countries that had become antagonistic to one another. There were many ways in which British diplomacy helped to create an atmosphere of normality in times when international relations were, in reality, highly fraught. In the EU, perhaps the most sensitive of Britain's external arenas, the comments of an Irish ambassador are instructive:

> British influence in the EU went well beyond that available to most member states. The UK's impact was exceptional due to several factors. The quality of its civil servants. The effectiveness of its coordination mechanisms. The reach of its diplomacy. The potency of its networking. The admiration for its pragmatism. The predominance of the English language.[13]

Of course, good diplomats and civil servants could not save the country from obvious diplomatic disasters such as the Suez debacle in 1956, or from the constant rebuffs of the European Common Market when Britain was seeking to join in the 1960s, or the political fallout from the failed military campaigns in Iraq and Afghanistan in the 2000s. But, whether successful or not, the international world generally recognized the traditional strengths of Britain's professional diplomacy. Its diplomatic voice was heard, and British diplomats were regarded as consequential and useful allies to have.

Another highly successful strand of modern diplomacy that has shown Britain speaking softly but in a way everyone can hear has been through the diplomacy practised by its secret intelligence services. That was demonstrated nicely in the years from 2012 to 2018, from *Skyfall* to Skripal, in fact. James Bond's 23rd outing in *Skyfall* in 2012 was, by general consent, his best since the beginning of the famous film franchise. It was released in the year of the London Olympics and the Queen's Diamond Jubilee. Like them it was confident, self-aware and looked to the future. The intelligence services, particularly MI6, always insist they have no truck with James Bond (he's actually a truly terrible intelligence officer), but it still suits them to have their real HQ filmed and, apparently, blown up more than once. For an organization that was still officially secret until 1994, it was happy to be named in Bond films that had already been going for more than thirty years. The glamour may be completely inaccurate but it is quietly helpful to the security services and gives them a certain cache around the world. And when, in 2018, Russia's GRU tried to poison ex-spy Sergei Skripal in Salisbury, the Kremlin reacted with blanket denials followed by a strong disinformation campaign. But the simple fact is that the world believed what the British security services said had really happened. And they believed it again over clumsy Russian attempts to hack into the chemical weapons laboratories in the Hague investigating suspected Russian chemical attacks and again in Russian attempts to hack into the records of the World Anti-Doping Agency in Canada. The weight of British intelligence led to new international rules to keep the Hague's international laboratories more secure and protect their work in detecting the use or possession of chemical weapons. British intelligence services speak very softly indeed, but they have worldwide credibility for what they say.

It is an open question how much of this international respect, still less glamour, has carried through broadly to British diplomacy in recent years. The intelligence services are one of the few instruments of the British state that has been able to maintain the confidence and verve of 2012 over the decade since. Britain's Diplomatic Service still embodies some of the best traditions of the civil service, and compared with many other countries, its own policy coordination and the coherence with which it presents government policy remains generally good. British ambassadors and their staffs still command some prestige in the world by virtue of a long-standing Foreign Office reputation for being competent and constructive.

Then, too, the current FCDO has made a notable effort to embrace the world of social media without falling into some of its more obvious diplomatic traps. Aspects of British diplomacy are increasingly presented in no more than 280 characters. In 2016, Britain's @ForeignOffice Twitter account had one of the largest 'Twiplomatic' networks. Interestingly, in 2020 the FCDO also created a unique post for the consul general in San Francisco, combining it with the new role of Technology Envoy to the United States – Joe White became 'our man in cyber-space, speaking in fluent code', as one might say.[14]

On the other hand, while the FCDO is still responsible for running the range of British overseas posts around the world, the fact remains that the community of 'HMG officials' who express British diplomacy is an ever-diversifying group. Britain sent a powerful message of gender equality around the world when, in April 2021, the UK's heads of Mission across the G7, Five Eyes and at NATO, as well as highly significant ambassadorial postings in China, Russia and key Commonwealth countries like Nigeria and Kenya, were all female.[15]

The reorganized FCDO itself, having incorporated foreign aid functions, has seen its formal headcount jump from fewer than 5,300 to over 10,400 people as it has absorbed the foreign aid community. The Ministry of Defence includes 57,000 civilians, a significant proportion of whom have to consider Britain's various external partnerships as they do their jobs; and though organizations like MI6, the Police's International Crime Coordination Centre, Border Force or HMRC have relatively compact teams to interface at senior levels with their foreign counterparts, over thirty different British government functions are formally represented abroad, aside from all the direct interaction that Parliament or ongoing military missions and operations have in foreign countries.

'British diplomacy' is now less the preserve of the Diplomatic Service than was the case at any time in the 200 years before the turn of this century. And during the years of the Brexit hiatus after 2016 the role of the Foreign Office was emasculated to reorganize Whitehall more specifically for negotiating the Brexit terms with European partners and seeking specific trade deals across the wider world. The Brexit decision initiated the biggest strategic shift Britain had undertaken for over seventy years – much greater than in originally joining the European Union in 1973 – and the Foreign Office was little more than an observer to it.[16] As the process of leaving the EU was concluded at the end of 2020, the Foreign Office, now as the FCDO, was reorganized and its role nominally restored as part of a strengthened policy-making core in the government's 'Integrated Review' of 2021.[17] It remains to be seen how the role of the FCDO will develop amid a governmental structure that has been highly centralized around No.10 by both of the previous two governments – uniquely so by modern standards.

There are, therefore, clearly plusses and minuses in Britain's current diplomatic standing in the world and in its ability to 'influence' – without appearing explicitly to negotiate or press – the direction of events or to provide a model of diplomatic style and behaviour that other states would like to imitate. It may all sound a bit glib. The ability of a country to have subtle effects on the international world and to deploy well-respected diplomacy is based on a great deal more than its own expert diplomatic cadre or the strong civil service ethos which still runs through most 'HMG officialdom'. There are bigger issues to consider.

The essence of speaking softly

The first and most obvious reason why British officials enjoy some heritage of influence in world politics – speaking effectively and softly to help shape the environment – is because the country was traditionally seen to be closely associated with existing power centres and structures. Its twentieth-century role in the Western alliance and closeness to Washington, its involvement in the creation and running of the major financial institutions of the world, its own once-powerful single currency 'sterling area' of seventy-four states, its privileged position at the UN, its empire and resultant Commonwealth of Nations all seemed to give Britain the potential to exercise hard power if it wanted to, which made its soft power influence all the more potent. Foreign officials might take more notice of how their British counterparts went about their work because they knew they were dealing with a country that was itself entrenched in the international status quo and who could call, if necessary, on a range of assets that might be used in hard power ways to help maintain it. In the decades after 1945 Britain was far from being the most powerful state in the world, but it was closely connected to those that were and was widely seen to be on the right side of history – a leading, Western democracy that could defend its interests with competent armed forces. Skilled officials can produce many useful soft power dividends if they have that sort of accumulated diplomatic capital behind them.

A second element that has facilitated the broadly influential style of HMG officials is the degree to which the outside world sees British governmental, and government-related, activities as consistent and coherent.[18] The British government is traditionally seen as speaking with a single voice, coordinated from the centre. The United States, by contrast, with its extensive policy community and its constitution of checks and balances embodies very dominant political power, but its allies and adversaries alike often comment that US foreign policy on any matter depends on 'who you speak to'. The views of Congress, the White House, the State Department or the Pentagon, let alone political opinion across fifty separate states, often create a fragmented policy response that would be more damaging to US interests if it did not also enjoy the margins of error that being a superpower allows it.[19] Equally, the diplomacy of many of Britain's key European partners has, for different national reasons, been noted as less coordinated and coherent than is normally the case in Britain.[20] That does not imply that German, French or Italian foreign policies, for example, on any given issue are necessarily inferior to that of Britain. But London's stance in international negotiations or conferences has often been noted by third parties as being clearer, more consistent and frequently more proactive than other major European countries, regardless of whose policies seem, in the event, to be more productive. The reputation of British EU diplomacy during the Brexit policy hiatus between 2016 and 2020 was, it must be admitted, almost the complete antithesis of these virtues. The Foreign Office would point out that it was largely a bystander throughout this process; from start to finish, Brexit diplomacy was driven from the centre of the machine and not much of it was softly spoken. But this should be regarded, hopefully, as an outlier to an otherwise good reputation.

In practical terms, a reputation for policy consistency goes beyond the boundaries of formal diplomacy. It encompasses how Britain's intelligence services interpret events around the world, how its foreign aid is used and the impact it has abroad. It also includes separate British financial, technical or training support for peace-building and conflict resolution activities in unstable foreign regions that matter to Britain. It encompasses Britain's ability to embrace the digital revolution, to develop accurate and powerful information about global trends and to show itself able to administer its own domestic affairs with bureaucratic competence – what these days might be termed as 'digital competence'. It also includes the ability to know quite a lot about what private British interests and UK citizens are doing abroad, to be 'info-savvy' and aware of how British society is interacting with international interests across the world – a much more challenging objective than it first sounds.[21] Internal governmental consistency, in other words, backs up consistency in policy that helps create images of competence and effectiveness from which other diplomatic machines draw their own conclusions and may try to imitate.

A third element refers directly to the values and ideas – the world view – of the country that it projects internationally. Values and ideas really matter in world politics, perhaps because – especially because – there is so little firm governance at the global level. And the values that Britain proclaims it stands for in world politics have been repeated many times.[22] They can be summarized as liberal capitalism as a source of national prosperity, the primacy of the rule of law both domestically and internationally, the protection of individual freedoms at home, the promotion of free trade abroad and a strong commitment to the international status quo that Britain was itself instrumental in shaping during the twentieth century. These may sound like political platitudes, and they represent ideals that Britain and other Western states have observed in the breach on too many occasions. But in presenting a basic national stance in world politics, such values still matter in creating a deeper and more persuasive style of diplomacy that cast ripples outwards from those particular international disputes or initiatives that diplomacy has to address. The 2021 Integrated Review asserted that Britain has 'the ability to turn the dial on international issues of consequence' – though others strongly disagree that such abilities still exist.[23] But these have nevertheless constituted attractive ideals to many peoples around the world, if not always to their own autocratic or dictatorial governments.

An autocratic state such as Russia under the leadership of President Putin, for example, certainly fields a coherent diplomatic machine, incisively directed from the centre with purpose and power, and emanating from a country that can exert a good deal of leverage through energy policies or by direct military means. In 2015 President Putin opened a massive, sci-fi style National Defence Management Centre on the banks of the Moskva river just a couple of kilometres from the Kremlin, where, in a quite astonishing hierarchy of screen-filled control rooms, Russia claims to be able to integrate all its policy instruments coherently and in real time.[24] Perhaps it can, since Western officials say they constantly see different elements of Russian foreign policy acting in mutually reinforcing ways.[25]

And yet, Russia's diplomatic relationships with its friends and allies in the world – Syria, Cuba, Venezuela, Belarus, Kazakhstan, Turkey – even with Germany on gas supply, are highly transactional and have not generated much wider diplomatic influence for Russia. It may be powerful and coherent, but Russian foreign policy since the end of the Cold War has not projected attractive political values or a view of the world from Moscow that has appealed much to the majority of the international community. Aside from those states who are evidently clients of Moscow, other governments that deal regularly with it are not anxious to imitate Russian diplomatic style, still less to come under its sway.

These are the three essential prerequisites for more influential diplomacy – to be able to say that 'HMG officials' embody a soft power benefit in addition to their primary roles in dealing with the particular issues before them. They can 'speak softly' but with effect and have a wider and subtle impact on global diplomacy as they go about their work.

But even setting out such prerequisites immediately raises the question of whether the conditions for them are changing from Britain's point of view. Is the country still closely associated with existing power centres; does it continue to project its own governmental and foreign policy style consistently and coherently; and does it embody in its actual behaviour the values and ideas it proclaims so loudly and regularly in official documents?

A bad couple of decades

British foreign policy has had a bad couple of decades. As we observed in Chapter 3, the soft power attributes of a country derive more from its long-term image and its traditionally understood presence in the world than from any immediate policy choices, successes and failures. This time lag may be fortunate for Britain as it embarks on the 2020s, since it may still be able retrieve some of the diplomatic damage done by exactly two decades since the 2001 terrorist attacks on the United States, after which British policy in the world has not been notably successful and its own self-confidence as a society took some considerable hits. To be sure, Britain has been affected by the more widespread political hiatus that diminished the power and influence of everyone in the Western world during these years, but Britain added its own uniquely national troubles to these challenges and did not maintain the diplomatic and strategic standards by which it traditionally claims to be judged.[26]

For the twenty years after the 9/11 attacks, Britain worked hard to stay close to Washington and paid some price for it – in the way the campaign against international terrorism was conducted, in the wars in Iraq and Afghanistan, the campaign to bring down Colonel Gaddafi in Libya, to contain the Syrian civil war, to combat the 'Islamic State' terror group or to push back against Russian blackmail and emerging Chinese pressure around the world. None of these campaigns were particularly successful since by the end of the Clinton Administration in the United States, Britain found itself closely allied not so much to the centrepiece of world power as to a quixotic and troubled American leadership at a time of great strategic drift within the United States. The Trump Administration was particularly stressful for Britain's self-assigned role as a close transatlantic partner. The arrival of the Biden Administration at least gave Britain a welcome chance to reset its relations with Washington in more traditional terms, though it still had more of a 'Trump legacy' to live down than most of its European partners.

It remains good strategic sense for Britain to align itself where possible with the United States, but there is nevertheless an evident shift of raw political power towards non-Western players in world politics, particularly in Asia. British diplomacy for the future, even where it can align more comfortably with Washington, as well as Berlin, Paris or Rome, cannot so easily be perceived as sitting on the right side of history in an era that now seems likely to put Western powers at a growing structural disadvantage.

Nor has Britain projected a very consistent or effective national policy image in the last two decades. Its military ventures have been small and tactically effective while the political strategies they served were tentative, often too ambiguous and not demonstrably successful. The world economic crisis of 2008 had a highly disruptive effect on the globalized British economy and the prospects of the break-up of the United Kingdom that dominated the Scottish independence referendum of 2014, and then the strategic and political shock of the Brexit vote of 2016, created a full-blown political and constitutional crisis that reverberates into the 2020s, notwithstanding a new government with a significant parliamentary majority and agreed deals with the EU.

Added to this picture, British governmental reactions to the Covid-19 crisis were patchy in showing policy at work. The government was successful in the way financial compensation was designed and administered to prevent an economic catastrophe arising from locking down the whole society. It was successful, too, in supporting the NHS so that it did not collapse under the initial pressure. But it was poor in the way it failed to learn from the past, or from the earlier experience of other countries dealing with Covid, and it did not administer many aspects of the public health challenge very well – or the wider social effects on matters such as education or public order. The arrival of approved vaccines changed the picture dramatically, however, and the government – which had made some shrewd early investments in vaccine development and supply – was able to preside over an unprecedented, and excellent, national vaccination programme that made it a global leader in immunizing its own population. After almost two years of the Covid-19 crisis, the net effect was that Britain had suffered almost the worst per capita Covid-19 death rate among the advanced nations, but it then emerged more quickly towards economic and social normality, thanks to its vaccine programme. The inconsistent policy performance stimulated an ongoing and largely introspective national debate.

Success or not, the debate seemed in keeping with the conclusions of many observers that there had been a steady reduction in British diplomatic confidence and vigour over these years, or sometimes a complete absence from many issues that were previously important to the country.[27] Even before the Brexit referendum, comments like that from Anand Menon were common: 'factors including fatigue following the wars in Afghanistan and Iraq, a recession, and a prime minister with little apparent interest in foreign affairs', he said in 2015, 'have conspired to render the British increasingly insular'.[28] The Brexit vote only added to this image, seeming to emphasize a prevailing governmental view that Britain was not leaving the EU for essentially economic reasons (all agreed there would be an economic price to pay for leaving) but rather because it was simply a cultural and political exception to the broad community of European states. Somehow, a new and more authentically British approach to the world should be devised outside the EU. And as the incoming government of Boris Johnson observed in 2019, 'Brexit Britain' had a lot of diplomatic ground to make up if it was to recover its former reputation. It labelled the revised strategic approach as 'global Britain' and spelled it out in the 2021 Integrated Review. As analysts such as Lawrence Freedman observed, a 'modest strategy' could be successfully based on the government's aspiration in the Review for Britain to be seen as a country that helped solve international problems and took its fair share of the necessary burdens. This could become a viable alternative approach to the one Britain seemed to want to relinquish. 'The United Kingdom has much to contribute', he said, but added ominously, 'so long as it accepts the limits of independence and, above all, abandons the quest for a unique, exceptional role.'[29]

And as part of this persistent policy hiatus, Britain has not performed notably well in terms of the third theme intrinsic to diplomatic influence. Its fundamental values and the attractive ideas British society embodies have not been consistently well represented under the pressure of twenty-first-century events. As an important capitalist country, the British economy has not done well since the 2008 crisis. More than ten years after the crisis personal income and GDP figures were still only just back to pre-2008 levels when the Covid-19 crisis struck; the country was clearly suffering all the social and political tensions created by the downsides of globalization. It has let its respect for international law slip on a number of occasions that have damaged its international standing.[30] The fact that the government drafted legislation in 2020 deliberately to break an international treaty it had concluded with the EU only the previous year – as such, a treaty deposited at the UN as an instrument of international law – appalled many senior figures inside and outside Parliament. Every living previous prime minister lined up against it. In the event, the Bill was withdrawn, but the international reputational damage was already done. And though the government made a number of policy decisions in 2020–21, particularly over China, representing some brave assertions of its liberal values, there was an evident problem of policy consistency and a lot of slippage to make up – all carefully noted and publicized by Britain's adversaries.

Perhaps the most important role for Britain in the 2020s and in the light of Brexit Britain's challenges will be to focus on the potential for it to be seen as a 'global broker' rather than an 'ex-great power' in world politics. Certainly, this is foreshadowed in the 2021 Integrated Review with its emphasis on those easy slogans that Britain should be a 'reliable partner' a 'burden-sharer' and a 'problem-solver'.[31] But that can only be achieved with a greater, and carefully calibrated, proactive approach to some key global issues that make a difference to Britain. It will need to reverse the trend towards introspection and retrenchment of the last decade.[32]

Researchers and innovators

Shaping the global stage

Any visit to Manchester's Museum of Science and Industry, the living Beamish Museum in County Durham or the National Railway Museum in York, let alone London's Science Museum, would confirm Britain's long-standing heritage in research and innovation. Individual inventiveness created Britain's agricultural revolution of the late eighteenth century and then founded the world's first industrial revolution that grew from it. Britain had already been the first to adopt the factory system, when John Lombe opened the earliest recorded example in Derby in 1721. British technology led in many aspects of the second industrial revolution and, driven by the pressures of fighting world wars and competing with France and the United States, it played a big role in the innovations that with the advent of computing led to the third. The British government has declared itself determined to embrace fully a 'fourth industrial revolution' – digitization, the internet and the knowledge-based economy – as it looks to the future.[1]

Leading research and innovation were always critical components of Britain's historical success story. For 300 years, from the founding of the Royal Society in 1660 until the 1960s, that success was based on a naturally laissez-faire approach to the way the scientific, educational and technical disciplines should facilitate the country's flourishing innovation, not just in the matter of invention but, just as importantly, the application and marketing of innovation. All over the world people protect their mobile phones and personal data devices from hacking and tracking with 'Faraday bags', without ever understanding the influence of British engineer Michael Faraday whose work contributed to turning electricity into a major motive force in the second industrial revolution – in electrolysis, balloons, electric motors, generators, dynamos and almost all the machinery that drove twentieth-century production processes.[2]

From the creation of the first railway to the world's first underground system in London, from the jet engine and splitting the atom or discovering the deoxyribonucleic acid (DNA) sequence up to the invention of the World Wide Web, Britain has greatly benefited from an intellectual and social environment in which creativity seemed to function and flourish naturally.[3] Nor was it all contained within the major institutions. In 1934 Percy Shaw from Halifax invented in his own home the 'cat's eyes' road safety studs that are used everywhere in the world. In 2006 his invention was judged by the Design Museum and the BBC to be among Britain's top ten 'design icons', alongside Concorde, the Spitfire and the Routemaster bus. In the early 1990s, Trevor Bayliss designed the wind-up radio after listening to a BBC programme on AIDS in Africa that lamented the difficulty of communicating safe-sex education in remote areas for lack of sufficient radio batteries.[4] The wind-up radio – so obvious that no one ever thought of it – was designed specifically for such a need. It doubly encapsulates a soft power advantage through both the winning innovation and the purpose of the design.

The economic and social environment in Britain and its prominence in world politics up to the mid-twentieth century favoured not just the innovation of British technology but also its practical application. Not many British scientific or technological breakthroughs were lost to foreign competitors for want of development finance or a bigger market. In those times, Britain's laissez-faire approach provided the environment that nurtured invention and also development and commercialization for its research talent. Its own market and those foreign and imperial markets in which it had so much influence were big enough to offer the incentives for vibrant research and exploitation in many socio-economic fields. They created a legacy of world-leading British research which still benefits the country's reputation today and remains a reality in a few particular fields – as disparate as medicine and biotech, aerospace, computing or renewable energy.

The conditions necessary for any country to engender the best international research are easy to state but hard to create.

They require a strong educational and research hinterland from which skills and innovation will naturally arise; freedom of action and movement for research communities; work has to be permeable and fluid, allowing for the transfer of people, skills and ideas across physical and intellectual boundaries – it should be open to international influences.

And while it is easy to see the difference between pure and applied research, those categories very often meld together, so a great deal depends on the quality of effective 'translational' research – where pure research can be directed towards application. That is a natural grey area and spotting where pure research can be most profitably applied is as much art as science and regular failures must always be anticipated.[5]

Britain's traditionally laissez-faire approach was never likely to be adequate to meet all these requirements. Outside of wartime there was never a settled relationship between British government and the national research base or its intensive technology sectors.

The Labour Government of 1964 famously dedicated itself to harnessing the 'white heat' of the technological revolution and created a new and large 'Department of Education and Science' alongside the landmark 'Ministry of Technology', which absorbed a number of separate Whitehall departments. It became known as the MinTech 'super ministry', explicitly designed to harness and direct British science and technology 'for national purposes'.[6] Later governments dismantled MinTech as being unwieldy and too politically driven. But they still could not find the right combination between government, education policy and the private research sector. Most governmental research was tied up in key sectors such as defence and there was little productive interaction with the private sector. These were difficult years for British science and technology, set against the 1970s backdrop when the British economy seriously under-performed, followed in the 1980s by the liberal economics of successive Thatcher governments which favoured explicitly market-based approaches to nurturing and funding British research.

There was also increasing unease within the British research community at what many interpreted as the 'abuse' of science and technology – the appropriation of objective knowledge for political purposes. Controversies around nuclear power, both for national energy generation and as weapons, were particularly vociferous.[7] At the same time, extensive investment in 'technical education' that had been so long promised was effectively lost in the controversies over selection versus comprehensive education.[8] During the 1980s calls from large groups of eminent individuals to 'save British science' were becoming routine.[9] And by the turn of the century, official white papers and anguished reports had all lamented the increasing gap between Britain's long-standing excellence in science and technology and its relative weakness in exploiting it for tangible economic advantage.[10] In 2007 David Sainsbury's *Race to the Top* examined the role science and innovation could play in enabling Britain to compete against low-wage, powerful, emerging economies such as China and India – the major technology challenge for Britain then as now.[11] It wasn't just a government problem, he made clear, but also a syndrome of over-conservative and unimaginative industrial management.

The approach that set up the essential philosophy and the structure of the government's research policy for the 2020s was articulated in 2015 by

Sir Paul Nurse.[12] Some ad hoc coordination bodies were closed down and in 2018 the whole government-funded sector was brought under the umbrella of UK Research and Innovation (UKRI), overseen now by the powerful BEIS. As such, UKRI includes the seven academic research councils alongside Research England[13] and Innovate UK. It's a big organization with around 7,500 staff and an annual budget of over £8 billion.[14] That makes it Britain's largest public funder of research and innovation with, it claims, 'responsibility to ensure the health of the system as a whole'. This structure was linked to the 2017 Industrial Strategy that focused, it said confidently in the pre-Covid-19 years, on the 'grand challenges' of the future: artificial intelligence and data; an ageing society; clean growth; and the future of mobility.[15] In accordance with this, the government committed itself in 2020 to reach a national investment level of £22 billion in public funding for research and development by 2024–5.

This represents the most coherent approach to government relations with the science and technology sectors that Britain has so far seen. It also encapsulates some key historical legacies. One is the recognition that there is an important difference between the applied research that governments might want and general free research, valid for its own sake as blue-sky thinking in the pursuit of knowledge and crucial to the maintenance of a healthy research hinterland. Governments understand that they must not just recognize and 'tolerate' this distinctive hinterland but actually nurture it, even as they are drawn naturally towards their interest (and translational research funding) for applied science and technology. The 'Haldane principle' of 1918, recognizing the need for government to respect pure science, has been repeatedly invoked, most recently in 2018 when the foundation of UKRI set out a future vision for British science and technology.[16] In 2020, UKRI's CEO, Professor Dame Ottoline Leyser, spoke of a future Britain where science is a normal part of cultural life: 'In the next 20 years', she said, 'we need to make the next step in the evolution of the place of science in society. It's not about science *and* society, it's got to be science *in* society.'[17]

A second historical legacy is the simple matter of government funding levels. Reorganizing central government structures to find the right policy levers to nurture British science and technology is one thing, but how much public money should be devoted to it is quite another. Though the government has ambitions to spend a good deal more in the 2020s, the fact remains that it is building public funding from a comparatively low base. For some years Britain's total research and development expenditure from both government and private industry sources amounted to less than 1.5 per cent of its GDP – well below the average for OECD countries and considerably below the recent levels of Britain's main competitors.

Comparative GDP levels on science and technology research have risen in recent years but fluctuated for a while above 3.0 per cent but then fell back to 2.7 per cent before the Covid-19 crisis scrambled meaningful GDP calculations as comparators.[18] In 2021 the government committed to devoting 2.4% of Britain's GDP on R&D by 2027. In light of its aspiration, this is a rather modest ambition. The fact is that whatever the comparative metrics may be, absolute levels of research funding matter, and there is a lot of ground still to make up.

Another legacy is the recognition that science, technology and innovation cannot be separated from the broader state of economy and society. In 1963, Harold Wilson's famous 'white heat' of the technological revolution also depended, he said, on 'far-reaching changes in the economic and social attitudes which permeate our whole system of society . . . the Britain that is going to be forged in the white heat of this revolution will be no place for restrictive practices or for outdated methods.'[19] It recognized both an anxiety that British innovation could no longer be taken for granted and a faith that there was enormous underlying potential for innovation in British society if only it could be somehow released from unnecessary constraints. Almost sixty years later, the government's statement in its 2020 'R&D Roadmap' was remarkably similar, albeit in somewhat breathless prose:

> We will need to be even more creative and innovative to adapt to the 'new normal', and to recover swiftly from COVID-19. It is our duty to build a future which is greener, safer and healthier than before. This means revitalising our whole system of science, research and innovation to release its potential – to unlock and embrace talent, diversity, resilience and adaptability, and to tackle our biggest challenges, such as achieving net zero carbon emissions by 2050. We have a once-in-a-generation opportunity to strengthen our global position in research, unleash a new wave of innovation, enhance our national security and revitalise our international ties.[20]

That was all echoed in equally fraught terms by the prime minister, writing in the 2021 Integrated Review: 'Our aim', he said, 'is to have secured our status as a Science and Tech Superpower by 2030, by redoubling our commitments to research and development, bolstering our global network of innovation partnerships, and improving our national skills.'[21]

The landscape of British research and innovation

History will decide whether the government can deliver on its 'once-in-a-generation opportunity' in 'revitalising our whole system of science, research and innovation'. It will certainly not be cheap, but the framework, and certainly the desire, appears to be there. If this is a reasonably settled framework, then what does the outside world see when it looks at Britain's research and innovation landscape? It initially sees a research base that falls naturally into three segments.

First, there is an active charitable funding sector, bigger and stronger than in most other countries, though concentrated on a few specific areas such as the biomedical and computing sciences fields. The Wellcome Trust and Cancer Research UK, for example, together put over £1 billion every year into the biomed sector. The majority of charitable funding, however, is directed towards research in the university sector, generally supporting both blue-sky and translational research projects. Charitable research money tends towards a concentration of expertise. The more successful an institution, particularly with high-profile research successes, the more charitable money it is likely to attract and the greater the concentration of expertise in that institution. Imperial College London, for example, the Crick Centre or many research centres at Cambridge or Oxford Universities attract major charitable funding. This exacerbates some important differentiation within the British university sector but the leading research colleges and universities are nevertheless prominent among the top fifty in the world. They are the main beneficiaries from the charitable sector's support for research.

Second, there is the commercial sector, which in annual cash terms, contributes considerably more than the government to British research and innovation. In 2019 British companies, both indigenous and foreign owned, put £26 billion into R&D, just twice the £13 billion that the government contributed, and even their combined amounts represented less than 2.4 per cent of GDP, certainly below the OECD average.[22] Research in the commercial sector, though it is extensive, is by definition applied – or at most translational – since it must ultimately serve the company's bottom line.[23] And far from being 'permeable' and allowing for the transfer of people and ideas across boundaries, such research is normally constrained by strong considerations of commercial advantage. Nevertheless, British commercial research is notably strong in the big areas of pharmaceuticals, aerospace, information technology, automotive products – and in some of the small, niche areas covered by high-tech early stage 'start-up' or university 'spin-out' companies. But it is a very uneven process. Among Britain's top twenty-five research and development spenders, the two biggest, AstraZeneca and GlaxoSmithKline alone, account for almost 80 per cent of the total, amounting to around £9 billion a year.[24] Governments are always trying to work with the private sector in generating research and innovation, however, without falling back into the grip of any more Whitehall 'MinTechs'.

Third, therefore, the government-funded sector looms larger than it ever did in the past. This in itself falls into two broad segments. The first is what might be called governmental strategic funding to nurture the development of the various research disciplines – the hinterland of applied research and technology. It does this through publicly funded research councils and supervisory bodies, and brigaded now under the auspices of UKRI. The principle of British research councils has a distinguished pedigree. The famous Medical Research Council was formed in 1913, but in the 1960s more centrally funded research councils for different sectors began to be established as changing academic fashion indicated – economic and social issues alongside national environmental studies in 1965, physical sciences, engineering and biotechnology in the 1990s, arts and humanities in 2005. All key areas are now covered by one of the seven research councils. Then as now, the councils are charged to take an independent view of research needs and proposals and to shape their policy by reference to the research leaders in their discipline. From start to finish, decisions are made through peer-review processes, though governments have periodically stressed to the different councils their own interests in applied research and asked them to direct their independent attention to certain thematic priorities.[25]

The second segment of the government's active involvement is where it funds – or part funds – several Public Sector Research Establishments, some of which overlap with the UKRI structure and are normally under the control of one or other Whitehall ministries. Such establishments cover everything from bodies like the Epidemiology Research Centre to the British Antarctic Survey, or the British Geological Survey, the Health and Safety Laboratory, the Atomic Weapons Establishment, the National Physical Laboratory, the British Museum, the Victoria and Albert Museum or the Met Office. The government officially lists over eighty Public Sector Research Establishments, a high proportion of them in different fields of medicine.[26] Some of these organizations have a relatively low profile in the world, regardless of the research they do; others have global reputations and are seen regularly to contribute to research and innovation that has universal importance.

At a recent count there were roughly 200 officially recognized Research and Innovation Organizations across the country.[27] There is no lack of research institutes or first-rate researchers or intellectual firepower in British universities or other institutions. The questions are rather whether the intellectual output still punches its weight in the applications of innovation – something Britain was naturally strong on in previous eras – how it translates into national economic success and what it contributes to the soft power virtues of magnetism and subtle influence in the world outside.

Research and innovation as soft power assets

Research and innovation can be judged in any number of different ways – for its international eminence or its highlights, its hard-edged contribution to the national economy or the sum total of what it adds to human happiness and welfare. There are many different standards. In terms of providing a soft power asset, however, two key questions dominate any assessment of the strength of British research and innovation.

First, regardless of how much is invested in research and how it may be spent, how does British research fare internationally, in ways that are recognized by the outside world? The most objective single measure lies in that which is published. This is the key to research 'permeability', to sharing, learning and ultimately to accumulating human capital from around the world as well as domestically – the only route to sustaining knowledge and application.[28]

Britain fields over 4 per cent of all the active researchers in the world, on the basis of constituting only 0.8 per cent of the global population. At least in gross numbers, Britain remains a major source of publications, of all descriptions. The United States leads the field with almost 700,000 publications a year (22 per cent of the global total), followed by China with 600,000 (19 per cent) and then Britain as the third greatest source of publications with over 213,000 a year (7 per cent of the global total).[29] In terms of the influence British publications may be having, however – in particular, how *influential* this country's 4 per cent of the global research community really are – the relative citation indexes are very revealing. Again, US publications receive some 37 per cent of the 'most highly cited' texts in the world, China 20 per cent and Britain 14 per cent – a figure that has remained consistent over more than a decade even as Chinese publications have grown rapidly in international influence throughout Asia. This strong performance is even more pronounced when 'field-weighted citation impact' is applied, which measures the average *relative* impact of a given publication, as opposed to the impact of absolute numbers. On this basis, British publications, one for one in their own fields of study, overtook their US counterparts in 2007 and remain the most influential within the G7 countries. Chinese publications are still below the global average on this weighted basis but will, presumably, begin to push hard against Britain's current lead.[30]

Another indication of influence is the degree of international collaboration involved in national publications. While 21 per cent of Chinese publications resulted from international collaboration of some sort, and 35 per cent of US publications, Britain, with 55 per cent of its publications – 117,000 of them – recorded as international collaborative efforts, was second only to France's 56 per cent. Germany recorded 50 per cent in the most recent statistics.[31] Britain's 'active researchers' were also second only to the United States in the world among the most internationally mobile researchers. In the twenty years up to 2015 over 70 per cent of British researchers were deemed 'internationally mobile' by commonly accepted definitions.[32]

Judged by its research publications, Britain distributes its outputs across all subject areas but puts significantly more than most into humanities, business and social sciences. Only the United States and Canada have a similar profile. By contrast, China's published research output is heavily weighted towards engineering, physical sciences and mathematics; Russia's only towards physical sciences and mathematics. Both have tiny profiles, by comparison, in humanities and social sciences. Likewise, in India, though it has much higher than average global profiles in environmental sciences, biological, health and medical sciences.[33] Whether or not it is better to have a 'well-rounded' research profile, as the British government likes to put it, not falling below the international average in any research sector, as opposed to having a sharp concentration on some areas, will only be resolved over time.

Particularly eye-catching is the fact that although Britain now accounts for only a relatively small total number of global patents, a high proportion of its available research is nevertheless cited in international patents. Of the nine research areas judged most relevant to industry, Britain is judged the world leader (at least for its published research) in four particular fields: genomics and synthetic biology, regenerative medicine, robotics and automated systems, and in satellites and other commercial applications of space.[34] Clearly, British research is well placed to be applied in commercially productive ways.

One major caveat hovers over this positive picture, however. The government's latest collaboration with the Elsevier organization to collate global publication figures was drawn from a baseline published in 2017, interrogating data that was available prior to 2016. This takes no account of the disruptive effects of the Brexit hiatus from 2016 to 2020, or the economic effects of the Covid-19 crisis, particularly on researcher mobility, research income in all sectors or the impacts of new public spending priorities and some big emergency investments in biotech. The national picture will assuredly change, better in some respects, worse in others, as the effects of Brexit and Covid-19 unwind in the coming decade and as changes in the international research environment reveal themselves.

The second major question in judging effectiveness in soft power terms concerns the degree to which British research and innovation has the effect of helping shape its particular sector on the international stage through its own prominence or success. We consider in Chapter 7 the more formal matters of regulation and standard-setting, but here we consider how Britain's reputation for research, technology and innovation has the power to influence the way certain sectors work internationally and encourage imitative behaviour within other countries.

No country, even the United States or eventually China, is likely to shape the global research stage in all areas. Britain has disproportionate influence for its economic size in some particular sectors. But the picture is uneven. In some sectors, there are big, important companies that have a major effect on innovation in their own domains. At the other end of the scale there is a burgeoning and successful constellation of small and medium British enterprises that are admired but whose international influence on their industries is naturally limited. And there is little in the middle that has significant international impact.

One of Britain's undoubted international success stories has been its biomedical sector. It always has been. The determination of the double-helix structure of the DNA molecule, at the Laboratory of Molecular Biology at Cambridge University in 1953, was the single greatest twentieth-century breakthrough in the field. 'Dolly the Sheep' was born in 1996 at the Roslin Institute near Edinburgh, bringing to life the first mammal clone from a somatic cell using the process of nuclear transfer.[35] In 1796 Britain's Edward Jenner had pioneered the smallpox vaccination, earning him worldwide acclaim as the 'father of immunology'. It was more than just symbolically appropriate, then, that in 2020 the Jenner Institute in Oxford became intrinsic to the worldwide quest for a safe and effective, viable and cheap vaccine for Covid-19. That potentially made its product – the 'Oxford/AstraZeneca' vaccine in shorthand – one of the 'workhorse vaccines' that could eventually offer the best chance of protecting the global population from the worst stages of Covid-19. And even in the midst of the Covid-19 vaccine programme, the Jenner Institute announced a breakthrough new malaria vaccine that promised game-changing effectiveness against the disease. In November 2020, both the Pfizer/BioNTech and Moderna teams in the United States, and the Oxford/AstraZeneca team in Britain, showed they had both created effective Covid-19 vaccines by different methods. The team working on the Oxford/AstraZeneca vaccine trials, it should be noted, comprised no fewer than thirty-six different nationalities. In total, at least 26 per cent of the scientists working on the Covid-19 vaccine were non-British. It was a national success in a deeper sense, displaying Britain's magnetism for international talent as well as its breakthrough research. According to Universities UK, 40 per cent of science, technology and engineering academics in Britain are from overseas.[36] So in the case of vaccine development, this sort of advanced and cosmopolitan research base, alongside Britain's pharma industry with its £41.8 billion turnover, and giant companies like AstraZeneca and GSK within it have kept Britain's biomed sector among the top in the world.[37]

That biomed industry exists, of course, within a deep pool of medical research and expertise. The Royal Society has been a cornerstone of UK scientific research and innovation in all fields since 1660 and currently has a global fellowship of some 1,600 of the world's most eminent scientists.[38] Major British scientific journals in medicine with international importance include *Nature*, *The British Medical Journal* and *The Lancet*. Less well known but very significant in international assessments of medical research is the Cochrane Library. Based on the pioneering work of Archie Cochrane and Oxford's Cochrane Centre, the library collates research reviews and trial data from around the world. Published now online by the John Wiley Company, the Cochrane Library's databases are acknowledged as a critical tool for international peer review in medical research. This non-profit organization, based in Oxford and accessing its data through a US publisher, 'has been producing gold-standard reviews of evidence on important questions in medicine since the 1980s', said Ben Goldacre in reviewing the somewhat dubious state of the global pharma industry.[39]

As we pointed out in the previous chapter, Britain's biomed and health sector may have rescued Britain's wider international reputation from its earlier failures in dealing with the Covid-19 pandemic. The government could credibly claim that if it lost too many of the early Covid-19 battles, it went on to win a more pivotal battle to create a rapid nationwide inoculation programme. Britain became the first big country genuinely to emerge from the first phase of the pandemic, employing a range of fully tested and approved vaccines and antiviral drugs. But it was not just biomed research that created this favourable result. The biomed research industry worked intensively with its international partners and kept vaccine research moving forward strongly as the Covid-19 virus mutated. The NHS was able to offer a nationally structured organization to deliver the vaccine, operating down to local primary care community levels. It was backed up by the flexible expertise of the armed forces and supported by a strong charity and voluntary sector. All this provided a shining example, finally, of what successful research really looks like in practice: how complex is the practical application of medical research and how it benefits society even under urgent pressure to perform. Such rapid innovation and application were previously only seen in times of war.

Of course, there are downsides in this sort of national mobilization. The displacement effect of the Covid-19 crisis on other research may be severe. Medical charities warned of annual shortfalls of over £300 million in their non-Covid-19 activities.[40] Other countries also have great biomed sectors that have been strengthened by the crisis. The US biomed sector performed heroically in producing the first vaccine approved for use, the Pfizer/BioNTech vaccine (though for a range of reasons the US government did not then roll it out efficiently). Other domestic vaccines were produced in China – Sinovac; in India – Covaxin; and in Russia – the Sputnik V vaccine, and widely distributed as developing countries did not have the luxury of picking vaccines based on political preferences or even whether or not full trial results had been published and scientifically peer-reviewed.

By mid-2021, the speed at which the United States, Britain and Israel were barrelling forward with national immunization programmes exposed the EU nations, and others, lagging months behind. This visible disparity inevitably led to flare-ups of vaccine nationalism, as enormous demand for approved jabs outweighed limited supply. At times Oxford's vaccine looked like the most promising hope for the developing world: relatively cheap to produce and easy to transport. Then in February 2021, the *Lancet* published a scientific peer review of Sputnik V that gave it instant international credibility. It was a leading British journal that gave Sputnik V the international stamp of approval that it had previously lacked. Almost overnight, no fewer than twenty countries were knocking on Russia's door. Despite the hope that the UN-sponsored COVAX programme would enable fair and equitable worldwide access, even poor countries were desperate to trade bilaterally with whoever could sell. It exposed a fundamental problem at the heart of the industry: the reality of price differentiation. Confidential contracts concealed different pricing structures for various countries because at a time when fair access to vaccines was akin to a human right, the immediate soft power prize was simply in delivering vaccines. The longer-term reputational gain, however, might lie in being seen to have done so fairly. This is deeply problematic. When Covid-19 can be managed more like a seasonal influenza, looking back on price differentials to supply the same vaccines to different countries may come back to bite the soft power reputations of some companies and supplier countries. Brazil bought into the Chinese vaccine, Hungary used the Russian vaccine and Bangladesh and the Philippines used India's Covaxin. Such decisions were controversial at the time since these vaccines had not been internationally approved and, in the case of China and Russia, the clinical trials data had not been made internationally available for scientific peer review before the vaccines were administered.

In the longer term, all these interventions will change the nature of the international vaccine industry that had been largely non-political and simply taken for granted in mainstream news coverage. Having been first out of the blocks in its national Covid-19 immunization programme, the 'first mover advantage' will only really be impactful if Britain can sustain its vaccination success. As it looks increasingly likely that populations will need regular vaccines over many years to outmanoeuvre Covid-19 mutations – like the annual winter 'flu jab' – domestic manufacturing capacity is critical to British access with surety of supplies to meet growing demand. Britain, therefore, needs rapidly to scale up the domestic manufacturing capacity of its own national companies (insofar as any pharma companies are national) and supply chains to meet the ongoing need for Covid-19 vaccines and antiviral medicines. This capacity would include access to raw APIs (Active Pharmaceutical Ingredients) through to resilient glass vials that can withstand significant pressure. The Pfizer/BioNTech vaccine, for example, being transported and stored at temperatures of –90 degrees, put pressure on the quality of glass required for vials. To ensure that Britain's vaccine success is not to be short-lived, ongoing research and innovation needs to be focused on sustaining the pipeline of science and technology that can develop and manufacture ongoing protection from Covid-19 mutations, particularly in times when multinational collaboration – formerly taken largely for granted in this field – may be inhibited by national policy decisions taken elsewhere. Britain needs an each-way betting approach to investing in future vaccination technology, creating the potential for greater national resilience, while also accepting the reality that big pharma companies work more efficiently when they use multinational supply chains and international research.[41]

Another example of successful research and its direct application to national prosperity that partly shapes the international market is the British aerospace sector. Britain plays a leading role in the industry. Rolls-Royce leads by a long way in the aero-engine market. BAE Systems is the third biggest military contractor in the world (after Boeing and Lockheed Martin)[42] and large companies including GKN Aerospace are major suppliers to the Airbus project.

In total, the British aerospace sector has an annual turnover of almost £34 billion and over the five years before the Covid-19 crisis had grown by 19 per cent. Critically, in terms of its soft power impact, some 94 per cent of all aerospace output is for export – worth almost £32 billion in 2020. Within those totals, space industries had a turnover that had grown to almost £15 billion by 2019.[43] Boeing, Lockheed Martin, BAE Systems and Airbus Industries all compete with each other *and* cooperate with each other in a series of consortia on particular projects.[44] These four, and the governments with whom they have major defence contracts, effectively structure their own global industry. The reputation of those particular companies, therefore, not just for business integrity but for efficiency, delivery and innovation, is a major national asset for the governments behind them.

Some 68 per cent of the 1,000 or more British aerospace companies claim to drive their innovation chiefly through partnerships, strategic alliances and joint ventures.[45] That can be regarded as a favourable 'shaping' response and also reflects the fact that British aerospace industries are more internationally structured than most of their continental counterparts. But the global Covid-19 crisis has shocked the international aerospace industry more than most and exposed some underlying flaws in Britain's own sector. Chief among them is a chronic skills shortage in most areas and some well-known cultural failings to embrace true innovation at the managerial level. Defence aerospace is often accused of missing the really new technological trends and exciting new commercial technology, it is said, may come to eclipse aerospace and defence as the cutting edge of high-end British manufacturing.[46]

Closely related, the business of 'defence' is sometimes regarded as one of the British sectors whose activities help shape the international environment in which it operates – offering a non-US example to other countries of how research and innovation can be integrated into many highly effective military capabilities. It is true that several aspects of the British defence model have been imitated by partner countries, though this has been more at the strategic than the industrial levels. Britain has more international influence in the way it thinks about defence and structures for it – particularly in the business of operating its separate armed forces jointly – than in its own defence industrial production.[47] Aerospace aside, British defence has real strength in naval ship-building, though little of that is genuinely exportable, whereas in armour, artillery, military vehicles, ordnance and defence electronics, the international record has not been noticeably good (or exported). The present government intends that to change as it tries to re-orientate Britain's defence capabilities to deal with new and complex security threats through investment in a series of 'sunrise technologies' and the early retirement of 'sunset' capabilities. It intends to show how different technologies can be integrated to produce new-tech synergies. But this will take some time, even where sufficient resources are allocated, though Britain's allies are certainly watching it all with interest.

At the other end of the scale, Britain has more SMEs than any of its main competitors and has been particularly innovative in creating university-based 'start-up and spin-out' enterprises on the back of its world-class niche research. In the university context, 'start-ups' refer to new business enterprises that employ the expertise of university staff and graduates, and 'spin-outs' to enterprises that are specifically based on the intellectual property generated by university research. Both are ways of taking something from the academic sphere directly to the market, usually to attract private investment into its development. Start-ups and spin-outs moved forward quickly after 2015, launching at a rate of around twenty-five every week and turning over an estimated £3.6 billion between 2015 and 2019.[48] The universities of Cambridge, Oxford and Imperial College always figure prominently when calculations are made about taking British research to the market. Nevertheless, Queen's University Belfast and QUBIS, its commercial arm, have been singled out as the most productive examples of a British higher education institution producing the most spin-out companies relative to its funding.[49]

Regional enterprise centres have arisen specifically to draw on the key research and staff expertise of their local universities. Trinity College Cambridge created the first British science park in 1970 to help apply its research to the business community and create a cluster of expertise from inside and outside the university worlds. Since then, the model has been widely adopted elsewhere. The University of Durham, for example, operates its own Orbit business zone inside the North East Technology Park in County Durham; the Birmingham Science Park draws naturally from Aston and Birmingham universities, among its private sector partnerships; the University of Plymouth is a founding partner alongside the City Council in the Plymouth Science Park. The Advanced Manufacturing Research Centre (AMRC) in Rotherham is a joint venture between the University of Sheffield, Boeing and over 100 industrial partners. Its residents include Rolls-Royce, McLaren, Nikken Europe and the UK Atomic Energy Authority, and there are eight universities close by that can feed into the AMRC – which, symbolically enough, sits on ground next to Orgreave, which saw some of the most bitter clashes between police and coal miners in the prolonged coal strike of 1984. Life moves on. The Catalyst science park in Northern Ireland sits in the Titanic Quarter of Queen's Island, Belfast.

One of the most impressive is Imperial College's White City Innovation Campus which now hosts Europe's biggest bio-incubator and provision of facilities for major technology and science-based businesses. Novartis, the huge Swiss pharmaceutical company, decided in 2019 to locate its British headquarters next door.[50] In 2016 in what was proclaimed as a 'masterstroke' AstraZeneca had already moved its headquarters into the life sciences hub in Cambridge, 'instantly changing the corporate atmosphere and offering immediate access to some of the world's brightest researchers'.[51] In the circumstances, the astonishingly rapid development of a Covid-19 vaccine was probably a more dramatic vindication of the decision than AstraZeneca management might have wished.

The government has tried to play its own incubating role in disseminating this sort of activity more widely. Since 2015 it has created more than twenty 'University Enterprise Zones' to promote similar initiatives and incentivize universities to create joint ventures with private industry, though funding for such an ambitious scheme was small – around £15 million in total – pending new targets in the light of the Covid-19 crisis recovery.[52]

Impressive as university interaction with industry has been in recent years, and notwithstanding the extent of the wider SME community in Britain, it is still the case that not much of this activity has the effect of helping structure the wider international environment in research and innovation. Britain's small-scale niche research is a player in the wider global game but not a pillar of it. The failure rate among all SMEs, including start-ups and spin-outs, is inevitably high. And when SMEs become really successful it is normally because they are bought out and absorbed by bigger companies who want their business and niche brand names. The chief soft power benefit of Britain's vigorous SME culture lies in the atmosphere of freedom and enterprise it transmits to the outside world – its implicit invitation to the commercially minded and the inventive of the world that Britain could be the place for them. In recent years, though British governments have said it repeatedly, it has sadly not always been the underlying message their tangible actions have communicated.[53]

There is little doubt that Britain has a fertile research and technology sector and has taken on the challenge of converting pure research in the universities into translational research that can be more quickly applied and shaped for the benefit of the wider economy and British society. The soft power image of Britain remains high as a country of research eminence, and it still attracts international talent in key areas. The problem of scale still remains, however. Britain is outclassed by the bigger players who can operationalize innovation in their own markets and earn exports from it more quickly than is often the case in Britain. Its generally successful laissez-faire research environment is also now under great pressure from a number of different quarters. Some of the big competitor nations have more centralized and governmentally determined policies for research and innovation. Russia and China engage in direct penetration and industrial espionage on a large scale, alongside big subsidies to their own industries. Even in the United States there is a heavy concentration on government-funded defence-related research, and a pool of EU research funding is available to Britain's main European competitors. As a soft power asset, Britain's research reputation remains high. But its ability to shape or influence the political structures that ultimately determine how technology will be used and who will benefit most from them is necessarily limited.

The case of graphene is a classic of its kind. The 2021 Integrated Review picked it out as a key example of Britain's 'strong record of innovation in S&T'.[54] Indeed it is. Graphene is a carbon allotrope that was developed by two scientists at the University of Manchester, Andre Geim and Konstantin Novoselov. The theory behind it had been known for decades but in 2004 they found a way of operationalizing a theoretical construct – translational research – to create a substance barely one atom thick, with high conductivity for heat and electricity that is, atom for atom, a hundred times stronger than the strongest steel. It is, by common consent, 'the material of the future' – theoretically as thin as a material can be, with potentially limitless applications in everything that materials science serves.[55] In 2010 the world woke up to graphene when the two Manchester scientists won the Nobel Prize for it. In 2011 the British government put £50 million into the development of graphene applications, while it was taking £1.7 billion out of the national R&D budget during the years of austerity. By 2013 the United States, China and South Korea between them had lodged some 5,100 international patents to protect their own development of graphene applications; a mere fifty had been lodged in Britain.[56] By 2017 graphene was being used in items as mundane as high-end running shoes. It all seems a long way from the breakneck development and confident application of Michael Faraday's discovery of what was then 'the energy of the future' – electricity generation.

Leaders and regulators

Setting the standards

Setting the standard for standard-setting

Lodged in a nondescript high-rise building on London's Chiswick High Road is an organization that regulates quite a lot of the world's day-to-day life, and most people take it for granted. It is home to the British Standards Institute. The BSI was founded in 1901, the world's first national standards body. Today it's a powerful organization that publishes over 3,000 revised or new standards every year to help guarantee good business practice, validate products and promote international trade. Its famous 'Kitemark', known to British consumers everywhere, was created as far back as 1903. And in 1947 the BSI was instrumental in the formation of ISO, the International Organization for Standardization, and then in 1961 for CEN, its European equivalent, along with a number of other standards regulators for Europe.[1]

More to the point during this era of globalization, the BSI remains one of the world's largest certifying bodies with over 80,000 clients – companies and organizations all over the world in fields as diverse as retail, insurance, engineering, cyber-security or environmental management. The standards that are deemed good enough for Britain are adopted by thousands of standard-setters and regulators in every continent among rich and poor alike. The BSI has held a Royal Charter since 1929, but it has moved with the times. In 1998, it became explicitly international as the 'BSI Group' and has absorbed over twenty other foreign regulators across Europe, in the United States, in Australasia and South Africa. And alongside the likes of Rolex, Google, BP, Microsoft, the BBC and Apple, it has consistently been awarded the status of a 'British Superbrand'.

The story of the BSI could be repeated in many fields. Britain's first modern building legislation was actually embodied in its various Public Health Acts between 1845 and 1875; and its building regulation regime was widely admired abroad by the standards of the time as 'brief, flexible, lenient, but strict and detailed where it had to be'.[2] By the late 1880s, the United States was following suit.[3] Modern copyright law began in Britain in 1710 and reached a watershed moment across the Anglophone world with the 1842 Copyright Act. The first meaningful 'Safety of Life at Sea' measures, the international SOLAS Convention, was adopted in 1914 in response to the *Titanic* disaster of 1912 and not updated until 1960. The International Maritime Organization that incorporated it along with other relevant conventions is now responsible for all aspects of maritime security and environmental control. The IMO is a United Nations specialized agency and it sits in a large building on the Albert Embankment beside the Thames in Lambeth.[4]

These are not just one-off historical landmarks, however, because 'standards' are never static. Whether in good old-fashioned product safety or in new concerns like demonstrating acceptable levels of environmental management or human rights among workers, standards are naturally dynamic and move with the times. Nor are they politically neutral or merely technical. When leaders and officials across the world sign up to some minimally acceptable standards or decide to harmonize their own national legal codes, they are exercising political judgement. And revising old standards, or working out thresholds for new ones, such as in cyber-security and the 'Internet of Things' (which the BSI does quite a lot), involves much consultation with leaders of an industry to arrive at a professional, peer-led consensus over how acceptable standards should be measured and monitored.

For historical reasons, many international frameworks naturally reflected British thinking about trade and services when it was industrially prominent. In the early twentieth century Britain created, or else greatly influenced, most international standards as they were evolving. Only seven of the nineteen UN specialized agencies and related organizations – dealing with everything from world health, food and agriculture, civil aviation, telecoms, meteorology, international labour standards and much more – were established after 1950. Britain was usefully over-represented in all League of Nations and UN matters before that time, while most of these agencies were drawing up their new regulatory functions. And Britain certainly had strong influence in the creation of some of the post-1950 organizations, such as the International Atomic Energy Agency of 1957 or the World Intellectual Property Organization of 1974.

Nevertheless, the real soft power benefits to Britain from these sorts of regulatory frameworks are more subtle. They reside in the professional and political judgements that are necessary in setting international standards and often in the way they are then legitimized – whether in the UN family or else as free-standing international conventions that are simply thought useful by their own members.

International standards are, for the most part, functional arrangements. Most cannot be directly or swiftly enforced by legal means or else – as in the case of the rules of the World Trade Organization – only as competing judgements that members can ignore for years. The real enforcement of an argument at, say, the International Civil Aviation Organization, or the International Maritime Court, lies in the prospects of retaliation or sanctions from other members. Such arrangements are 'functional' partly because they are largely self-policing – on the basis that the parties to the agreement value the functions such arrangements perform and take a dim view of disruptive behaviour. Such arrangements 'stick' internationally (at least more often than they fail) because they are credible. They represent hard-nosed, practical arrangements between fellow professionals who know how to make cooperation work and alongside a mature political framework that holds the ring for it and lets an organization get on with its job. The International Maritime Industries Forum that existed from 1975 to 2018, for example, brought together the shipping owners, charterers, bankers, insurance, oil and freight industries as a meeting of professionals to help regulate the fluctuating supply and demand for world shipping. It was based on the personal drive of Jim Davis and when he retired, the IMIF merged with Maritime London that had also evolved over these years. Jim Davis had, his obituarist said, 'helped to shape the government's shipping policies and steer the industry through busts and booms'.[5] A national reputation for being professional and practical goes a long way in such functional organizations. Britain has a good record in helping make international regulatory organizations credible and in being a credible player in them itself.

The internationally accepted standard for good quality management is defined by the International Organization for Standardization in the 'ISO 9000' serials for which international accreditation and certification is available. They are updated every seven years and are widely recommended by organizations like Britain's CBI, the Institute of Directors and their international counterparts elsewhere in the OECD countries. These standards were introduced to the world by the ISO in 1987 and are accepted as the right approach. Compliance with them helps get a company onto 'approved supplier' lists that all modern governments operate. Not many managers who follow them realize that they are based on the British Standards Institute's own BS 5750, the world's first quality management standards published in 1979. That British standard had arisen from British defence procurement policy during the Second World War – ensuring that defence companies dealing with the government met certain basic management criteria. It was all codified in the late 1950s at a time when the Pentagon in Washington was taking a similar approach to dealing with its own defence suppliers. These British and American defence-orientated standards went into NATO on behalf of the whole Western alliance, thence into BS 5750 and then, more than thirty years ago, became the bedrock of the world's famous ISO 9000 serials. No organization has yet improved on them as a workable standard for companies everywhere; they reflect long-standing British and American thinking about what 'quality management' should look like; and being compliant with ISO 9000 serials helps win contracts.[6]

Nor is this sort of influence all a thing of the past. The Grenfell Tower fire in 2017 was a tragic wake-up call to the dangers of potentially flammable cladding on buildings around the world, and yet another reminder of how different, and poor, international fire safety standards were from one country to another. Even while controversy still raged around the aftermath of the tragedy, the Royal Institution of Chartered Surveyors (RICS) in London took it upon itself to create an 'international coalition' to promote what became the International Fire Safety Standards Common Principles, known by its snappy title as the IFSS-CP. This process is designed to help guide a greater codification of fire safety regulations across different national jurisdictions and set higher common standards. In 2019 it had recruited more than eighty other professional bodies from around the world to join the initiative.[7] RICS is coy about its role as the instigator of this free-standing 'coalition' – even though its global building standards director in London is the coordinator for it. But in November 2020 the UN in Geneva made the IFSS-CP its European fire safety standard, and from 2021 it was adopted at the UN in New York as the first-ever common global standard for fire safety.

Nevertheless, British influence is up against some coherent and effective competition from the big players who are flexing their political muscles more obviously these days. The United Nations is an important arena for international standards; it is where so many complex, functional regulatory frameworks are negotiated and legitimized. And though Britain's role within the various UN agencies was historically strong, the contemporary picture for British influence at the UN is becoming more mixed.

There was a major setback in 2017 when Britain lost its place on the UN's International Court of Justice in The Hague having had a British judge in the court since its foundation during 1946. London mishandled the choreography of getting its sitting judge re-elected for a second term when he unexpectedly had to go head-to-head against an Indian candidate for the seat. The British candidate had the support of the UN Security Council but clearly would not have the necessary votes in the General Assembly – India was a more popular proposition to the majority of states. To avoid further embarrassment Britain withdrew its candidate and took the (considerable) hit to its international prestige at the UN.[8] Nevertheless, it still has influential roles and chief, deputy or senior presence at the International Monetary Fund, the Bank for International Settlements, the International Labour Organization, the International Seabed Authority, the World Health Organization, the International Telecommunications Union and the International Maritime Organization. On the other hand, there are almost forty significant UN and related organizations of this functional kind and as one of the Permanent Five of the Security Council Britain might increasingly wish it could play a bigger role than is apparent here.

The reason is that the UN's functional organizations are changing. The UN is, by its very nature, a political arena. Country and regional representations have to be balanced, roles have to be invented to avoid national offence, and so on, endlessly. But that sort of international parish pump politics has been increasingly overshadowed by the general indifference in the United States over recent years to what happens at the United Nations, coinciding with Beijing's strategically coherent approach to using every diplomatic avenue the organization offers.

China is now the second biggest contributor to the UN budget at 12 per cent and its deeper influence – apart from being another of the Permanent Security Council members – is felt right across the organization. By 2021, for example, Chinese officials headed four of the thirteen UN specialized agencies and had established a permanent deputy role in the Department of Economic and Social Affairs (DESA).[9] It has purchased its way to securing many votes among African states, by offering incentives or cancelling debts, and has shown itself skilful – in the way British diplomats always thought themselves skilful – at shaping the diplomatic vocabulary that everyone else in the organization uses. The practical effects of this have been that Beijing has integrated its 'Belt and Road Initiative' objectives into the UN's own global 'Sustainable Development Goals'. It has changed the terms of debate to make it increasingly difficult for genuine human rights concerns to be introduced into any UN agenda. It has used its role in the DESA to prevent Uyghur voices being heard over the racial repression in Xinjiang province. And it provides several routes into UN institutions for blatantly anti-democratic governments – not in itself unreasonable (the UN is not meant to be a club for democrats) – but certainly not in Britain's national interests. The fact is that Britain always played a diplomatically effective role at the UN and for too long took that fact for granted. Now it is anxious to retain its professional, pragmatic influence at a time when Chinese policy is turning the functional organizations of the UN into politicized instruments of its own.[10]

The principles of good standard-setting

The flexible British economy boasts a plethora of around 400 significant trade associations and regulatory bodies, all upholding their own professional standards. There are more than ninety regulatory bodies in the UK and together they spend more than £4 billion a year. The Office of Communications (Ofcom), the Civil Aviation Authority (CAA), the Office of Rail and Road (ORR), the Water Services Regulation Authority (Ofwat) and the Office of Gas and Electricity Markets (Ofgem) can all apply aspects of competition law in their sectors, which are concurrent with the Competition and Markets Authority (CMA) – not an economic regulator itself but it has overall responsibility for the UK's competition regime.[11] There are no fewer than seventeen important regulators in Britain's health sector, eight in the finance sector and a mix of regulatory or standards bodies in many others. They range from the CBI and the Chamber of Shipping to the Association of British Travel Agents, all the various Chartered Institutes, the Society of Master Saddlers or the Gin and Vodka Association.[12] The Department of Business, Energy and Industrial Strategy is responsible for coordinating the work of these organizations through the framework of its National Quality Infrastructure, wherein it works closely with the BSI.

Good standards-setting is justified by its measurable long-term impact, both for individual companies and for the national economy.[13] The Centre for Economic and Business Research analysed almost a century of British standard-setting across the national economy and concluded that Britain's improving standards underpinned around a third of all annual productivity growth between 1921 and 2013.[14] This proportion was maintained even in the years of peak economic crisis between 2008 and 2013. The benefits vary from sector to sector; mass production in the food and drink industry, or in the automotive sector, for example, finds it more beneficial than bespoke producers in sectors such as aerospace or defence. And bigger companies get more direct economic benefit out of official standards than smaller ones.[15]

From an international perspective, the benefits of agreed standards are that they facilitate trade in creating interoperability between different national products and services. They promote efficiency and drive exporting costs down by allowing production at scale which avoids falling foul of separate national regulations. Standards can also help promote innovation where they make it easier to share knowledge and can take much of the compliance cost out of new production processes and product innovation. And while compliance costs are less onerous for big companies than smaller ones, international standards nevertheless have the effect ultimately of lowering costs across the board for SMEs.[16] Not least, international standards can be a substitute for more onerous regulatory regimes that would otherwise be needed.

To be effective, international standards have to perform a number of functions. They must decide on metrics to measure and assess the outputs of a given sector – much easier where the output is a discrete product, like a retail item or a food product; harder in the case of a service, say in finance or law. But such metrics also apply, these days, to many of the processes of production – the guarantee that it is environmentally sensitive, energy efficient, compliant with human rights and so on. Such international standard-setting is not something that can be done by governments. It can only be properly achieved by professionals from all parts of an industry, agreeing in some detail on which standards are realistic and – critically – how a threshold for reaching them should be determined.

The system must then have the specialized means and the expertise to test any sector's outputs at regular intervals. There is the certification of members to the standards they have agreed and usually a process of accreditation to keep standards open to new adherents.

The hard-nosed objective for all members of a standards regime, of course, is to create the best competitive edge for what they do, whether in commerce, professional agencies or in the workings of government itself. Governments can rationalize and legitimize the international standards they want the national economy to uphold – and they can make a point of observing important standards themselves – but they cannot create or maintain them. That is a matter for the professionals within the sector.[17] Professional credibility is intrinsic to all levels of national and international standardization. The Chartered Institute for Archaeologists, for example, has international credibility, not because Britain is brimming with archaeological sites but deriving from long-standing scholarship in the field and an excellent reputation for professionalism. And it works hard to establish and enhance global and professional standards in archaeology.

Standards can only be successful if they embody high levels of international credibility and legitimacy. That is why the specialized agencies of the United Nations can play a big role in recording and legitimizing harmonization where it occurs. The same applies to the European Union, and in the post-Brexit process it is not yet quite clear how ongoing British standards-setting will mesh with similar processes within the EU. And it varies. Harmonization is more evident in sectors such as electrical product safety, for example, than in more diffuse areas like food processing or textile production.

Professional standards should be apolitical, but they are not. The technical management of the World Wide Web may be handled non-politically through ICANN,[18] but the licensing of internet companies such as Facebook, Twitter or TikTok and the standards they uphold from one jurisdiction to the next has become massively political. The 'autocratic internet' – driven for political reasons by quite different professional standards that apply to the 'global, free internet' – seems set to become the norm for most of the global population as the majority of the three billion people yet to join the system will do so in states that are currently autocratic and aligned with Russia or China.[19]

The political challenge to Western liberalism posed by the current governments in Russia and China, and in the autocratic regimes that are heavily influenced by them, also plays out in its own ways within the world of more mundane international standards. Russia does not feature greatly in global manufacturing; its exports are predominantly in energy and raw materials and it has a large domestic market for its own manufactures that has not varied very much since the Soviet era when it ran, in effect, self-sufficiently. Where it manufactures or offers services to the global market, it does so on the basis of existing agreed standards, though Russia also has some niche and highly unregulated trade with its economically eccentric clients like Belarus, Syria, Venezuela, Serbia or Cuba.

In contrast, as the Chinese economy achieves parity with the United States, its extensive manufacturing now largely underpins global consumerism. Chinese manufacturing cannot ignore quality and safety standards for its products that have been laid down by predominantly Western standards institutes. As its international telecoms companies like Huawei and ZTE have discovered to their cost, they can be excluded from lucrative Western markets because their own product standards cannot rule out the possibility of political control from Beijing. But this also highlights the deeper political problem the Chinese economy poses in the directions that standards-setting are moving. While its product outputs can be assessed and tested, and Chinese companies certainly need to have their products certified to international standards, it is much more difficult for standards institutes to guarantee that production processes within China are compliant with international labour, human rights or environmental standards. Successive scandals have emerged of forced labour being used in cheap garment manufacturing. China has hit back with consumer boycotts of Western brands. It is the beginning of a proxy war over who controls standards in textile production.

Nor is it only about China. Supply chain scandals and labour standards are a major headache for a number of Western companies, many of whom have been unable to monitor, still less control, all the processes in their long supply chains. Even Marks and Spencer found itself caught up in an Asian sweatshop scandal in 2010 because of its own complex supply chain. In the same year H&M suffered a massive factory fire at one of its Bangladesh suppliers where all the fire exits had been blocked. In 2013 Walmart found it was being supplied by a factory in Bangladesh that collapsed with its workers inside. Nike had a very bad supply chain reputation in the 1990s, which it claims to have fixed, and companies such as Gap, Sears, La Senza, Disney or Victoria's Secret have all featured on naming and shaming lists for their inability to apply proper standards in their low-cost supply chains. The fact is that the credibility and inclusiveness of standards regimes in many manufacturing sectors is patchy, for both political and non-political reasons, as supply chains have lengthened.

The fields of British influence

Global soft power, as we have observed in Part One, is fundamentally driven by an overall image of liking and trust. And this applies not just at the national level in the image the British state projects but from sector to sector in the commercial world as well. In the case of regulation and standardization, the international metrics favour Britain.

The OECD assesses the regulatory performance of its thirty-seven members on a continuing basis as part of its mission to keep markets as flexible and free as possible. In 2018 it rated Britain highly for its investment in regulatory policy, its consultation and oversight mechanisms and the strong emphasis on evidence-based policy. In its comparative country studies – though the OECD is too careful to say as much – Britain provides a model of modern approaches to regulation. The OECD particularly notes the 'innovation office' in the medicines and healthcare regulator and the 'regulatory sandbox' in the Financial Conduct Authority (FCA) where new products and services can be properly live-tested before they are offered to the market. On a scale of 0–4 it scores Britain between 3.0 and 3.5 – significantly above the OECD average – on different measures of productive regulation.[20] Britain's scores in this respect are almost identical to the EU average, though that average disguises much lower performances from Germany (2.0–2.5), France (1.8–2.0) and Italy (2.5–2.8), where the OECD observes politely but somewhat devastatingly that the country needed systematic direction to 'connect the dots' and 'develop a culture of evidence-based user-centric policy-making'.[21] Interestingly, though the United States performs well above the OECD average, it still scores lower than Britain.[22]

It is, at least, a tangible indicator of Britain's commitment to free and fair markets and it helps underpin Britain's business reputation overseas for upholding – and itself sticking to – international standards. In this respect, the overarching role and the effectiveness of Whitehall's Department for Business, Energy and Industrial Strategy deserve due credit.

Beyond the official metrics, however, the image of pragmatic and professional competence is also extremely important. In January 2021, as the country adjusted to the realities of Brexit Britain, a major independent report commissioned by the City of London argued that British government urgently needed to restore its reputation and image as 'more predictable, stable and strategic' in the way it does business after the hiatus of the Brexit process and its unsure handling of the Covid-19 crisis.[23]

It is self-evidently true that general images of competence matter, but the most important foundation for Britain's soft power in any given sector is likely to be its own demonstrable success. There are some fields in which Britain can certainly demonstrate that its own standards – of both performance and regulation – are globally acknowledged.

Financial services in the City of London constitute the most prominent sector in Britain's international economic image. It certainly demonstrates success. This arises not just from the financial institutions of 'the City' itself – the different types of banks, the investment houses and the various exchanges – but also London's 'central business district' where all the insurance, legal services, accountancy and facilities management also exist. It remains a cluster of institutions of 'global importance' that can still claim to be a 'global powerhouse'.[24] The City generates the second greatest international financial activity in the world behind only New York. It remains the global capital for fintech and, importantly, for innovation in financial services. Based on ninety-one separate metrics assessed during 2020, London's financial centre was still objectively ahead of New York, Singapore, Hong Kong and Frankfurt. Its strongest competitive offerings were seen to be in 'leadership' and 'innovation', in its 'reach of financial activity', 'resilience', 'business infrastructure', 'talent, skill and regulation'.[25]

In the matter of regulation, the FCA alongside the Prudential Regulation Authority (PRA) are prime examples of international sectoral influence. They were both established in 2013 as a rationalization of the previous arrangements. They are both independent of the British government but the FCA works closely with the Treasury and alongside the independent Bank of England, while the PRA is an arm of the Bank of England, acting as a quasi-governmental regulator to monitor standards for banks, building societies, major investment firms, insurers and credit unions.

They are both funded through money levied from institutions among the financial services industry. The FCA receives around £600 million a year and monitors standards across its £65+ billion industry with its 58,000 businesses and 2.2 million employees nationwide. As such, it has strong international influence in setting standards, through ESMA and through its chairing or co-chairing of the International Organization of Securities Commissions and the various committees of the Financial Stability Board.[26]

The FCA is not without its critics and there are calls for it to be abolished or replaced by something else again as the City tries to resettle itself into a level of regulation that will maintain its reputation for upholding standards while not dulling its competitive edge as a financial centre. Controversial or not, the FCA represents a classic example that incorporates the hard power of London's sheer financial weight and the soft power of being able to set standards for the City that the rest of the world has to take seriously.

Inevitably, the current direction of travel cannot be taken for granted. Brexit, it was always clear, would not destroy the City, but it might administer a 'slow puncture' if it does not remain genuinely dynamic.[27] Early in 2021 it appeared that Amsterdam had rapidly overtaken London as Europe's share-trading centre since Brexit.[28] More importantly, Brexit exacerbated worries over a skills gap and especially over immigration policy that created an image that the City may no longer be the top destination for the best foreign talent. And the need for more government investment in Britain's digital and transport infrastructure remains a running joke in the coffee shops and wine bars around Lombard Street. The particular challenge for the regulatory framework is to keep pace with technological change and innovation. While Brexit offers the City the opportunity to be more internationally competitive outside the EU in the regulatory regimes it runs, it has still 'missed the boat' in the view of some, regarding important new markets: for example, in setting green investment standards on the 'ESG' (Environmental, Social and Governance) criteria oversight.[29] Britain risks lagging behind, it is said, as Brussels pushes hard to create the world's first 'green gold standard' for future investors.[30]

Another sector that promotes strong international images of success and high standards is architecture. The building and architecture of a country symbolize the cultural achievements of a civilization. The number, and the geographical distribution not just in London but around the country, of Britain's great public buildings and engineering structures is an enduring record of architectural eminence. Castles and Jacobean houses are one thing, but Christopher Wren's seventeenth-century Cathedral at St Paul's marks an epochal change in British architecture, which takes in so much from the Hawksmoor churches, the Palladian grandeur of country houses and the great civic architecture of Britain's nineteenth-century industrial cities.

Most analysts would agree that twentieth-century architecture was led by the United States. Architecture was one of America's most confident and triumphant expressions of its own culture. But British late-twentieth-century architecture has also been highly international. In the early 1970s, Britain's Richard Rogers with Italian Renzo Piano won the international competition to design one of Paris' great cultural landmarks, the Centre Pompidou. In the late 1970s, Britain's Norman Foster won the bid to design 'the most expensive building in the world', the HSBC headquarters in Hong Kong. The Foster global brand was cemented by the time it won the commission to reconstruct the German Reichstag in the 1990s.

British-Iraqi Dame Zaha Hadid (1950–2016) was the creative firepower behind the London Aquatics Centre for the 2012 Olympics; Michigan State University's Broad Art Museum; the MAXXI Museum in Rome; the Guangzhou Opera House; the Beijing Daxing International Airport; and, before she died, the Al Wakrah Stadium in Qatar for the 2022 football World Cup. British-Ghanian Sir David Adjaye, along with Philip Freelon, won the international competition to design and deliver the National Museum of African American History and Culture in Washington DC. And Adjaye also designed the Skolkovo Moscow School of Management in Russia, wanting, he said, 'to disrupt the old order of a school as a series of houses and instead to prioritise student interaction and reflection'.[31]

Such modern British architects have also helped build an image of multicultural Britain; huge and impressive design desired by the world and made possible by successful collaboration among architects who can reach across cultures. Not surprisingly, the Royal Institute of British Architects is not embarrassed to offer global architectural awards to champion 'buildings that change the world'.[32] This eminence does not disguise the fact that domestic architecture in Britain, flawed planning laws and its long-standing housing shortage have between them created something of a state of anarchy in British building and architecture that has been the subject of fierce criticism in recent years.[33] It seems a curious juxtaposition to the high reputation that British architecture and big project engineering enjoy and the otherwise high international standards they have showcased over decades.

Publishing is another field in which British conventions blend strongly with the power of its tangible outputs. Cambridge University Press is the oldest university press in the world.[34] Oxford University Press is the largest.[35] Britain is also home of some of the largest book publishers anywhere. The RELX Group, Pearson, Bloomsbury, all headquartered in London, are repeatedly ranked among the top global publishing houses by worldwide revenue. Pearson – the British multinational publishing and educational company providing assessment services to schools and corporations – began publishing books in the 1920s and now operates in over seventy countries. Britain's publishing industry is worth over £6 billion annually, marginally more than India's (even with its 9,000 publishers). The US publishing market is worth about £21 billion, but Britain exports over 60 per cent of the books it publishes and still produces the third biggest absolute total of books in the world – about 190,000 volumes annually, compared to a little over 300,000 in the United States and around 450,000 in China. Even Russia or Germany only publish around 100,000 volumes a year. In fact, Britain publishes more books per capita than any other country; and that is not because Britons are greater readers than anyone else but because British-produced books, in English, are in demand internationally.[36] And British-based publishers structure the type and quality of their outputs to catch and influence trends in the global market. As a result, Britain is the largest book exporter in the world.[37]

We have described elsewhere the international prominence of Britain's medical and pharmacological sectors, particularly in the extensive national research base, the big pharma companies that operate in Britain and the way they have worked together effectively. The importance of this sector as a soft power influencer for international standards lies not so much in the global reach of its own national medical regulation but more in the power of British medical research to be rated highly and imitated in other countries. High standards and demonstrable performance go together; one reinforces the other.

We have mentioned the effect on Russia's Sputnik V Covid-19 vaccine of a single inclusion in *The Lancet* on 2 February 2021. More significantly, Britain's genome sequencing research remained second to none, at a time when understanding the genetic data of SARS-CoV-2 and its evolution was critical to the development of diagnostics and therapeutics. Through the work of Genomics England, the 100,000 Genome Project and specialist laboratory hubs across Britain's 'Covid-19 Genomics UK Consortium' (COG-UK) had sequenced over 450,000 viruses by the start of May 2021.[38] Britain's expertise and linked infrastructure made it, undoubtedly, the world leader in this particular field. It seems remarkable that the Gambia, Equatorial Guinea and Sierra Leone had a higher rate of sequencing than the likes of France, Italy or the United States – in part due to their previous experience of domestic epidemics.[39] Key to British success was that it worked at remarkable speed and scale, shared this critical information internationally and created the New Variant Assessment Platform to do so more effectively.[40] There was never any questioning of Britain's scientific credibility.

The impact of the UK's medicines regulator, the MHRA, is another case in point. The European Medicines Agency (EMA) was, until Brexit, headquartered in London. It is now in Amsterdam. The EMA operates the Committee for Medicinal Products for Human Use (CHMP) where medicine developers submit their applications for authorization to take products to the market. CHMP works by taking two different national committee members – rapporteur and co-rapporteur – to lead each assessment, picked for their therapy area expertise and their reputation for conducting rigorous scientific evaluations. In 2016, prior to Brexit, Britain's MHRA was selected more times than any other EU Member State.[41]

Finally, a quite different dimension in which British standards can be seen as a soft power asset – creating a sense of trust and acknowledging underlying national professionalism – lies in the realm of accountability and transparency when standards fail or are breached. In Britain, there is an assumption that failures will be thoroughly investigated and in public, not covered up by state agencies. There is an expectation of transparency in the public interest and a quick resort to law if victims of a failure feel that relevant information is being withheld.

Of course, there is a great deal of public cynicism as to whether this degree of accountability and transparency is actually present in modern Britain, if it ever was. Critics point to Royal Commissions that take years to report: of banking scandals in 2008 that seemed to be swept aside. They point to celebrated cases like the Hillsborough stadium disaster in 1989 that was still subject to legal judgement in 2020; the official inquiry into Britain's Iraq war that was not initiated until it was finally over and then took more than seven years to report; the lessons of the Manchester terrorist bombing in 2017 that was still being assessed in 2021; the shocking Grenfell Tower fire in 2017 and the deadliest residential fire in Britain since the Second World War, which remains a subject of continuing review and bitter controversy and which uncovered failures that the press habitually refer to as 'Britain's housing scandal'; to endless incidents in the Northern Ireland emergency as far back as 1972 that remain the subject of fierce discord and open-ended calls for greater transparency and (still) for private prosecutions.

On the other hand, it is easy to remember the labels we give to national disasters and forget about some of the effects they had. The Flixborough explosion in 1974 led to new legislation and extensive changes in chemical industry standards in 1975. The Heysel Stadium disaster in Brussels in 1985 was rightly blamed mainly on British soccer hooligans and all British major league clubs changed their procedures and began redesigning their grounds from 1986. The King's Cross fire in 1987 was followed within months by sackings and an extensive programme of tube refurbishment to reduce the combustibility of materials used on the underground. The massive Piper Alpha oil rig explosion that killed 167 men and cost £2 billion in 1988 was followed by an exhaustive report on the disaster in 1990 and a new Offshore Safety Act in 1992 that changed procedures across the international offshore oil and gas industries. Just as the *Titanic* disaster in 1912 led to new international safety standards at sea, the Grenfell Tower fire – for all its controversy in Britain – led to the adoption of new UN global standards for international fire safety.[42] Even in the financial sector, the LIBOR scandal that came to light in 2012 led to Serious Fraud Office charges and convictions and some important changes in the international procedures, and law, governing inter-bank setting of average interest rates (LIBOR rates) between them. However unsatisfactory British 'lessons learned' exercises may sometimes be, the fact is that the external world sees that a process almost always does take place, that the law does bear on it and that it fully recognizes the rights of victims of a malpractice or disaster to continue to press their case.

Nor may it be lost on the external world that, in some contrast to Britain's forensic and anguished breast-beating, the disastrous Ponte Morandi bridge collapse in 2018 was Italy's eleventh collapsed bridge since 2013. The frequency of repeated and similar disasters in major countries, and in many smaller ones, is indicative of how many governments evidently do not conduct meaningful enquiries, transparent or not. Between 2010 and 2021 there were three serious building collapses and two civil site collapses (a bridge and a major dam) in India; and four buildings, three bridges and one power station collapsed in China during the decade. In the United Arab Emirates there were two major fires in the same seventy-nine-storey Dubai Torch Tower in 2015 and again in 2017. Then a disastrous blaze in the Zen Tower at Dubai Marina in 2018 and another in the forty-eight-storey Abbco Tower in Sharjar in 2020.[43] It goes on.

There is never room for complacency or self-congratulation in this field, but the long-run image of a country in which such failures are actually unusual, and which tries to learn the important lessons, should command at least some respect from analysts.

Cosmopolitans and diasporas

Reflecting global cultures

There was a 44-minute period on 4 August 2012 at the London Olympics – 'super Saturday' as it became known – when the confidence and achievement of multicultural Britain seemed to be triumphantly on display. At the memorable Olympic opening ceremony eight days previously a striking pageant of British history had been beautifully presented in the stadium. In front of a global audience of over a billion people, the pageant had fun with the sensibilities of American free-enterprise disciples by showing children bouncing up and down on hospital beds in celebration of the NHS. It cocked a snook at religiously conservative countries by showing inter-religious and interracial groups dancing joyfully to brash British music. It confronted audiences of many countries in Africa, Asia and the Middle East with gay couples, intrinsically part of a vibrant British scene. It was unapologetic, assured and comical; even the Queen appeared to parachute into the stadium to open the games. And then, in the final 44 minutes of super Saturday, with two rowing gold medals already won by men's and women's crews earlier that day, red-haired Scottish athlete Greg Rutherford won gold in the long jump. A few minutes later Jessica Ennis-Hill, a mixed-race Jamaican Briton and 'face of the games', ran a storming 800 metres to win the Heptathlon gold. And just before ten o'clock, Mo Farah, who had arrived in Britain in 1995 as an eight-year-old Somali refugee without a word of English when his family fled Mogadishu, won the 10,000 metres gold with an imperious performance. Around 80,000 ecstatic spectators in the stadium cheered his every lap as he became the most successful British track athlete in modern Olympic history. None could have been more proud to be British athletes than Rutherford, Ennis-Hill or Farah that night. It seemed like a decisive vindication of all the cheeky vignettes the opening ceremony had presented, and a lot more besides.

Of course, it was all the highlight of a flag-waving showpiece, not a considered reflection of Britain. But it mattered nonetheless, because it captured at least the aspiration that 'Britishness' was not really defined by ethnicity but more by a certain way of doing things – in this case very successfully. The opening ceremony had presented Britain as a naturally multicultural and multiracial society, something baked into its own long history. During the polarized political arguments over Brexit that followed the 2012 Olympics, there was some pushback against this characterization and much controversy over how Britain should express its fundamental identity. Whatever identity modern Britain feels comfortable with, however, the evidence also suggests there is a more long-standing public acceptance that the very nature of British society is multicultural, multiracial and cosmopolitan, even though in practical terms that can be very hard to handle.[1]

As Andrew Marr puts it, 'If there is a genuinely tolerant and successful multiracial Britain somewhere in the future, the journey towards it is a long and twisting one.'[2] But few seriously dispute that the country is on – has always been on – such a journey. It is the speed of the journey over recent years, not the fact of it, that generates such political sensitivity.[3] There was widespread public alarm at the effects of the foreign refugee crisis that built up across Europe after 2010, and some real anger at the influx, legally and illegally, of refugees and asylum-seekers coming into Britain as a result of it. In fact, the numbers involved were dwarfed by those arriving in Germany, Italy and many smaller and poorer European countries and Germany, at least in 2015, shamed the rest of Europe by opening its borders to hundreds of thousands of people in genuine distress.[4] This ongoing crisis of uncontrolled migration affects all European countries one way or another. In Britain, what is most notable is a difference of public attitudes between fear of immediate large-scale migration alongside the widespread, sometimes even proud, embrace of British multiculturalism. It currently appears to be an unresolved identity question that will play out in British politics and society in the near future.[5]

In response to the 'Black Lives Matter' movement that gained public traction in Britain from 2016 and then again in the wake of the US movement in 2020, the government created a commission of enquiry that reported in March 2021. 'We no longer see a Britain where the system is deliberately rigged against ethnic minorities', it said, but 'we take the reality of racism seriously and we do not deny that it is a real force in the UK'.[6] The report set off a fierce debate about whether racism in Britain was 'structural', and had not been shaken out of the system, or else 'incidental', in that it arose through more particular processes of social failure. For all its ferocity, the fact of the debate may be regarded as encouraging but the picture of inequality with clear racial overtones, at the very least, remains unsatisfactory.

As an asset of soft power, however, the longer-term perspective of Britain's tolerance and multiculturalism is more important to the image of what British society fundamentally represents than its fluctuating policy responses to Europe's migration crises or the demands of the Black Lives Matter movement. But the underlying and historic reality of British multiculturalism, for all the undoubted tensions along Andrew Marr's 'long and twisting' road, creates a tangible reality. And different communities of British persuaders describe to the rest of the world, warts and all, what from their perspective British society is really like.

Multiculturism and cosmopolitanism

In the 2011 census, Britain's multicultural make-up revealed a country where 87.2 per cent of the population described themselves as 'white British'; 3 per cent as 'African/Caribbean/Black British'; 2.3 per cent as 'Indian'; 1.9 per cent as 'Pakistani'; 2 per cent as mixed and 3.7 per cent as various other descriptions classified generally under the collective title of Black Asian Minority Ethnic (BAME) individuals.[7]

These figures are the stark statistics of a very long and distinctive story. As has been observed many times, Britain is a country of immigration and cultural mixing, from the time of the Roman occupation onwards (which, incidentally, brought many Africans – soldiers, traders and slaves into Britain). A Londoner in Tudor times complained that 'Tottenham has turned French'. Traditional, iconic British fish 'n' chips appears to be, in fact, a cultural innovation of *pescaito frito* (fried fish) brought by Sephardic Jewish immigrants fleeing pogroms in Lisbon via Amsterdam before reaching England, with a love of fried potatoes brought to England by Protestant Huguenots who could not live under Louis XIV's Catholic decrees. There is a long history of toleration towards not just Huguenots but also Greek Christians, Dutch, Italian and German immigrants moving to Britain, usually to avoid persecution. At least 150,000 Jews fled to Britain from Russian Tsarist pogroms in the 1890s. And the Second World War created some distinctive communities from the occupied countries of Eastern Europe that persisted after 1945, particularly among Polish groups.[8]

But the census figures tell a much bigger story than that of Britain's long-standing toleration and refuge, and one that is more uncomfortable for many Britons to acknowledge. It is the story of the empire. The BAME population of Britain makes up about 14 per cent of the total, 7.5 per cent Asian and 3.3 per cent Black ethnic (mainly of African and Caribbean descent). While there has been a long tradition of BAME people in Britain for several centuries, it was the end of the empire in the mid-twentieth century, plus the advent of mass and affordable travel, that brought people to Britain and created these numbers – about 9.3 million among a 68.2 million total population – as families settled into second- and third-generation citizenship. Much of the multicultural pattern is determined by the erstwhile patterns of British colonialism and by the domestic labour shortages in the 1940s and 1950s, which led to extensive job advertising across the Commonwealth, inviting workers to come to Britain, especially to take up jobs in the transport and health sectors. And in the 1960s it was natural and inevitable that when racist leaders in Kenya and Uganda drove out the Asian communities that the empire had settled in their countries as a nascent merchant class, some 83,000 'Kenyan and Ugandan Asians' would resettle in Britain. As the popular refrain runs at times of inter-ethnic tension in this country, 'we are here because you were there'. It's a natural consequence of empire.

Britain's multicultural make-up therefore leans heavily towards the different peoples of the Indian subcontinent, East Africa and the Caribbean. In the case of France, the equivalents are ethnic minorities from West Africa and the Maghreb countries of North Africa. In Italy, multiculturalism is driven from North Africa and the Balkans. In Germany, its 'multikulti' – the slogan of the progressive approach to multiculturalism – is dominated by immigration into Germany from many other European countries, two-thirds from within the EU, and by its *Gastarbeiter*, guest workers, particularly from Turkey. In contrast to Britain, with its 14 per cent of BAME citizens, Germany's more continental pattern of cultural diversity is driven by the 25 per cent of its population – some 20 million Germans – who now have a migrant background in their immediate generation.[9]

Multiculturalism in Britain with its centuries-long pedigree has only emerged in the last sixty years as one of the sensitive issues that surround the recent questioning of national identity. It has been marked by many scandals and failures, like the 'Windrush issue' and some disturbing race riots in British cities. Some minority communities have become ghettoized. It has been challenged by the Black Lives Matter movement and the focus on historic slavery in Britain's imperial prosperity. The spectre of implicit racism or hidden prejudice against ethnic minorities still stalks British policing and the upper echelons of sectors such as education, law, sport or entertainment. The charge of institutional racism, true or not, doesn't go away. In 2011 even the then prime minister, David Cameron, joined other European leaders in questioning whether multiculturism, at least in the laissez-faire way it had been followed in Britain, was capable of withstanding the levels of stress that had been put on it for more than a generation.

But British multiculturalism has also had its underlying successes – its predominantly tolerant form of eventual and unforced integration into a society that generally accepts the benefits of cultural renewal and managed upheaval. Overt racism has never pushed its way onto the political mainstream in Britain, as it has in the United States and several European countries, big and small.[10] There is still an inbred faith among the majority of the British public that, given enough time, the laissez-faire approach will evolve to maintain an inclusive national culture.[11] It will change Britain one way or another, but the result will still be 'British' because of the evolutionary way it works. Britain's history, says Robert Winder, 'is the sum of countless muddled and contradictory experiences' in absorbing migrants.[12] Most would accept this view, though others regard it as complacent. A key problem in resolving differences between these views is that the imperial basis for Britain's current pattern of multiculturalism is neither well understood nor calmly discussed as the country edges towards a new expression of its own national identity: post-imperial, post-war and now post-EU. British popular culture seems not to want to acknowledge the importance, for both good and bad, of the British Empire in its twenty-first society. As the Sikh-born writer Sathnam Sanghera put it:

> I'm glad empire gave us our multiculturalism, our internationalism, a certain tradition of anti-racism, and laid the foundations of the welfare state, and while I delight in the fact that our language, art and cuisine reflect our complex history, our imperial legacies and the way we fail to see them are a burden. . . . We can progress only if we confront them.[13]

That stands as a good summary of the relevance of British multiculturalism as a soft power asset. The very concept is under the microscope because of the speed with which numbers of citizens who define themselves in BAME categories have grown since the 1960s.[14] It is also under the microscope for other reasons as British society suffers stresses from elsewhere. Multiculturism and its successes and failures become symptoms of deeper doubts about social cohesion.

It is constantly affected, for example, by Britain's poor record on social mobility – 'one of the poorest rates of social mobility in the developed world', says the Deloitte consultancy – and certainly by common perceptions that it has not improved. The Social Mobility Commission's 'State of the Nation' report in 2019 showed that social mobility in Britain was static in virtually every sphere: birth chances, education, occupation, pay, gender and so on. Interestingly, the one area in which there was some slight improvement was in 'differences of ethnicity', where those from '*privileged* ethnic backgrounds' had become almost as socially mobile as those from '*privileged* white backgrounds'. But this was swamped by the lack of mobility in every other dimension, so that, for example, there was a significantly higher proportion of working-class people among 'ethnic groups', whose own occupational chances were no worse than for white working-class people, but who saw the far bigger gap between themselves and the better jobs privileged ethnic people were getting.[15] In 2020 the Commission's surveys revealed stark regional disparities throughout the country, especially in relation to the difference in life prospects between London and everywhere else. This had the effect of putting social mobility overall into decline.[16] It remains an unsatisfactory picture which, in any case, is unlikely to improve until the national economy is in better health.

Certainly, the realities of poor social mobility create powerful images of exclusion. When the Covid-19 pandemic affected public health disproportionately within ethnic minorities or the vaccination programme met resistance among those same communities; when the broad economic damage of the pandemic fell most heavily on the most deprived regions of Britain, the success of British multiculturalism is always in question. The incongruity of a National Health Service that is disproportionately staffed (over 20 per cent) from the BAME communities, where health provision is nevertheless substandard for those communities, is self-evident. And Sathram's point is that multiculturalism is not a challenge because Britain was somehow so attractive to foreign minorities – still less a soft touch for some sort of parasitic foreign pressure. It is multicultural because that is what made the country what it was, and is now, two centuries ago.

So, multiculturalism is both a force to drive soft power magnetism and a phenomenon that can diminish the sense of a country's social cohesion and stability. It depends how it is handled. Germany's opening of its borders to distressed migrants in 2015 eventually damaged Chancellor Merkel's political standing and hastened her retirement from leadership as more hostile reactions set into some of the social consequences. But though Germany rowed back from many aspects of this 'opening' policy, it has enhanced its status over the longer term as an ordered, humane and effective society in addressing global problems – exactly the images in which Britain wishes to be seen in its post-EU manifestation.[17]

Multiculturalism creates cosmopolitanism and that is a very attractive quality for any society to project abroad. London is a long-standing and shining example. 'When I arrived in Britain 30 years ago', wrote Bettina Schultz in

2020, 'London was freedom for me, a living utopia, a model for how people from all over the world could live together, work together and love together. There were no foreigners. Everybody belonged.'[18] This may be a sentimentalized view and within Britain it could probably only apply in London – Europe's only truly global city. But we know what she means. London itself creates powerful images of Britain for the rest of the world. In the nineteenth century Benjamin Disraeli observed that 'London is modern Babylon'. To Paddington Bear from Peru, 'In London everyone is different, and that means anyone can fit in.'[19] Such cosmopolitanism is not only captured by individual anecdotes. A significant perspective is provided by London's Muslim population of over 600,000 people, which is thought to be the most diverse concentration of different Muslim communities anywhere in the world, outside Mecca itself.[20] Or again, the Notting Hill Carnival which began in 1966 has filled the streets of West London with Caribbean dancers, calypso and zouk music every August – in recent years involving 2.5 million revellers, 40,000 volunteers and 9,000 police – some observably dancing along to it all.

London's own cosmopolitan image, however, must also be set in a broader national perspective. Tourist chiefs may make much of it, alongside the other great capital cities of Britain – Edinburgh with its international festival, Cardiff with its new media prominence, Belfast with its Titanic Quarter and the famous shipyard where it all began. But the fact remains that London has for some time been a Fourth Kingdom within the UK. It encompasses 13 per cent of the national population, produces over 20 per cent of the national output, has by far the highest proportion of BAME residents among British cities (it crossed the 'majority–minority threshold' in the 2011 census) and it effectively refreshes its resident population every decade as 'incomers' and 'leavers' almost balance each other out – around seven million in and out within a city population that fluctuates between eight and nine million. And London is still eight times bigger than the next biggest British city.[21] Capital cities are seldom like their own national hinterlands but in London's case – though it is a bright jewel in Britain's multicultural and cosmopolitan crown – the inescapable fact is that over the last forty years it has become increasingly untypical of the Britain over which it presides.

Within the United Kingdom London is in effect a socio-economic kingdom of its own. In addition to Britain's four de facto existing kingdoms – Scotland, Wales, Northern Ireland and London – we should also recognize a Fifth Kingdom of 'England outside London' where the difference between the capital city and everywhere else in England has become economically greater and certainly *perceptually* greater. The Fifth Kingdom contains around 72 per cent of the total population of the UK, and it certainly has its economic bright spots: in the Thames Valley, Bristol and the Oxford/Cambridge corridor or the sparkling city centres of the midlands and the north. But as the Brexit vote in 2016 and the collapse of the Labour Party's erstwhile 'red wall' in the 2019 general election showed, it was a kingdom where many people were exasperated with the state of British politics and for a long time had felt largely 'left behind' by Britain's success as a globalized economy. The great cities that arose when northern businesses powered the industrial revolution, commanding significant political weight within Britain, were distant memories by the mid-twentieth century. The Fifth Kingdom, as the Conservative government of 2019 readily recognized, was politically volatile, untrusting of Westminster and needing to be nurtured. So it was that the government stressed its 'levelling up agenda' for most of the Fifth Kingdom. It would revive the 'northern powerhouse' initiatives of its predecessors. And when that was blown apart by the Covid-19 crisis, it stressed that the post-Covid-19 economic maxim would be to 'build back better' and make a perceptual difference to how people in the Fifth Kingdom felt about their own economic future, their immediate environment and their place in the United Kingdom of the twenty-first century.

And on that matter, the government found itself facing the post-Covid-19 world with a stick or twist option. The very concept of the Union of the UK is now at issue for the decade to come: an argument about whether the United Kingdom can serve the interests, and command the loyalties, of all its people. The government's 'stick' option is to assert the virtues of the Union as it is and defy separatist movements in Scotland, Northern Ireland and Wales that seek to gain enough support to break it up. The 'twist' option is to take dissolution as a challenge that cannot be faced down and more fundamentally reform or rebuild the Union along new lines. This is not the place to discuss Britain's constitutional future, which the authors have tackled elsewhere.[22] But it raises the government's stick or twist stakes a great deal, specifically in relation to the Fifth Kingdom. If London and the Westminster establishment – the Fourth Kingdom – is to fight separatists in the first three kingdoms successfully, to either preserve the Union as it is or reconfigure it to be more flexible and acceptable, then some new deal for the Fifth Kingdom is unavoidable. If London's 13 per cent of the total population is to argue with Scotland, Wales and Northern Ireland's combined 15 per cent of the total population over the fate of the Union, then the 72 per cent in the constitutionally passive Fifth Kingdom of the Union will want their voices heard. A dissolving Union, a reforming Union or a new Union will become constitutionally a new Britain – and perhaps a socially and psychologically new Britain too.

Diaspora communities in Britain

Whether, in the event, British governments go for the stick or the twist option, the country will be embarking on some daunting social and constitutional challenges in the near future. We return to this in Chapter 14. As it does so, however, Britain will be able to draw on the potent weapon of its own diasporas – potent in the sense that they can have very important impacts on others' essential perceptions of the country, and a weapon in that diasporas can work either for or against a national image depending on the opinions and ideas of the individuals and families who comprise it. The image its diasporas convey of Britain in all its 'five kingdoms' as it moves towards some sort of constitutional reckoning will have an important bearing on the country's soft power standing in the world.

As we discussed in Chapter 3, the most potent transmission mechanisms of soft power are through 'lived experience' and 'human contact'. Diasporas are the most direct and authentic mirrors on another society that any group will probably have to make its own judgements and form its opinions: people whom they themselves know and whose direct experiences will be of interest to those living in the home country of origin. People who also identify, perhaps in their second, third or even fourth generation, with another country or culture along with the British identity they were born into have the effect of conveying very personal and specific human images and ideas to their heritage communities overseas.

The United States, for example, is heavily criticized in all parts of the world, sometimes ferociously, as by Iran – every week at official Friday prayers. But as top of the soft power tree, populations around the world that have contact with their diaspora communities in the United States, usually with the exception of Germany, report favourable views of 'life in America'.[23] Even, perhaps especially, among Iranians in America, where the biggest portion of the Iranian diaspora in the world actually live. If the 'United States' is not popular everywhere, 'America' still is, thanks largely to the transmission links of the different diasporas.

As a result of its own patterns of multiculturalism, Britain has very particular sorts of diaspora communities that are similarly important in communicating an image of Britain as a prosperous society and also as a stable and tolerant one. India's Prime Minister Modi described the Indian diaspora in Britain as a 'living bridge' between the two countries.[24] He well might. Even excluding those of mixed ancestry, the 1.4 million ethnic Indians living in Britain are regarded as the single largest BAME group in the country. In 2019 the Hinduja brothers led the list of the richest six people in Britain with their £12.8 billion fortune.[25] The annual Diwali festival in Leicester is one of the biggest outside India.[26] 'Prosperity', 'opportunity' and 'respect for law' are important attributes in the eyes of others and remain key organizing principles for most people's more nuanced views. Naturally, some diaspora communities also react against certain aspects of law, toleration or opportunity where it may go against particular cultural norms. Some diaspora communities are deeply socially conservative and kick against the social mores of modern Britain. The principles of applying aspects of Sharia law to intra-community relations within parts of Britain's Muslim communities, for example, may go down well in some home countries observing their friends and relations in Britain, but it will always be an uneasy fit with English law. Arranged marriages back in the home country for British women who may not have consented were made a criminal offence in 2014 by bringing it under existing domestic law. Nevertheless, over 1,000 cases of forced foreign marriages are reported most years, about 40 per cent of them concerning Pakistan and Bengali women, with Somali communities also featuring prominently.

Diasporas also work in both directions. It has been estimated, for example, that counting emigration from Britain to other parts of the world just in the nineteenth century, some 200 million people around the world are of direct British ancestry.[27] And around six million British citizens are living and working abroad at any one time. In terms of the international access it provides, the British passport is rated seventh in the world in 2021, though it had been rated first in 2010.[28]

Most British diaspora communities abroad work within all levels of their adopted society, encapsulating both rich and poor within them, establishment figures and outsiders, parochialists and internationalists. The influence and value of a nation's diaspora abroad is not lost on the Dublin government that appointed a minister with special responsibility for the Irish Diaspora.[29]

Diasporas can act as important agents of development. The UN's Institute of Migration notes the transfer of knowledge and skills that is potentially involved: the opportunities for investment in both directions and the development of entrepreneurship in a home country alongside the humanitarian and voluntary potential to mobilize sometimes powerful help from diaspora communities to their heritage countries in times of crisis and distress.[30] Not least, prominent diaspora members can act as convenors and 'track 2 diplomats' in conflict prevention and mitigation. As Warwick University's European Research Council observed after five years interviewing members of diaspora communities across Europe,

> This resourceful, entrepreneurial section of the population are important actors in the conflicts and post-conflict reconstruction processes of their homelands, be that Iraq, Palestine, Bosnia or Armenia. Conflict-generated diasporas can have a huge influence on war and peace, and it is often something that is under reported in the media.[31]

Cosmopolitanism and hospitality

Next to natural diaspora linkages, global tourism is the most powerful form of lived experience and human contact that soft power can bring to bear. Hospitality and tourism, going in both directions, are key elements in mobilizing a natural cosmopolitan sense that builds lasting personal images of any society.[32] A British Council survey in 2018 asked young people in the G20 states what they rated most highly in their estimation of any country's 'attractiveness and trust'. They found that 'cultural and historic attractions' and 'cities' were together rated most highly out of nineteen possible variables.[33] To a new generation of travellers and curious young people, tourism and hospitality matter a great deal. They are also big business and have always figured prominently in Britain's modern economy. In the last pre-Covid-19 year, the 40.9 million overseas visitors who came to the UK spent £28.4 billion, with London accounting for 55 per cent of inbound spend, the rest of England 32 per cent, Scotland 9 per cent and Wales 2 per cent.[34]

But while the income and employment it generates is important, the overall image of Britain through its tourism and hospitality is of more lasting impact in soft power reckoning. General standards of hospitality, quality, friendliness and efficiency are always important. Cornish pasties, Devonshire cream, Cheddar cheese, Somerset cider, Scottish salmon, whiskey, Irish butter, Welsh rarebit, and so on, are desired in far corners of the world. English wines have been coming up in the world, for example winning some best in shows for the 2020 Decanter World Wine Awards.[35] Both quality and economy hotel accommodation has expanded greatly across Britain in recent years. In this respect the Anholt-Ipsos annual Nation Brands Index is interesting. It assesses 50 nations each year on the basis of 20,000 consumers across 20 different countries. Its focus is therefore not on politicians or elites but on *customers* and their own various experiences of different countries, however they have been garnered. In 2020 it ranked Britain second behind Germany as a 'nation brand' among consumers, measured against their views on tourism, culture, the welcome of people, governance, exports and immigration/investment perspectives.[36] And this assessment among consumers was made during some of the most stressful months of 2019 when the Brexit process was unpopular with leaders and elites in many of the twenty countries polled.

If high general standards are important, notable highlights are also key to soft power imagery. Visitor numbers cluster inexorably around London. Within Britain's top twenty visitor attractions in 2017, only four were outside London – three of them in Scotland – with heavy predominance in numbers around London's big four: the British Museum, the National Gallery, the Tate Modern and the Natural History Museum. Interestingly, the Tower of London was only just in the top ten; Westminster Abbey and St Paul's Cathedral near the foot of the list, probably because the big four are more suitable for families and younger children. Outside London, Scottish attractions rated highly in four of the top ten non-London venues: the National Museum of Scotland, Edinburgh Castle and Kelvingrove Art Gallery in Glasgow – strong suggestions of Scottish diaspora links among Britain's foreign tourists. Leading English attractions included Chester Zoo (top of the non-London destinations in 2017), Stonehenge, the City of Bath, Stratford on Avon, Oxford, and the Eden Project in Cornwall.[37] In the ninth and tenth centuries, Viking invaders moved all over Europe and the Caucasus settling in some regions, like Normandy, and leaving their heritage everywhere. But with its 50,000 visitors, York's annual Jorvik celebration is the biggest Viking Festival anywhere in Europe.

Less obvious tourism highlights are also possible and seem set to be more strongly promoted. Coventry, for example, was the 2021 City of Culture. It has a multicultural demographic profile, it is a prolific city-twinner and it opened the world's first air hub for flying cars and delivery drones to serve cities and towns radiating out from its central position within the English manufacturing regions.[38] These sorts of attractions – part of the deeper fabric of British society alongside the established tourist trails – will be highlighted at the 2022 Festival of the UK. The festival intends to stamp a certain sort of diverse, innovative and attractive identity on Britain, in both its own eyes and those of the rest of the world. As we pointed out in Chapter 3, it is part of a year that offers some big opportunities in the realms of British soft power.

Educators

Pursuing truthful minds – and truth

'Education', said Albert Einstein, 'is what remains after one has forgotten what one has learned in school.' Quite so. True education is less concerned with what to think than with how to think it. At its best, education is designed to excite human curiosity and wonder. Knowledge and facts come and go with changing requirements, but the urge to want to know more and the confidence to handle more, much more, is the product of an educated mind. Deprived children in Africa, or those whose futures are blighted by conflict and war, repeatedly say that their greatest wish is to 'go to school'. Privileged children in rich countries often said the same after living through the Covid-19 pandemic. To be shown how to learn is a deep human instinct. As former UN Secretary-General Kofi Annan once observed, 'Education is the premise of progress, in every society, in every family.'

In this respect, Britain has both the benefit of English as the lingua franca and its own well-developed education sector, at least some of which provides an attractive model that many others would like to share or else imitate. Many people act as educators, whether they know it or not. What makes educational persuaders in some societies more influential than others is the reputation they inherit for being able to show people *how* to learn – and as a natural corollary to that, how to understand and pursue truthful knowledge. Ultimate truth may be a grand abstraction, but truthful knowledge is not – that human curiosity to want to learn more and to understand better, to be educated constantly throughout one's life.

Insofar as British society maintains some reputation in the world for integrity and ultimate truthfulness, its educators also enjoy a degree of international influence. A highly pluralistic society may sometimes have an eccentric relationship with truth and accuracy, particularly in a social media era of conspiracy theories, and the British establishment is as venal and evasive as most others. But an inbred, even bloody-minded, British commitment to pluralism offers a guarantee that people learn and judge for themselves as they choose. Britain's technical, medical and scientific achievement has something valuable to pass on, and its pluralism underpins any number of different ways the arts and humanities can be explored.

If this is a true reflection of Britain's educational reputation, then it has the ability to be rather persuasive in the global education sector. 'Education' goes a good deal wider than the formal process of offering structured learning programmes. For our purposes, Britain's educators might be described as 'formal', 'incidental' and 'advocative'. And they all have the soft power to be persuasive in their own different ways.

The formal educators

The formal institutions of British education have long been thought of as an excellent source of soft power in presenting and promoting Britain's values throughout the world. In 2018 no fewer than fifty-five 'current world leaders' had studied at British universities.[1] In 2021 the government calculated that more than 25 per cent of the world's serving heads of state or government had 'been educated' in Britain.[2] Then too, British universities are well ranked by international standards – 4 out of the top 10 in the world and 18 out of the top 100 in 2021.[3] In most years, 750,000 foreign students study in Britain – the second biggest international cohort next to the United States.[4] Correspondingly, British university research outputs are regarded as globally significant.[5] There has, however, been a relative drop in the overall international ranking of most British universities since 2016 for a number of different reasons, not least as the benefits of increased investment in Asian universities begin to show up in the calculations.[6] The competition is becoming very challenging, though Britain can still face it from a robust position that continues to reflect a powerful higher education sector.

In international terms, British schooling and education prior to the university level is not notably distinguished across the board. There is a vigorous debate over whether, as a whole, Britain ranks within the international top ten, nearer the fifteenth place (or even below), or whether rankings for school education are a meaningful exercise at all.[7] The vehemence of the debate certainly represents the unevenness, the growing inequality, of educational provision and opportunity in Britain. As a symptom of poor social mobility, it certainly does not reflect well on British society. But the inequitable educational system does have a top end, and from the perspective of soft power, that is the part of the educational sector that draws international attention.

Britain's best schools and specialist educational institutes are well regarded globally, both the famous private schools and many others that recruit increasing numbers of pupils from abroad. In the last twenty years there has also been a considerable growth in schools establishing satellite institutions abroad, particularly in Asia where the growth prospects are so enticing. There is, for example, a Harrow International School Bangkok, a Harrow in Beijing and a Harrow in Hong Kong. There is an Eton International School in Manila and Beijing, an Eton International Pre-School and an Eton Global Institute. There is a St Paul's International School in Queensland, Australia. In fact, some 4,000 British schools operate internationally one way or another. British schools abroad are, of course, hostages to political fortune, and in 2020–1 there were loud controversies over what should be on the syllabus for British schools in China and a degree of pushback as some of those schools feared the reputational damage of being seen to be restricted by the state. But the elite schools operating abroad project a general image of British education that makes the most of its reputation for quality and is trusted for the individual values it is felt to embody. They all claim, naturally, to be nurturing the 'leaders of the future'. On their domestic track record in Britain, many of them probably are.

The strongest trend in modern international education, even before the Covid-19 pandemic, has been the popularity of online and distance learning. Online and distance learning offers education and career development to an unlimited number of people, and in particular, it holds out the prospect of gaining accreditation from a prestigious institute. Britain was one of the original leaders in the online education business with the establishment of the Open University in 1969. With over 175,000 students it is now by far the largest university in Britain and one of the biggest in the world. With physical bases in many European countries and over two million graduates, it can look traditional universities in the eye over how many top politicians and officials it has educated, in the knowledge that the OU has turned out more CEOs across the world than any other British university, including Oxford, Cambridge and the LSE.

The exponential growth of online and distance education has gone far beyond the early work of the Open University, however. In 2018, before the Covid-19 pandemic, the global value of online learning was put at $200 billion annually. By 2025, in a post-pandemic world, it is confidently expected to reach around $350 billion.[8] The pandemic had the effect of making many more people and institutions aware – and able – to absorb education online. It also changed the economics of mass education and made more niche subjects viable options again. Courses that could not recruit enough students in person to make them economically viable, or which were otherwise too expensive to offer in their entirety, can be more easily broken down into modular form and potentially offered to any number of students. The only real limiting factors are an institution's capacity to supervise and examine the students it serves online. Mass online education, ironically, could have the effect of rescuing some of the niche courses in British higher education that are otherwise facing effective extinction.

Interestingly, online innovation may also favour a different group of British universities. Many of the most eminent institutions in Britain and the United States are only prepared to put particular technical courses online and are careful how much they will offer for fear of reputational damage. An independent assessment rates University College London, Edinburgh, Manchester and King's College London as Britain's top four distance learning universities, judged overall by quality in relation to what they offer online.[9]

The current fashion among emerging economies in Asia and the Middle East has been to invite (and subsidize) prestigious educational institutions to establish their own satellite campuses abroad and service them through a mixture of online material and rotational staffing with the home institution. In principle, this reverses one of the great standard assumptions of classical education, since it delivers courses to the students, rather than students to the courses. But if satellite campuses can partly compensate for what students lose in not being able personally to absorb the glamour of some of the great seats of learning, many British and other Western universities and colleges have been happy to run foreign satellite campuses – though there have also been some spectacular failures.

The demand remains for British educational institutes at all levels to deliver their products as widely as possible and, more importantly, to *accredit* them on the basis of their own international reputation. Aside from the university sector which sets and maintains its own standards, the British Accreditation Council which works across the independent, further and higher education sector in Britain also operates in twenty foreign countries. Most significantly, its accreditation is accepted by the Home Office for visa applications and immigration status.

The incidental educators

In addition to the formal education sector, however, considerable British prestige is also embodied in the work of other organizations and individuals who have a direct influence in educating people around the world, though their prime focus may well be somewhere else. They also embody, in their own distinctive ways, the underlying objective that education is not only about qualifications but also about the more fundamental objective of encouraging curious minds and upholding certain standards of truth simply for its own sake.

Education and entertainment fit well together. An individual like Sir David Attenborough, for example, emerges as one of the world's great educators on the natural world and few individuals have done more to add public credibility to the scientific warnings of climate change. He is both loved by a global viewing public and trusted for the integrity of his judgements. He began presenting programmes in 1954 and alongside his astonishing range of broadcasts, the scope and sheer ambition of the ten documentary series in his *Life* collection from 1979 to 2010 is regarded as his core global contribution to broadcasting. These series are in themselves masterclasses in natural history film-making – a great advertisement for the BBC, which leads the world in natural history television. 'The peerless educator', as Giles Smith called him, few of whom have ever had twenty or more species and genera named after them.[10]

Professor Brian Cox is often cited as the natural successor to Attenborough – indeed Attenborough voiced the thought himself.[11] Brian Cox, an eminent particle physicist of the University of Manchester, working at CERN's Large Hadron Collider in Switzerland, is a prolific presenter and author who has done a great deal to project popular science to an international audience as well a domestic one. Or again, Lord Martin Rees, Astronomer Royal since 1995 and internationally famous astrophysicist and cosmologist, has written and spoken with authority and passion on researching climate change solutions as well as on many ethical and political challenges raised by science. And, not to be outdone by Attenborough, he has had an asteroid – number 4587 – named after him. Self-taught amateur Patrick Moore was one of the curious English eccentrics who popularized astronomy through books and television and became an international figure whose abilities to explain astronomy to children and ordinary viewers were rated alongside those of Arthur C. Clarke and Carl Sagan. He was honoured by groups as diverse as the International Astronomical Union and the Astronomy Society of the Pacific; and he claimed to be the only person to have shaken hands with a unique trio – the first aviator, Orville Wright, the first man in space, Yuri Gagarin, and the first man to step on the moon, Neil Armstrong.

The distinguished ethologist and evolutionary biologist Richard Dawkins became an internationally famous (and infamous) figure in his scientific denunciations of creationism and an insistence on the rational acceptance of atheism. The title of his most famous book, *The God Delusion*, spoke for itself. And in explaining how people collectively act and believe, he coined the now universal concept of the 'meme' – a social version of the gene – as an idea or behavioural trait carrying symbolic meaning that passes from one person to another. Stephen Hawking, the world-famous theoretical physicist at Cambridge, was the epitome of the popular scientist. His *Brief History of Time* was in the best-seller lists for over four years, and he himself found time to appear, as himself, in *Star Trek*, *The Simpsons*, *The Big Bang Theory*, and to feature with Pink Floyd and be the subject, in his own lifetime, of a biopic film.

People like Martin Rees, Richard Dawkins, Stephen Hawking or Brian Cox built international fame on the basis of their professional scientific eminence that stood in its own right. The outsiders and amateurs in Britain have also made an international impact over many years. In the nineteenth century Elizabeth Garrett Anderson set new boundaries for women in medicine right up until her death in 1917; self-educated and repeatedly spurned by the male establishment, she became an apothecary and then the first female physician and surgeon, founded the first hospital for women, was a passionate educationalist and reformer and has several medical and teaching institutions in her name. Engagements with the girls' school in London named after her became a repeated feature of Michelle Obama's time as US First Lady. Florence Nightingale – not a terrifically effective nurse during the Crimean war – was spurred by her failures to become a whirlwind social reformer, the founder of modern nursing and creator of the world's first secular nursing school – now part of King's College London – and an international writer who believed in hard data and graphics in presenting evidence for modern approaches to hygiene.

Perhaps the most poignant British individual who continues to have lasting educative influence around the world is completely anonymous. The Unknown Soldier, entombed in Westminster Abbey in November 1920, continues to provide inspiration to other societies, to represent not just the unnamed dead but also the deeper principle that war dead is the price society pays for conflict.* His unknown namesakes join his constant and silent witness in at least fifty-seven other countries from Argentina to Zimbabwe.

Many national institutions also perform educational functions of international significance. The British Museum, using its practical reach across the world, helps

---

* The initiative was originally agreed with France. The 'Tomb of the Unknown Warrior', as the British grave is named, was set in November 1920. France followed with a similar ceremony in January 1921. Other allied nations quickly followed suit in the 1920s as it became a wider international gesture.

uphold vital knowledge under threat from political destruction. It was proactive in trying to recover, replace or repair some of the destruction to heritage caused by conflicts in Afghanistan, Iraq and Yemen. And in 2018 it launched, with government money, the CircArt global platform to help the whole system – museums, private collectors, dealers, police – check the provenance of artefacts coming onto the antiquities market.[12] This 'circulating artefacts' initiative offers e-learning and training to upskill the international antiquities market to help meet the growing challenges to authenticity – an international investment in truthful education.

In different fields, other initiatives stand out, such as the Eden Project in Cornwall with its massive biomes that houses 'the largest rainforest in captivity'.[13] This is not simply an attraction but an avowedly significant, international educational project. Or again, Kew Gardens in South-West London is many things, including a repository of knowledge and research on plant and fungal life. It also partners with over 400 institutions in more than 100 countries to act as an international educational centre for plant and fungal diversity.[14] The Millennium Seed Bank Partnership at Wakehurst in West Sussex made Britain 'the first country in the world to have preserved its botanical heritage', and it is now the largest and most diverse wild plant species genetic resource in the world, as a result of its partnerships with over ninety-five countries.[15]

In a completely different field, British open-source intelligence (OSINT) organizations have made important international contributions to expertise and truthful research. New spin-out companies like Ridgeway, or its charitable offshoot, Faros, are committed to promoting the expertise for individuals and organizations to be able to organize and interpret for themselves the plethora of information confronting them. The most prominent and successful of these organizations is undoubtedly Bellingcat, based from Leicester, which in just seven years has made some astonishing and globally acknowledged contributions to standards of truth in world politics. Bellingcat is a small, cyber investigatory organization established by journalist Eliot Higgins. It describes itself as 'the home of online investigations – an intelligence agency for the people'. Working across the echo chambers and alternative realities of social media, it has been highly successful in using OSINT to uncover incontrovertible facts around politically explosive issues. Bellingcat is cautious in drawing conclusions but very clear in presenting evidence it can demonstrate is true. It has hit several jackpots and established factual truths that most of the world's journalists – rather few of whom are now foreign correspondents or real specialists – acknowledge are accurate. The approach is transparent and cooperative between those who know how to access OSINT and take a rigorous approach to corroboration and verification. Being good at OSINT requires real skill and experience.

Using those skills, Bellingcat has established some vital facts in (to name only a few) the chemical attacks in Syria, the conflict in Ukraine, the downing of the civilian Malaysia Airlines flight, the poisoning of Sergei Skripal in Salisbury and Alexei Navalny in Tomsk, the Capitol Hill riot in 2020, the QAnon conspiracy theory leaders in the United States, Emirati drones operating in Ethiopia or the EU's FRONTEX border force apparently behaving illegally while policing Mediterranean waters.[16] Bellingcat specializes in fact-checking and investigating war zone events, human rights abuses and the criminal underworld, wherever it feels it can unearth something important.[17] Its volunteers have created a decade-long archive of 3.5 million pieces of digital content from the war in Syria. Dates and metadata have been carefully preserved to assist any future war crimes prosecutions. Bellingcat is funded (and now quite well funded) by donations about which it is transparent. The organization won six major international journalism prizes between 2015 and 2020 and none of the mud its adversaries have predictably thrown at it has stuck. Bellingcat is what it says it is: no more and no less.[18]

As one of Britain's incidental educators, Bellingcat believes not in protecting its own expertise for commercial advantage but rather in teaching its techniques so that more people and organizations can become competent with OSINT. It runs regular workshops and shares its own techniques online to help create a wider network of fact-checkers and corroborators. Its influence, said the *New York Review of Books* in 2019, was already being felt in other areas of international journalism and research. Bigger organizations like the *New York Times* or the Berkeley Human Right Investigations Lab, and human rights organizations like Amnesty or Human Rights Watch, were learning from Bellingcat's techniques and imitating them. Bellingcat guides are recommended by journalist training centres in the United States and across Europe.[19] Indeed, Bellingcat's website is now included in the US Library of Congress' web archives. All this conveys important images of the way Britain values a pluralist culture where the pursuit of truthful investigations is not monopolized or directed by the government.

A very different example of a powerful incidental educator with global reach is the collection of businesses that form the Heritage Alliance.[20] The independent heritage sector has an interesting impact overseas. The 'heritage industry' estimates that it directly generates at least £10 billion in 'gross value added' revenues and indirectly generates another £21 billion in GVA, about

2 per cent of GVA nationally – 'more than the agriculture and aerospace sectors combined'.[21] Despite an image of British 'heritage' as a series of cash-strapped country houses and distressed attractions in need of refurbishment, the reality of the sector is that it witnessed an underlying economic upswing in recent years even as it suffered with the rest of the economy from more recent downturns.

As an important part of British tourism there are many examples of the heritage industry working individually, or collectively, with international partners on projects of global importance. These have included working and cooperating with the World Monuments Fund, or working with the world-renowned scholarship programme of the Society for the Protection of Ancient Buildings, or being part of the Venice in Peril campaign or the Antarctic Heritage Trust.

The advocacy educators

As a pluralistic society Britain is a place where many advocacy groups exist. This is a healthy symptom of strong civic culture. Britain encourages proactive pluralism and it is a country with a well-developed charity sector –'one of the busiest and most generous in the world', according to one observer.[22] Most advocacy groups are established, or operate closely with, charities, and this has an interesting bearing on the ways most of them frame their campaigns.

The long history of charity/advocacy groups in Britain led to a fairly sophisticated understanding that to be effective, long-term advocacy had to be based on truthful information and reliable reporting. Advocacy is often not an argument over the existence of evidence but rather over what interpretation should be put on it. The most professional and successful advocacy groups understand the benefits of setting out their stall on the basis of factually correct evidence. For them the struggle is not to keep information honest but to get it heard. And those British groups that, over a long period, established good and effective international reputations have all contributed to the promotion of British values of open-mindedness and respect for truth. They were educators even as they were advocates.

PEN International began in London in 1921, known then as PEN, and now welcomes poets, playwrights, editors, essayists and novelists of any kind. It was to be a club that would connect writers worldwide: a 'common meeting ground in every country for all writers'. It claims to be the first worldwide association of writers and one of the world's first NGOs advocating for human rights –

pointing out that freedom of expression and literature are inseparable. Within 4 years there were 25 PEN centres in Europe; by 1931 there were centres in South America and China, and now it is represented in over 100 countries.[23]

The Save the Children charity was founded in London by Eglantyne Jebb in 1919, to help the lives of children devastated by the Great War through better education, health care and economic opportunities, alongside emergency aid. It soon became 'the first global movement for children'.[24] Jebb went on to draft the historic 'Declaration of the Rights of the Child', adopted by the League of Nations in 1924. It is a distinguished pedigree for a world-renowned aid organization. Today, the publications and factual statements of Save the Children, their situation reports on the effects of conflict in Yemen or Syria, for example, are widely regarded as empirical and truthful. They are not doubted around the world, except by those who seek to falsify facts on the ground.

Oxfam (the 'Oxford Committee for Famine Relief') was founded in 1942, originally campaigning for food supplies to get through an allied naval blockade to reach starving people in enemy-occupied Greece. After the Second World War, Oxfam moved its focus firmly to developing countries and grew to be one of the biggest aid charities in the world, working in more than ninety countries with thousands of partners, allies and different communities. Oxfam's reputation has suffered greatly in the last five years with repeated revelations by whistle-blowers of internal corruption and sexual scandals. It may have a long journey to recover the respect it had too easily taken for granted as well as the confidence of British government as one of its core funders. Nevertheless, its commitment to the truth of what it sees in the world, how it reports human distress – and now reflecting on its own personnel failings – has remained robust. The same robustness applies to the Disasters Emergencies Committee (DAC), formed in Britain in 1963. The DAC has launched sixty-seven separate appeals since then, raising around £1.4 billion in charitable donations. It needs publicity to do this, but it has always seen its honest relationship with the world's broadcasters as an essential part of success. Its objective reporting has allowed it to maintain a non-political reputation that gives it access on the ground in many sensitive natural and man-made disasters.

Another major British advocacy group that deals in accuracy and truth among its 10 million followers is Amnesty International. It was founded in 1961 by British lawyer Peter Benenson, after he read about Portuguese students in a bar being sentenced to prison by the Salazaar dictatorship for raising a toast to freedom. Benenson wrote a famous article for *The Observer,* 'The Forgotten Prisoners', calling on every reader to put pressure on governments to push for the release of political prisoners worldwide.[25] The public response was spontaneous and overwhelming, going well beyond Britain, and an international letter-writing campaign was suddenly underway that seemed to have the effect of getting political prisoners released in a number of countries. The Amnesty approach was intuitive – to mobilize international public pressure to have detainees either brought to trial, under proper judicial procedures, or be released. And in between, it worked to try to bring some comfort to those who were detained unjustly. In 1977 Amnesty International won the Nobel Peace Prize, specifically for its work uncovering human rights violations. Its voice remains authoritative because its material is regarded as truthful and as accurate as possible. Amnesty's campaigns are often unwelcome to British government ministers where they may raise questions about British support for a repressive regime, but ministers never publicly argue about the information Amnesty brings to bear.

These days the most activist, and often most fierce, advocacy is found in the different campaigns to demand more effort in tackling climate change. The field has been awash for more than twenty years with research and information, almost all pointing in one general direction. The argument over whether climate change is happening and that it will greatly impact all our lives has effectively been won. But the argument about how, and how urgently, it should be addressed – what political priority to accord the problem – has only recently begun. Two particular advocacy initiatives in Britain devised a concept, and found the right words, to make their powerful, intuitive point.

The 'Stop Ecocide' campaign was founded in 2017 by a British lawyer, the late Polly Higgins and the environmental activist, Jojo Mehta.[26] They wanted national and international law to be redefined to establish the idea that destroying the natural environment should be regarded as akin to genocide, since it would cause at least as much indiscriminate death and misery. The visual imagery of the Stop Ecocide logo was a deliberate reflection of the anti-nuclear CND movement. The message was clear; environmental destruction should be equated with a nuclear war. It was an idea that immediately resonated with another group of activists.

In April 2018 in the Cotswold town of Stroud, a handful of long-time environmental campaigners and academics gathered at the home of Gail Bradbrook to thrash out how they should go for broke in tackling, once and for all, the multiple crises of climate change, biodiversity loss and ecological collapse. In October 2018, some ninety-four environmental academics signed an open letter and with that, Extinction Rebellion (XR) was launched.[27] Within a year it had turned into a global environmental movement. It was joined and supported by Greta Thunberg, the young Swedish activist, and it made headlines around the world. It was briefly deemed 'extremist' by counter-terrorism police[28] but was prepared to stage acts of public disruption across London (for two weeks in 2019) and in other city centres to make its point. Many argued that such actions were a tactical mistake. But the XR movement maintained it was amply justified by the real nature of the threat and pointed to its success in raising public awareness of it, in both Britain and abroad.[29]

Extinction Rebellion had found the simple, motivating phrase. It encapsulated both the threat and the response and it gave them an international brand name. It will be an interesting question to see how the XR movement, and doubtless offshoots from it, reconciles the urgency of their demand with the need to maintain the educator's credibility to draw a wider public, by its own learning and volition, into their consensus.

Hard power and education

In terms of soft power, these three types of educational activity, taken together, are second only to tourism, hospitality and the influence of diasporas in the direct effects they can have on the lived experience, and hence of the impressions, of those outside Britain. As we discussed in Chapters 3 and 4, authenticity, involvement and having skin in the game are critical elements in being able to exert the magnetism of effective soft power. The self-evident maintenance of essentially truthful ideals, through a pluralistic society, might be regarded as Britain's skin in the education game at a time when it has never been more difficult to uphold truth globally.

In this broad sense, education is a very big and open window on British society as it evolves.

As one of the soft power magnets, it interacts very directly with the harder end of the spectrum. The willingness of the world to be either educated abroad or pay particular respect to the education of any particular country – to want to imitate it – is also based on a view that it is on the side of the politically powerful. People generally want to be educated in the language and culture of the evident winners, not the 'declining' or the likely losers. During the Cold War many young professionals from third world countries were educated in Russia, including around 60,000 African students who attended Russian universities, in the 1970s and 1980s. And though Russia's currently small (6 per cent) foreign student intake has increased in recent years partly as a result of economic distress in Western countries, it is not the place where 'the leaders of tomorrow' choose to go anymore. The Kremlin aspires to achieve a foreign student intake of around 700,000 by 2025. That would still be 50,000 lower than Britain's current average total.[30] At the People's Friendship University in Moscow, where most foreign students study, there is a big mural on the wall in the main refectory. It says, 'Make the World Better' – and it says it in English. Whether this vignette would still hold true in Chinese or Indian international universities in the not-too-distant future remains a moot point for now.

Creatives

Opening new ideas

In 1994 Sony produced its PlayStation 3 games console offering new standards in computer game graphics. Core Design, a small company in Derbyshire, saw the opportunity to create a different type of interactive game. Toby Gard, a young designer with Core Design, created a new genre of treasure-hunting challenge amid Egyptian antiquities. And he broke all the rules laid down in US marketing by having a British female character as the adventurous protagonist. So began Lara Croft's *Tomb Raider* career, as a tough and resourceful British girl taking on the world. It became a brilliant global marketing success in computer games, a series of joint production Hollywood films and all the related merchandising. The game itself sold seven million copies and even now is cited as one of the greatest video games ever produced.[1] It made multiple millions for Sony PlayStation products and Eidos Interactive, its British developers, even though in the process Lara Croft had taken on US citizenship and flirted with the soft-porn fringes by turning herself into a Barbie doll action figure.[2] Whether or not, in its outcome, this seems to be an encouraging or a cautionary story, it could be told in many different genres. British creativity is very real – sometimes it remains characteristically British, in other instances it morphs into something more foreign. But creativity and the ability to offer the world new ideas, to break down established boundaries, is not something in which Britain has ever been lacking when its national morale and self-confidence are high.

In that respect, the late 1980s and 1990s saw Britain recover some of its creative mojo after many difficult years: finding again that same verve of the 1960s that had shown the world a different Britain to the one recovering from a world war. The economic story of the 1960s was not a happy one, but the sense of creative break-out within that decade was palpable. In the late 1980s it was back – first in music, where London could again claim to be the pop musical capital of the world, even as orchestral music was showing new development in provincial centres and London still fielded its four major orchestras (alongside over forty others in the city). In the 1990s the brash Britpop bands had become a global phenomenon, courted by Britain's own political classes in their quest for street credibility: a 'strange foxtrot of showbiz democracy', as Andrew Marr puts it.[3] They flew an assertive Union Jack flag for Britpop. In the case of the Spice Girls they regularly wore them, creating for one historian 'a new ersatz patriotism'.[4] Something similar was evident in the London fashion world, and in the opening of arts galleries and exhibition spaces, particularly outside the capital. New galleries in Salford, Walsall, Cardiff and Edinburgh stood out; and in London, the conversion of the massive Thameside power station in 2000, looking straight at St Paul's Cathedral across the river, became the Tate Modern and has been among the top four visitor attractions ever since.[5] New festivals sprang up. The Glastonbury Festival, which had been an intermittent event during the 1970s, became from the early 1980s an annual set piece in the British cultural scene – no longer an alternative muddy pop gig but a 'festival of contemporary performing arts'. And everywhere, local towns and communities rediscovered (or in many cases invented) ancient celebrations that were worth marking again with new community events. They took inspiration from the doyen of all arts festivals in Edinburgh. World famous even in 1947 as it began, the Edinburgh Festival (actually a collection of ten overlapping festivals) has become bigger, many times over, than the next biggest arts festival anywhere in the world. Its famous 'Fringe', which began when eight companies simply turned up, uninvited in 1947, to perform in the streets, symbolizes its creative freedom at the centre of a global movement of over 200 other fringe festivals, all following in its footsteps.

'Creativity', of course, is entirely in the perception of the beholder and is a desirable feature in any field of human endeavour. It is absolutely intrinsic to the world of entertainment, which we will discuss in Chapter 11. Our purpose here is to outline some of the ways in which British 'creatives' – both individuals and organizations – have the proven capacity to push or change international boundaries and become subtle persuaders for British approaches to global culture and international connections.

The persuasive creators

Advertising is one of the most unashamedly persuasive occupations and Britain has always been a leading international player in the field. In the mid-nineteenth century, while consumerism in the United States was still in its infancy, British entrepreneurs made the most of growing common literacy to exploit the advertising potential of new magazines and newspapers. In the twentieth century the growth of direct mail, radio, film and television created the advertising landscape that became so familiar in daily life. Sport and its followers have always been a natural target for advertisers. The British soup stock company Oxo was the first to use the enormous potential of big sporting events, even before the advent of mass communication. At the 1908 London Olympics all the athletes were provided with Oxo beef stock drinks.[6]

Alfred Leete's famous image of Lord Kitchener in September 1914 looking out from a poster, pointing an accusing finger and declaring 'Your Country Needs You', was reproduced to fit the particular national images of the United States and Canada during the war. It was adopted by both Germany and Russia in 1919, by Brazil in 1932 and by the United States again in 1985, when Smokey Bear campaigned against forest fires. The original image, over a century later, remains a global brand, a standard English catchphrase and a vehicle for innumerable jokes.

The launch of radio in Britain was dominated by the creation of the BBC as a public service broadcaster – a fairly distinctive situation compared to other countries. Britain did not licence a commercial radio station until as late as 1973, goaded into it by the offshore 'pirate radio' stations. The first commercial station, the London Broadcasting Company (LBC), began operating, with its first advertisement for Bird's Eye frozen food.

Despite the monopoly on public service broadcasting, there was nevertheless a surging expansion of the British advertising industry during the 1920s and the creation of a number of interesting clubs and trade associations to promote certain values in the way it operated. Their titles indicate that they intended to set standards as well as profits: the Creative Circle, the National Advertising Benefit Society (NABS), Women in Advertising and Communications, London (WACL), the Publicity Club of London, the Regent Club, the Solus Club or the Thirty Club – all to shepherd the burgeoning advertising industry into the consumer economy future.[7]

The breakthrough moment for the industry occurred in 1951 with the prospect of commercial television opening up. Critical government discussions took place up to 1954 over whether to allow competition with the BBC's broadcasting monopoly. The launch of commercial television at that juncture was the key to the future for advertising in Britain. Both Labour and Conservative leaders were sceptical that commercial TV would be in the public interest. But a coalition of advertising executives and government critics, the Popular Television Association, emerged to create a counterbalance to the BBC's own arguments.[8] It was a powerful lobby and commercial TV was launched in 1955, despite a BBC attempt to spoil its opening by killing off one of its best loved characters in *The Archers* that evening.

Nowadays, Britain is host to the fourth biggest advertising market in the world behind China, the United States and Japan.[9] British advertising services grew 15 per cent year-on-year to reach a new record level of £7.9 billion in 2018. In fact, advertising has overtaken telecommunications and engineering services to become the second-largest services sector export behind computer services. As the Advertising Association points out, this performance was recorded over years that spanned the uncertainties created by the Brexit decision, where there was still 'robust growth' in British advertising, reflecting, among other virtues, its own digital and data skills.[10]

The persuasive capabilities of the British advertising industry are well demonstrated in its many celebrated campaigns. Government public information efforts during the Second World War – 'keep calm and carry on'; 'walls have ears' – have been internationally iconic ever since. Guinness launched its advertising campaign, controversially at the time, in *The Daily Mail* in 1929. A cartoonist from the Newcastle Evening Chronicle was engaged to do the artwork, and he created a series of simple, arresting images – among them the Guinness toucan – that are still seen today and launched one of the most long-standing international brands of our era – masterclasses in sustained advertising. The slogan 'Beanz Meanz Heinz' created by Maurice Drake in 1967 is still rated the single best global iconic advertising phrase, not least for its musicality (a novelty at the time it was launched). Since then, Nike's 'Just Do It' American iconography of 1988 or Audi's 'Vorsprung Durch Technik' have firmly cemented their places in global psychology. But Saatchi & Saatchi's 'Labour Isn't Working' campaign of 1979 proved to be a game-changer in British election advertising, adopted in 2012 by US presidential candidate Mitt Romney as 'Obama isn't working'. Channel 4 made an important breakthrough in 2012. Having won the broadcasting rights for the Paralympic Games the channel worried about the possibility of public indifference to them. The Blink Studios in Soho and their own C4Creative came up with a series of 'Meet the Superhumans' campaigns. It was brilliantly successful, won awards at Cannes, delivered Channel 4 an international audience and its biggest in a decade and 'changed the way Britons viewed disability. Maybe forever.'[11]

Ultimately, advertising is a servant of the art of marketing. As a natural 'nation of shopkeepers' in the words of Adam Smith, and with a retail sector that is so economically prominent in the national economy, Britain has traditionally been good at it.[12] The art of marketing is driven by some hard metrics – what market penetration has been achieved, levels of total market share, bottom-line sales trends and so forth. But marketing also draws heavily from the worlds of art and design, communications, psychology and game-theory. In a thriving market, whether high-tech aerospace, wholesaling or mass retailing, good marketing relies on creativity and access to inventive threads from many different sources.

It mostly comes down to successful branding, which in any sector is key to long-term commercial success. Short-term marketing is designed to sell products and services. Long-term marketing is designed to establish a brand that does quite a lot of selling on its own. In the globalized world, with its vast potential markets, successful branding has never been so important. The 'corporate message', 'the image', the association with like images or personalities are all critical components to achieve the ultimate accolade – a global brand that has currency everywhere and among those who can afford to buy. A global brand can integrate its appeal in a unified strategy, precisely because it establishes a brand for something that has a distinct attraction to a customer in one recognizable form – like Coca Cola or Macdonald's. The American Nike brand or Germany's Adidas have global recognition in mass sportswear with a universal appeal. British sports brands like Dunlop, seen on an array of sports equipment, Mitre on footballs or Gilbert on rugby balls, also have a global reach and gain huge brand awareness from big sports events. Burberry clothes and Aston Martin cars still convey a top-of-the market cache, whatever their sales levels. But the world's most visible brands now lie with the tech companies. The four most valuable commercial brands anywhere in the world are Amazon, Google, Apple and Microsoft. Others in the top ten include Samsung, PingAn and Huawei.[13] In Europe, the two most valuable brand names are Germany's Mercedes and the British-Netherlands Royal Dutch Shell.

Throughout the twentieth century, the dominant marketing approach revolved around print and broadcast media, to create effective messaging and advertising. In the digital age, however, and in the growing era of online retailing and powerful artificial intelligence, the quest for global brand status is becoming easier. That exalted strata in the marketing stratosphere is more crowded since the tools of effective marketing have changed so quickly. More than half of all the world's consumers – those connected to the internet – have a greater or lesser electronic signature of some sort and many more ways in which marketeers can interact with them, whether they are aware of it or not. As Eric Schmidt, chairman of Google's Alphabet parent, famously (and now infamously) declared: 'We know where you are. We know where you've been. We can know more or less what you're thinking about.'[14] Social media, in particular, enables this two-way communication between business and client.

Digital marketing strategies offer the opportunity to leverage search engines, email, websites and blogs. They are able to use social media platforms directly and plug into the rapidly growing 'influencer marketing' where individuals with a big social media profile, like sports people of old, will promote sponsored products and services. Aside from pursuing global brand status, the new tools of marketing also allow for more subtle 'relationship marketing', whereby the marketeer works to establish a long-time and loyal client base, managing a brand name to create a bond between customer and brand. Client preferences ('needs' in the marketeer's lexicon) can be identified quite precisely and products customized for them with flexible product development.[15] It also allows for 'societal marketing', 'green' or 'sustainable' marketing, to associate brands and products with causes a customer believes in, even if the product has little direct relevance to such issues.

The British marketing industry is well placed to make the most of these new techniques and opportunities, drawing as it does from so many related fields, particularly in advanced computing services, data management and design. It has the power and the drive to integrate new thinking from all these areas into different styles of discriminating marketing.

It can draw from the creative eminence of Britain's design studios that attained international recognition some decades ago. The London Fashion Week is acknowledged as the 'European showcase' for the clothing industries, in Britain's case with a noted focus on retail outlets. It ranks favourably alongside New York, Paris and Milan. During the 1960s when Britons were already deep into experimental music, fashion, photography and graphic design, the Design and Art Direction (D&AD) organization was founded in London's Spitalfields. The 'D&AD Pencils', its annual awards, have become famous in the field and today D&AD represent creative, design and advertising communities worldwide.[16] *Campaign* in the late 1960s was struggling to find a market, until Michael Heseltine acquired it for Haymarket and hired Maurice Saatchi to rebrand and relaunch it. It is now a global business magazine covering advertising, media, marketing and commercial creativity. Headquartered in Britain, it also has editions in the United States, Asia-Pacific, India, the Middle East and Turkey. The Haymarket Media Group owns more than seventy brands worldwide including FourFourTwo, Stuff, Autocar, What Car? and PRWeek.[17]

The flexible growth of consultancy in Britain is also a source of creativity that feeds into marketing and advertising. The arrival of US consultancy firms in Britain during the 1950s fuelled a growth in the industry, alongside a wave of new management techniques and growing demand for specialized skills. Britain's consultancy expertise lies in a number of overlapping levels. The majority of British consultants work in big or medium-sized firms, and they are led by the 'Big Four': Deloitte, EY (what was Ernst and Young), KPMG and Price Waterhouse Cooper (PWC). Since the profession has grown rapidly to cover the general fields of management, company strategy, finance, operations or technical capabilities, giants like America's McKinsey's have figured prominently as worldwide management consultants. But the Big Four, originally as auditors, have expanded their remit into every major management domain for both private industry and government. They are ever present in all the 'best of' lists within the industry. They are judged not only by their size and profitability but, more importantly in the soft power equation, for their influence on the industry, reputation and trust with clients and their scope to be innovative in new services and products.[18] They are all global operators but EY is headquartered in London, as is PWC. KPMG is an Anglo-Dutch firm headquartered in the Netherlands. And Deloitte, founded by William Welch Deloitte in 1845 and expanding to the United States in 1890, is an Anglo-American company headquartered in London, still running the biggest professional services network anywhere in the world.

Though the Big Four, and some of the other major companies, like PA Consulting or RAND Europe, together employ most of Britain's consultants, around 85 per cent of businesses in the sector are actually SMEs or small group consultancies among freelancers. It is another significant layer to the overall picture and reflects something of a revolving door between individuals and companies. Most significant firms try to develop their own in-house advisory and implementation units, where ideas transferred from the external world are most relevant to them. They also draw in freelancers – often ex-employees from somewhere else in the sector – which generates newspaper criticism of an endless 'gravy train' but nevertheless has the effect of exchanging creative approaches.

The story creators

Those who create stories can have universal appeal, and the most celebrated British storytellers from Shakespeare to Dickens to J. K. Rowling gave the world stories that set new literary boundaries and offered their audiences different ways of viewing life.

The most technically advanced British story creators these days are undoubtedly the computer game authors. In addition to the global success of *Tomb Raider*, British designers also originated the global entertainment phenomenon that is *Grand Theft Auto*. It is the fourth highest-selling game of all time and it began life in DMS's small development studio in Dundee.[19] DMS had released its game to PlayStation in 1997 and by 1999 the game had been acquired by Rockstar Games in New York. Its latest iteration, *Grand Theft Auto V*, sold more than 11 million copies in its first 24 hours – generating $800 million for Rockstar Games and its parent company, Take Two Interactive. The game is, according to the industry, 'Famed for its anarchic, satirical humour and huge, fully-realised open worlds'. Probably appropriate that it was all inspired in Dundee.

In fact, two other game developers in Dundee, Chris van der Kuyl and Paddy Burns, joined the Times Rich List in 2020 after they took over from a Swedish developer the *Minecraft* game for their 4J Studios. Like other successful products – *Minecraft* has over 480 million players around the world – it is carefully designed to be both interactive and addictive.[20] It has generated a widespread global franchise, films and merchandising. Its global success has made a number of developers all over the world very rich. They earn their vast rewards because successful game designers are storytellers who create narratives that allow the audience largely to set its own boundaries and then keeps challenging them personally. For all the arcade-style aggression that characterizes so many successful games, the underlying principles are not so different to science fiction or magical realism in literature, but they generate stories in a new medium and give the audience more control over where their imagination and skill wants to take the narrative.

Britain has long been a leader in computer game design. In 1989 it was the first to establish a trade association for the video games industry anywhere in the world and it has attracted global talent into Britain ever since.[21] In 2020 about a third of core games production, art and programming roles were taken by foreign employees, most of them from other European countries.[22] BAFTA recognized the importance of the gaming industry as an artistic genre in 1998 when it began to make 'interactive entertainment awards'. And the government recognized its importance to export success when it offered the industry tax breaks to encourage development within a sector that was growing by double digits from 2012 to 2018 and is worth well over £5 billion a year. That is expected to double by 2023, particularly since the industry has been boosted by the effects of global lockdowns in response to the Covid-19 crisis. The gaming industry in Britain is restructuring towards an even more online future. Its hardware sales are declining, as are boxed sets, books and magazines, while its software sales in digital and online platforms are growing strongly. It scores highly in particular areas of what the industry refers to as 'game culture', growing robustly in movies, soundtracks and merchandising, while also waiting for the post-Covid-19 bounce in gaming 'events and venues'.[23]

Britain's more conventional storytellers are also a source of global influence and internationally acknowledged creativity. Britain is the largest exporter of books in the world. Its internationally popular authors are all standard names: Shakespeare, Jane Austen, the Brontë sisters, Charles Dickens, Thomas Hardy, D. H. Lawrence or Evelyn Waugh. Particularly popular twentieth-century authors with an international following include literary luminaries such as Agatha Christie – still the most translated author – Beatrix Potter, Terry Pratchett, Salman Rushdie, John Le Carré, Pat Barker, Sebastian Faulks, Giles Foden, Phillip Pullman and J. K. Rowling – who produced the fastest-selling book in publishing history with 8.3 million copies of *Harry Potter and the Deathly Hallows* shifting in its first 24 hours. Writers from Britain's BAME communities have also achieved international recognition. Zadie Smith's *White Teeth* or Monica Ali's *Brick Lane* stand out as examples of writers who can demonstrate the creative freedom of the British literary scene, even if their own experiences and perspectives on it are less than complimentary.

Books and films go together naturally in popular culture. British books have been behind three of the world's biggest film franchises – *Harry Potter*, *James Bond* and *The Lord of the Rings*. Within Britain, in the decade up to 2016 more than ten of the top twenty British box-office hits were based on British published works. Authors tell stories, producers film them and game designers fantasize from them in a simmering soup of artistic creativity.

The Publishers Association claims:

> Publishing has helped make the UK a centre of thought, discovery and creation, projecting our values and culture into the hearts and minds of billions around the globe. The collective endeavour of authors and publishers has enabled the UK to exert unprecedented soft power, helping to shape laws, politics and perspectives around the world. Our publications and publishing brands are a global beacon of accuracy and authenticity.[24]

The PA makes a series of rather grand claims that are impossible to prove, but it has to be admitted that the anecdotal evidence is certainly encouraging.

The fine arts represent other creative storytellers. They may seem to occupy the opposite end of the spectrum to computer gamers or marketing executives.

But they tell their own stories, visually, in their own genres and contribute more than most people might think to the imaginative drive behind everyday activities. The world of the fine arts is a vaguely defined, but important, sector in the landscape of Britain's persuaders who not only contribute to the economy but have a significant effect on the country's international image. In 2020 around 135,000 people were estimated to be working across the fine arts, including in related music professions.[25] That number has been growing steadily through the last decade.

Britain's status in the fine arts world – normally, paintings, visual arts and sculpture – is internationally high. Since the onset of the global economic crisis, the market has lost around £1 billion in auction sales and the number of what are defined as 'artistic creation enterprises' has contracted by 18 per cent. Nevertheless, there are still 15,400 of them in Britain, down from almost 19,000 at the onset of the crisis.[26] In monetary terms, the fine arts and antiques market is naturally volatile from year to year but has been worth between £8 billion and £9 billion to Britain in most years. London stands as one of the world's three fine arts market hubs. The United States has 40 per cent of the global fine arts market trade by value, Britain 24 per cent and China 20 per cent while France and Germany have about 9 per cent between them. Sotheby's, Christies and Bonham's are themselves an iconic presence in the market, and most of Britain's trade is also notably high value – over half of it in items individually worth more than £1 million, and the majority of it is generated by contemporary and modern art. Britain's fine art trading is also overwhelmingly global. More than 90 per cent of it is with the world beyond European Union countries, though British businesses within the sector still worry about the knock-on effects of any restrictions to cross border trade with the continent.[27]

More significantly, this market hub position backs up the international visibility of British artists. The country's leading contemporary artists are high earners in the auction houses. In 2020, sales of Damien Hirst's work were worth almost $700 million, Peter Doig almost $500 million, Cecily Brown and Banksy over $100 million, others such as Anthony Gormley, Jenny Saville, Tracey Emin and Jack Vettriano ranged from over $90 million to $23 million.[28] Artistic judgements are a matter of taste, but global market values of that order are a vindication of the international standing of such artists. And that does not include the international reputations of other recent figures who reflect British work in contemporary art such as the late Lucien Freud, Grayson Perry, Chris Ofili, sculptors Rachel Whiteread and Anish Kapoor or conceptual artists Jeremy Deller or Gilbert and George.

There are many high spots worth mentioning when thinking about soft power influences and Britain's natural 'creatives'. The creative drive in the different sectors of society we have discussed here is not primarily a matter of how well-funded or profitable they are – though to be sure, income and funding always matters. But creativity in these fields arises from a broader commitment to openness and intellectual freedom: the creation of an atmosphere that encourages experimentation and does not punish failure too harshly, that attracts foreign talent and concentrates human expertise in tight hubs and loose networks where ideas bump up against each other. Creativity is infectious and it naturally invites imitation. To do something first is often not the most profitable – ask Toby Gard of *Tomb Raider* – but in soft power terms it can create influence and mystique and become the building block of a more subtly powerful reputation. The iconic Mini automobile, designed by Alec Issigonis and first produced by the British Motor Corporation in 1959, was the most successful car in British automotive history. It did not cease production until 2000 and in that time it changed both the design and the building blueprints for the whole international car industry; it created a completely new trend in design, construction and economy. But though more than one and a half million Minis were produced and sold it was not the commercial success that many expected and it did not save the independent British motor industry. As anyone who has watched the film *The Italian Job* will know, however, the Mini projected a lasting image of British chic and cheek that has endured long in the memory.

For all the social conservatism, the British reserve, the aloof attitude to the world, that many foreign observers say they discern in British society, recent history indicates something different. In some important respects, as in its official institutions and some of its social organizations – say from Parliament, across the corner of St James's Park to the Reform Club on Pall Mall – Britain holds doggedly onto its social conservatism. That can be seen the length and depth of the country. But in so many other respects British society not only nurtures creativity and even disruptive change, but it positively embraces many aspects of the socially anarchic. Toleration of eccentricity is almost a matter of national pride, and British society extends it to bloggers and influencers, charity fund-raisers and activist protesters, alternative life-stylers and offensive entertainers. Being unafraid to embrace the socially anarchic is a symptom of a creative society, whether or not any particular strands of such anarchy turn out to be creatively productive.

The confidence to do this is also affected by prevailing national moods. The 1960s became a decade of dizzy and anarchic change that built creative confidence radiating to the rest of the world. It diminished in the 1970s but was back in the late 1980s and much of the 1990s. Apart from a bright, shining moment in 2012, that national confidence gradually rowed back again in the wake of the 2008 global economic crisis.

As we have tried to establish here, Britain's creatives are in good shape and can certainly sustain significant roles, even if not dominant ones, in the world of the 2020s. There is not much any government can do to mobilize this creative imperative; it runs on its own dynamics. But in the wake of the Covid-19 crisis the drive to exploit British creativity in all these areas, and the international regard in which they are held, will be one of the routes to full recovery. The most important thing any government can do is pay particular attention to the requirements for openness, the attraction of talent and constant experimentation. The 'creatives' can do more than most in British society to generate that sense of national confidence that may dispel the gloom and national angst of recent years.

Entertainers

Feeding a human need

Dinner for One is an 18-minute, black-and-white skit performed by British comedians Freddie Frinton and May Warden. Hardly anyone in Britain has heard of it. Yet across Germany, Switzerland, Austria and Scandinavia it is legendary and broadcast nationally every New Year's Eve. It is the story of an old butler, a retainer for an even older dowager aristocrat, trying to match her eccentric British determination that he should represent all four of her – long deceased – friends as well as serving a meal to them all. He becomes progressively more incapable with all the drinks he consumes standing in for the non-existent guests. Frinton and Warden had been doing this sketch in British music hall theatres since 1945, until German TV filmed it in 1962, and ten years later it gained a fixed spot on foreign TV schedules that it has never relinquished. It would not be apparent to most British citizens how much this annual 18-minute vignette affects foreign perceptions of British society, at once social commentary and slapstick funny. It stands as a little example of a big phenomenon – the persuasive international importance of entertainment.

In Britain's modern society a discrete 'entertainment sector' is hard to define, still less an exclusively British one, as might have been the case when *Dinner for One* was filmed in 1962. But there are some strong lines of British identity and creativity in the burgeoning world of global entertainment. Entertainment comes in all shapes and sizes. From our perspective the elements of most international interest include film and television, theatre, music, the performing arts and sport. They constitute some of the most important soft power players in the world politics arena and they interlink with each other. They draw strength from a larger British 'creative industries' sector which is economically impressive, even if it is not fully acknowledged within politics or society at large; rather it is somehow taken for granted by both public and politicians.

Prior to the Covid-19 crisis, the whole creative industries sector in Britain was estimated in 2019 to be worth £116 billion in gross value added (GVA) terms.[1]

Film and TV was the biggest portion of this (£21 billion) but 'music arts and culture' was worth £9 billion, publications of all kinds around £12 billion, and there was a big spread of activities that account for many smaller proportions. Overall, 3.2 million jobs were tied up in creative industries in 2019 – that's three times more than in London's finance and insurance, four times more than in the automotive industry and eight times more than in defence. Its total export value is calculated at £35 billion a year – more than three times the value of annual British weapons sales – and it is estimated to account for 12 per cent of all service sector exports.[2]

At least in the eyes of the external world, the hard statistics indicate that Britain is clearly a nation of myriad entertainers more than it is a nation of soldiers, financiers or car-makers. In soft power terms, however, the importance of this big sector is not in its economic contributions to the economy – they are indicative but not the central point. Our interest, rather, is in those particular parts of the creative industries sector that most explicitly present Britain to the world and have some effect in promoting images and values: the ideas and atmosphere of British society that attract admiration and imitation. While the world of quiet diplomacy, or standards and regulations, may have underlying influence on the way power is structured in world politics, entertainment represents the most explicit window on society. That is not to say that entertainment has got to be 'about Britain', still less to 'present Britain' in a favourable light. That approach has been tried, for the most part unsuccessfully, by a century of dictatorships around the world. But entertainment feeds a deep human need. It structures the way people think and react, and they experience it directly far more often than they experience political discourse – however entertaining that frequently turns out to be. Entertainment has the ability to open many political doors, at home and abroad. But more than that, societies that create and influence global entertainment are on the right side of its deep structural power. They may not be able to manipulate it directly, but their lives will be easier and probably safer for being intrinsically involved in this sort of amorphous network of influence, which has only recently become truly global. Entertainers of all kinds are some of the most important persuaders in Britain.

The silver screens

British film and television is worth £21 billion to the British economy in GVA, and it accounts for £8 billion of exports in services collectively of film, TV, radio and photography, plus another £500 million in hardware exports of one sort or another. Before the Covid-19 crisis there were around 240,000 jobs in this sector, though it may take some time to get back to these numbers.[3]

The British film industry has been very successful over the last forty years. Film-making has become a more decentralized, international and high-tech process, less dependent on the big Hollywood studio complexes.[4] British studios are attractive to foreign film-makers for their concentration of specialists and the tax breaks on offer for foreign film production. The large British sound stages still operate at studios like Pinewood – James Bond's movie home – or at Leavesden in Watford, a big British studio bought by Warner Brothers to operate Europe's biggest collection of sound stages and tanks alongside a 100-acre backlot – 'Built by filmmakers for filmmakers', as the Warner Brothers slogan runs. The Leavesden studios are where Harry Potter grew up. Ealing Studios, the oldest in the world (astonishingly, having opened in 1902), still operate and provide those parts of Downton Abbey that Highclere Castle cannot manage. Shepperton Studios in Surrey is home to a Netflix hub as well as to Captain America. These days Shepperton is part of the Pinewood Group, a major British multinational that also runs studios in Canada, Germany, Malaysia, Dominican Republic and, until recently, in Atlanta. Since it was founded in 2001, the Pinewood Group has hosted over 1,500 film productions. And there are over thirty other significant British studios, generally concentrated in London or Hertfordshire, though studios are also busy in Wales; the *Game of Thrones* weaves its dastardly way at the Titanic Studios in Belfast, and the famous Aardman Animations, where Wallace and Gromit live, is still based in Bristol.

The real attraction for international film-makers, however, is not just the sound stages or the crews available, or Britain's posse of leading actors and directors. Britain's most distinctive attraction really lies in the skills and frontier technologies of its post-production facilities.[5] There are about 3,000 post-production enterprises in Britain, ranging from fashionable companies like Goldcrest Films to self-employed individuals with particular skills. Many of them cluster around tiny offices in Soho and Bedford Square where they edit, grade and 'finish' visual and audio rushes, internationalize a product or make it nationally compliant. Above all, the 12,000 people in British post-production are known for their world-leading VFX – the visual effects that have become so important in film and television production. In 2018 it was all worth almost £2 billion, just in direct services, not counting any credit for bringing film companies into British studios. They are the best in the world at VFX; Hollywood would not be Hollywood without Wardour Street.[6]

The pre-pandemic year of 2019 saw the second-highest level of spending by international film-makers in Britain ever recorded – almost £1.8 billion spent directly in the studios. The production hiatus across the industry caused by the crisis appeared not to have seriously dented this growth in 2020.[7]

If Britain gets great credit for what goes into the silver screen, how much credit does it get for what comes out? When British screenwriter Colin Welland picked up his Oscar for *Chariots of Fire* in 1982, he famously warned Hollywood 'the British are coming'. That might have been a little premature but it eventually turned out to be true enough. In the 2019–20 international awards season British talent had an average year, which is to say that twenty-six major awards were secured, more than one in eight of all those available. Awards at the Cannes and Venice film festivals, the BAFTAs, the Oscars or the Golden Globes covered everything from producers, directors and performers to composers, cinematographers and costume designers. British stars and actors certainly get their fair share of acclaim in the industry, as do highly rated directors like Ridley Scott, Danny Boyle, Sam Mendes, Steve McQueen, Christopher Nolan, Kenneth Branagh or Mike Figgis.

International recognition for British talent on both sides of the silver screen is evidently high. It is interesting to note that two-thirds of box-office returns for British films are earned abroad.[8] But this also reveals the tip of an iceberg of real change in the global film market that poses many future challenges. The British film industry, in all its economic strength, and its 7 per cent of global market share, has grossed roughly the same as the Indian film industry since about 2015. But India is far and away the biggest producer of films in the world. The second biggest producer is Nigeria, third is the United States and fourth is China.[9] Britain is overwhelmingly tied to the US sphere of film-making, both economically (it is still the most profitable) and artistically.[10] The five key distributers for films that project British talent are all American: Paramount, Sony, Disney, Warner Brothers and Universal – 20th Century Fox has already gone. Amazon and Netflix are upending even the big five's domination of the market, as the major distributers increasingly see movie-making not as an end in itself but as the entry point for the other merchandise and services they really want to offer. There is very little room for independent films or distributers in this brutal picture (which is why creatives turn increasingly to TV and the boxed sets to express themselves).

The same is true for artistic judgements about the most marketable themes. Even in the United States, only about a third of film income now comes from the domestic market; films succeed or fail economically on their international, cross-cultural appeal. Which is why blockbuster films fighting against space aliens, fantasy villains or natural disasters are a much safer economic bet than films that appear to make cultural distinctions – still less set up any racially stereotypical baddies. A different version of one of Disney's *Pirates of the Caribbean* films had to be made specifically for the Chinese market, cutting out the actor Chow Yun-fat because he was portraying an unsympathetic character in the version the rest of the world saw.[11] Culturally challenging, edgy and penetrating films certainly win awards, but the big money is made by either screwball comedies or non-specific explosion-fests. In 2020 the highest-grossing films produced by the US market were *Bad Boys for Life, Sonic the Hedgehog, Jumanji* and *Star Wars: The Rise of Skywalker* – though a very honourable mention should also be made for Sam Mendes's ambitious all-British film *1917*, which was second in the top five list. To date, the highest-grossing films of this century have been – in order – *Avatar* (2010), *Avengers Endgame* (2019), *Star Wars VII* (2015), *Avengers Infinity War* (2018) and *Jurassic World* (2015), which together grossed over $11.1 billion.[12]

Asian and African film-making has already overtaken Hollywood in the volume of its output, though Hollywood, backed with British talent, remains very profitable because it is so thematically dominant – it still entertains the world. But 'Hollywood' is in trouble, both in its own world, caught between cinemas and home entertainment, DVDs and streaming, and in defining its global market for the future. It is not difficult to see how the structural influence of global film entertainment might be moving in less Anglosphere directions. The British film industry has been on the right side of this type of structural soft power – largely uncontested – for over a century. But that might change quite quickly. The British film industry – far more flexible and diverse than Hollywood and not weighed down by top-heavy management or power-crazed moguls – certainly has the capacity to be agile. It may need to be.

Overlapping with the film industry, British television is another soft power entertainment asset. But though its production processes are very similar, its international market dynamics are somewhat different. British TV has produced any number of signature programmes that demonstrate its international appeal. The fourth season of 'Sherlock' – trading on the tropes of Arthur Conan Doyle's famous detective, alongside fashionable modern-day London – sold to 230 territories around the world.[13] Many British critics became scornful of Julian Fellowes's 'Downton Abbey' as it went into successive series after its original launch on ITV in 2010, but NBC Universal estimated that by 2013 it had achieved a global audience of over 120 million and that was before it was dubbed into mandarin.[14] David Attenborough's two 'Planet Earth' series had been licensed in 233 territories by 2016. The enigmatic 'Dr Who' who first appeared in London in 1963 now materializes in over 200 different territories. And no fewer than 22 series of 'Top Gear' accumulated 350 million viewers in more than 200 countries.

'Top Gear' and other winning entertainment formulas are frequently franchised for home-grown production. There are national versions of 'Top Gear' in countries as different as Australia, Russia and China. 'The Great British Bake Off' format has been reproduced in over twenty countries. There were fifty national versions of 'MasterChef' showing around the world in 2020. 'Who Wants to Be a Millionaire' began on ITV in 1998 and was franchised to over 100 countries from Afghanistan to Vietnam. It was the essence of Danny Boyle and Loveleen Tandan's *Slumdog Millionaire*, a 2008 'Bollywood blockbuster' movie that swept the awards. The BBC's 'Strictly Come Dancing' has been replicated in sixty other countries, licensed by BBC Worldwide as 'Dancing with the Stars'.[15] Even more dramatically, 'Pop Idol' in 2001 and 'X Factor' in 2004 both created cascading international franchises that traded on 'Idol' and 'X Factor' brand names to create stables of programmes, and even dedicated channels, and changed the economics of programming – where audience telephone voting, for the first time, became a major source of programme revenue. Those brands created a new business model in participatory entertainment shows that has been replicated around the world in the last twenty years.

The fact that stands out in this success, however, is that the foreign demand for British TV is more in the programmes than the format ideas, though the formats – for good and bad – have proved to be highly influential in the global broadcasting world. In 2019–20 British TV exported £1.5 billion of its products, the majority of it as finished programmes. By comparison, selling the formats and co-production rights was worth about £250 million. Whereas Hollywood comes to British studios and facilities to make its films, the world wants British TV programmes as they are: a direct window on the artistic and domestic TV scene in Britain. Half of that trade for finished programmes is still with buyers in the United States. France and Australia are the next biggest markets. Asian markets, as to be expected, are comparatively small (though, of course, BBC World Service radio and British TV services, BBC World, BBC Prime and Sky TV, have enviable coverage for their regular broadcasting across Asia and Africa).

In this respect, the BBC is a special issue. It is a considerable force in world broadcasting at all levels: in film production and co-production, TV, radio, websites and global merchandising. But in addition to its role in the entertainment world, it is a massive soft power communicator of news for foreign audiences in addition to what most domestic audiences see of it. The BBC World Service Group includes World Service radio, which broadcasts in forty-two languages, World Service TV News which is broadcast in 200 countries, the BBC News website which receives around a billion hits a month and BBC monitoring, which acts as the BBC's own information and intelligence service. In all, the broadcasting services of the BBC World Service Group reach some 438 million people every week somewhere in the world. Some have called it simply 'Britain's strongest tool of soft power'.[16] In May 2021 the FCDO confirmed that it would increase its funding to the BBC World Service to a level of £94 million.[17] More than that, the BBC is one of the most trusted news sources in the world, particularly in times of crisis. It is the service to which many people in the emerging countries turn when they are confused by a crisis that affects them personally. In Iran the BBC is banned, jammed and ridiculed. But still some twelve million Iranians, almost 15 per cent of the population, regularly tune in.

Despite all this, however, for a number of reasons – not least its national broadcaster status as an arena of Western culture wars – the corporation has been going through an identity crisis for more than a decade. It is distracted by many issues outside the realm of production and broadcasting and it is ideologically opposed by different strands within modern British conservatism and free-market thinking. The BBC's licence fee income is worth around £3.5 billion annually – far more than it can earn commercially. And it is due a mid-term review of its Royal Charter licence fee terms in 2022–4, before the original Royal Charter expires on its centenary in 2027.[18] For all its international prestige, the BBC has to justify itself as a public service broadcaster, even as it is being urged to find ways of collaborating more deeply with on-demand subscription channels and/or to rebalance its heavy reliance on licence fee income.[19] The BBC model as an independent, licence-paid, public service broadcaster is admired and imitated in many parts of Scandinavia but not directly replicated in many other countries around the world, and certainly not much outside Europe.[20] By common consent, the BBC is struggling to adapt and in the new landscape of international broadcasting possibly even to survive.

The bear pits

British theatre has always enjoyed an unrivalled international reputation. Modern drama, alongside modern theatres, effectively began in Elizabethan England

and it was, from the very first, highly cosmopolitan. William Shakespeare, the world's playwright, set his scenes in no fewer than twelve countries across Europe, Africa and the Middle East, spanning history and cultures in his thirty-eight surviving plays.[21] British pantomime – as mystifyingly British to foreign visitors as cricket – developed in the eighteenth century as a hybrid of the English medieval morality plays and the anarchic Italian sixteenth-century street theatre of the Commedia dell'arte. In a sense, the present-day Shakespeare's Globe Theatre on the banks of the Thames recognizes and celebrates all this amid a 'west end' of no fewer than 45 principal theatres, among 200-odd other theatre venues in the capital – and more than 1,100 active theatres nationally.[22] In 2018–19 British theatre income totalled almost £1.3 billion, £800 million of it earned in London. Indeed, it is estimated that on any given day, around 3,000 artists somewhere in London are gearing up to perform in one of the capital's theatre venues.[23]

British theatre's output, if not always its audiences, increasingly reflects British society's multiculturalism. It is also notable that the subsidized sectors, such as the National Theatre or the Royal Shakespeare Company, are not reluctant to criticize the establishment or the government in their works. Publicly subsidized theatre has tackled Northern Ireland issues many times. It has produced 'factual drama' over the Iraq War of 2003; it has dramatized the Hutton Report on the death of scientist David Kelly, the role of the police in the racially aggravated death of Stephen Lawrence, even the events of the Potter's Bar rail crash. Some regarded British theatre, notwithstanding all its big production musicals and rock operas, as Britain's 'substitute forum for political debate'.[24]

In reality, the reputation of British theatre feeds into most other areas of British entertainment, aided by the fact that there are two billion English speakers in the world these days. It incorporates music of all genres and the other performing arts from opera to musical theatre, from ballet to street dance. It is said that humour doesn't travel well, but British comedy traditions also remain strong in the wider world, where it is often regarded as 'quintessentially British'. In reality, the comedy scene is much influenced by comedy trends across North America, though in Britain it is set within less deferential, robust, social mores – another tradition for which we can thank Shakespeare and his contemporaries.

More than in most other service industries, however, the Covid-19 crisis devastated the theatre industry and, unlike its Elizabethan forebears, moving it out of London during the plague years was not an option. More than a year of dark theatres exposed even more starkly the financial vulnerability of an essentially itinerant industry. The international reputation of British theatre certainly won't diminish quickly, but its outputs might. And a talent drain elsewhere is certainly possible.

British music in the global entertainment scene is naturally strong, thanks in no small measure to two generations of US cultural pre-eminence and the power of the English language. English is the lingua franca of global pop music, much to the chagrin of successive French governments. It is, at least for the time being, the cool foreign language even among very different cultures. It is the language of major brand names and protest banners everywhere in the world, so it is also the language of rock and pop.

That does not automatically translate into success or influence, of course. The global pop scene is extremely variable and the fashion for British music and pop superstars comes and goes. Over the first ten years of this century the 'streaming revolution' undermined CD sales and took a lot of income from the British pop scene and its artists. Morale was low and the industry was worried. Then in 2015, Adele (whose album, *25*, that year sold 1.71 million CDs in its first week[25]), Ed Sheeran, One Direction, Coldplay and Sam Smith were all named by the industry's international federation as among the top ten recording artists in the world. But by 2020 the relative dearth of British pop superstars was again a topic of discussion. The essential point, however, is that the British pop industry *expects* to be second only to that in the United States and becomes fretful during the downtimes. The fact is that even in the more anarchic streaming era, where individual songs rather than a collected work of the artist (an album CD) are being accessed on a highly selective basis, one in every ten songs streamed anywhere in the world is by a British artist.[26] The sense that Britain is still the hub of European pop music is supported by *UK Music*'s calculation that in 2017 over 800,000 'music tourists', mainly from the continent, came to British concert venues, the vast majority for pop and rock gigs.[27]

British jazz, it has been said, is like a minority sport in relation to the glitz and reverence that jazz is traditionally accorded in the United States. That may be true, but it also gave it license to experiment in some creative ways, as Anton Spice pointed out in 2015: 'Immigration to the UK has been the catalyst that made sure this experimentation was not relegated to the cultural margins. Instead, it fed into and borrowed from the wider musical and social movements that swept through the country after the Second World War.'[28] And artists like Joe Harriott, Stan Tracey, Humphrey Littleton, John Surman, Ronnie Scott or Steve Williamson developed their own inspirations between the 1950s and the 1980s and bequeathed a vibrant tradition to contemporary artists such as Courtney Pine, Kishon Khan, Mabel Ray, Jools Holland, Martha D Lewis or Sam Brown.

Meanwhile, the institutions of classical music and opera in Britain are as strong as in any of the Germanic or Italian states of Europe. Most of its great orchestras were established around the mid-nineteenth century – the Royal Academy of Music in 1822 – and the world-famous Proms concerts go back to 1895. The Royal Albert Hall was opened in 1878 and has been the venue for wonderful national events ever since, though it has to be admitted that from a classical music perspective, it still embodies the acoustics of the inside of a gasometer. Attendances at classical concerts in Britain are vulnerable and have been for some years. But classical recording for CDs and streaming services is at an all-time high and in most years the major British orchestras – like the Hallé, the London Symphony, the Royal Liverpool, the Bournemouth Symphony – can expect to be on tours that collectively take in about thirty-five foreign countries.

Like most sectors in Britain's strong entertainment world, each feeds constantly into the work of most others and should not really be assessed as free-standing activities. British music and British musicians – rock, pop, classical, jazz – can be heard in films, TV, computer games, advertising, backing soundtracks and at events and venues of all kinds. It has international appeal and even those around the world who would not think of attending anything other than a pop concert might be surprised if they knew just how many classical and jazz musicians and singers had actually entertained them.

Finally, there are the most obvious entertainment bear pits that lie in the realm of international sport. Sport naturally carries with it the most direct identification of national character and performance in its global competitions. Just think of the medal tables and the flag-raising ceremonies even, perhaps especially, in the purist atmosphere of the Olympics.[29] Sport matters so much to so many people precisely because it doesn't matter; it doesn't matter to other more critical parts of their lives. Sporting heroes can win or lose on Saturday, but the fans still go to work, as normal, on Monday morning. Sport matters because it is the most exquisite form of live theatre, where triumph and disaster, grace, nobility and Schadenfreude are all given as much scope to reveal themselves as in 'King Lear' or 'Star Wars'.

Britain had a founding role in so many of the global sports that currently provide this exquisite live theatre to the world, and British sports people remain significantly involved in the international management of many of them: from soccer to sailing, from F1 motor racing to international rugby; from lawn tennis to golf or cricket; from modern athletics to boxing. Britain has been internationally pre-eminent in the development and codification of many modern sports. In 2006 Melvin Bragg judged the publication in 1863 of the *Rule Book of the Football Association* to be among the most seminal works in the world, since it codified – along British lines of thinking – an attitude to playing and spectating a game that has become the most popular single sport in world history.[30] British sports administration has also been in the lead supporting the rights of women's teams to compete internationally in sports that were formally all-male at the top competitive level, particularly in cricket, soccer and latterly, rugby. And despite a self-image that British teams and sports people are plucky losers – a nation of sporting amateurs and underachievers – the facts are that in the last decade British competitors featured in the top international echelons of athletics, rugby, cricket, F1, tennis, boxing, golf, cycling, rowing, field hockey, shooting, even – just about and just occasionally – in soccer. And allowing for the disappointing performances of the national team, the interesting truth is that the English Premiership is still, by some considerable margin, the biggest and richest league in the world even though over 60 per cent of its players are from different nationalities and do not qualify to play for England.[31]

The English Premiership's global coverage through its licensing of TV rights makes it available to watch for around a third of the world's population. This means it is a global leader in the field in every sense. It's an economic sporting powerhouse as well as a cultural hub. The Premiership is a genuinely international, and multicultural, league and the merchandising of its teams and its individual players can be seen on children's shirts from the suburbs of Hanoi to the favellas of Rio de Janeiro. What it says, good and bad, about British society as large portions of the world watch games week in and week out, and all the hoopla that surrounds them, is a matter of some discussion.[32] Does it anchor the image of soccer as something essentially British? Probably not. Does it show Britain's inventiveness or demonstrate its progress in multiculturalism? Perhaps, but not always. Does it create a sense of place – Manchester, Liverpool, Leicester – to people outside Britain? It would certainly seem so.[33]

Golf has a claim to be the world's greatest participation sport (though how 'participation' is defined in any mass sport is a delicate matter). It is estimated that there are between 50 and 60 million regular players globally, at least 24 million in the United States, 13 million across Asia, 7 million in Europe and 1.5 million in Britain.[34] The earliest record of modern golf is dated to 1457 when King James II of Scotland banned it – along with football – because it interfered with archery training necessary to fight the English. In 1502, however, after the Treaty of Glasgow, King James IV lifted the ban and had a beautiful set of clubs made for himself by a bow-maker in Perth. The town of St Andrews in Perthshire was –

and emphatically remains – the home of golf. In 1820 the first golf club outside Britain was founded in Bangalore, then in 1888 in New York.

British golfers like Dai Rees, Peter Oosterhuis, Bernard Gallagher or Peter Alliss established strong international reputations in their day. More recently, England's Nick Faldo held the number one slot in golf's world rankings for 97 weeks, winning three US Masters and three Open Championships. Northern Ireland's Rory McIlroy spent over 100 weeks in the world's top spot.

At the opposite end of the scale, British sports also embrace the more individual or dangerous pursuits like scuba-diving, climbing, gliding or skydiving. These are not high visibility mass sports, and not often broadcast, but British qualifications, as with the British Sub-Aqua Club or British Skydiving, to be allowed to pursue them safely are normally well respected around the world. Occasionally they hit the headlines. Cave diving is one of the world's classic minority sports. Yet it was a British-led international team of cave divers that worked to rescue twelve boys and their teacher when they were trapped for many days a mile and a half underground in Thailand's Tham Luang cave complex in 2019. As an Australian who was key to the rescue put it, 'There are probably a few hundred cave divers in the world, but only a very few at that level. The guys on the British team, they are the first guys you call.'[35]

Not least, the Paralympic Games began in earnest in 1960, thanks to the tireless work of British neurologist Ludwig Guttman, a Jewish doctor who fled Nazi Germany in 1939 and took up work at the Stoke Mandeville Hospital in Buckinghamshire. He organized the first Stoke Mandeville Games in 1948 when the Olympics were staged in London and by 1960 was able to get his ninth Stoke Mandeville Paralympic Games organized alongside, and acknowledged, at the 1960 Olympics in Rome. The 2012 Paralympics in London were the biggest and most successful ever, and they were followed in 2014 by the Invictus Games for injured and disabled military veterans from around the world. Initiated by Prince Harry, they quickly became a regular biannual event. As a group of athletes, British para athletes regularly rank among the top three in the world. Every nation nods to the significance of para athletics and the Paralympic sports, but Britain has always done much more than most to make the concept a reality – and to believe in it.

Entertainment is part of the human condition and all the mainstream forms of entertainment mentioned here are, in their own ways, effective transmission belts for British soft power. They convey images of British society; and they have direct links to foreign audiences, since all of these activities are internationally recognized in one way or another. The various worlds of entertainment also demonstrate the potential of soft power influence to operate simultaneously at different levels. Individual achievement for artists, sportspeople or teams brings its own national accolades. Their success is made to seem in the eyes of the world like the success of the nation, something of which all citizens can be proud and which other nations might envy. This is the sort of soft power benefit the British Council writes about – the international eminence of British artists or sportspeople, the success of its bands, orchestras or teams.

There is a largely unspoken level on which entertainment success also operates, however. International acclaim is simultaneously an implicit acknowledgement of the *way* a society produces its successes. It is a vote of confidence in the social and institutional hinterland that creates the achievement – that which appeals so entertainingly to the wider world. Opprobrium has rightly been heaped on governments who have created state-sponsored doping and cheating to win sporting recognition or to rig international award contests in favour of their national artists. On the other hand, like many governments in free societies that would not dream of state-sponsored cheating, successive British governments have put tax breaks and public money – and indirectly a great deal of lottery cash – into supporting growth for many British entertainment sectors, film and theatre, and other Arts Council clients. Britain may feel like the natural home of the gifted amateur, but some British sports bodies, in particular, have shown themselves to be ruthlessly focused on funding 'performance' directed at the natural cycle of the next Olympics, the next world cup, the next world championships or whatever. Gaining the societal benefits of winning is an attractive political goal even for free world laissez-faire systems, and there is always a demand that governments 'should do more' to support the nation's various creative industries and sports sectors.

There is only so far any government can go, however, before it risks undermining the talent and the credibility of its own entertainers. Since entertainment is an essential human need, there is ultimately a basic honesty that eventually emerges in what peoples of the world do, or don't, find entertaining – what they are happy to watch and pay for. British achievement in the sectors mentioned here is a powerful vindication of some aspects of British society. The particular achievement is not the point; Britain is not fundamentally characterized by the *type* of rock music or the genre of films or the particular division of sport in which international success is recognized. In its achievements the country is characterized by the more basic fact that British society can breed this level of success through virtues like opportunity, freedom, openness and human endeavour. It shows it can be successful in many different fields of entertainment and they will not always be the same from one era to another.

And then there is the structural power of having influence in the markets that organize and distribute access to various entertainments. They all have their own arenas of global power – films, music, TV, theatre, soccer, rugby, motor racing – and Britain has been historically important in establishing most of those arenas. It also remains an influential force, if not a dominating one, in many of them. Of course, as globalization matures further, influence in all these sectors will move towards the money. That should be expected. It may be that traditional influences have already been diluted as global society shifts towards the greater concentrations of population in Asia and the Indo-Pacific regions and the money follows non-Western, indigenous cultures. The ill-fated attempt of six English Premiership football clubs to join a new European super-league in 2021 was not so much a bid to take their fans with them to a new competitive level, so much as to exploit a vast new fan base in Asia and the TV franchise money that would go with them. Less clumsy attempts to exploit these new fan bases will almost certainly be made in the future. It is a cautionary tale which emphasizes the premium on those entertainment areas that are capable of crossing cultures, as many sports and genres of popular music certainly do.

If it does not become complacent about its range of achievements, Britain can still follow the money and be a part of new cultural power alignments as they may take shape. It will, in any case, still have the considerable English-speaking and European markets to address, and those markets may have a lot of structural power left in them even as growing income levels across Asia and Africa allow for more individual choice. If it is adaptable, Britain can build on its underlying strengths as a nation of natural entertainers.

Stars and bloggers

Embracing the anarchic

On 13 July 1985, the first Live Aid music concert fundraiser blasted around the world, led by an Irish rock-singer. 'Bob Geldof's genius', said CNN's Graham Jones,

> was to use the latest TV satellite technology to link up Wembley in north London, JFK Stadium in Philadelphia and a host of smaller venues in other countries to blitz the world's TV networks. It was the first truly global concert, and people felt empowered and exhilarated. They felt they really could help change the world. About 1.9 billion viewers in 150 countries – the biggest-ever TV audience.[1]

Live Aid was quite something and it started a global movement in aid-giving. It had begun in late 1984 when the BBC's Michael Buerk broadcast a 'biblical famine' in northern Ethiopia that was re-broadcast by 425 television stations worldwide.[2] The artist Boy George first came up with the idea of a simultaneous international charity concert. Bob Geldof took it on and challenged millions of viewers to make donations over the telephone. 'We took an issue that was nowhere on the political agenda', he said, 'and, through the lingua franca of the planet – which is not English but rock 'n' roll – we were able to address the intellectual absurdity and the moral repulsion of people dying of want in a world of surplus.'[3]

Twenty-five years later an Australian living in London, Julian Assange, was catapulted to fame when the WikiLeaks organization he had founded dumped a first tranche of over 250,000 leaked US diplomatic cables onto the world's press for simultaneous publication in the *New York Times*, *The Guardian*, *El País*, *Le Monde* and *Der Spiegel*. Assange successfully embraced the anarchy offered by the internet, creating WikiLeaks as a vehicle to publish leaked material. Both he and WikiLeaks were immediately world famous and deeply controversial. Many claimed the organization was a servant of true democracy, others that it was a malicious disrupter that endangered US and Western diplomacy specifically. Even now, WikiLeaks has never published any leaked Russian material.

The point, however, is that in either case, an Irish singer and an Australian journalist, from homes they had made in London, worked at the edge of communications technologies of the time to create events of global significance that changed the international landscape of their businesses. Their paths were different. Geldof joined the British establishment with a knighthood; Assange began a legal odyssey to avoid extradition to the United States on espionage charges. But the world saw that Britain was a suitable launch pad for anarchic activities that were, according to taste, creative or disruptive. Britain has always seen itself as a natural home for individualism and projects that self-image to the world. Unlike its neighbours, Britain has never been subject to any significant anarchist outrages – for instance from France's Emile Henry to Germany's Baader-Meinhof gang. But it has played host to some outrageous anarchism all the same, in all spheres from arts to science. Britain likes to think of itself as a society that embraces ancient institutions as willingly as it smiles on non-political anarchic behaviour, if only as expressions of the individual's right to be individual.

It accords with a British toleration, sometimes celebration, of 'honest eccentricity' – which is a term, after all, that derives from the Latin meaning merely 'away from the centre'. The essayist George Santayana wrote in 1922 that 'England is the paradise of individuality, eccentricity, heresy, anomalies, hobbies and humours'.[4] Edith Sitwell wrote a great deal about eccentricity. Her own father placed a sign above the entrance to their home stating, 'I must ask anyone entering the house never to contradict me or differ from me in any way, as it interferes with the functioning of the gastric juices and prevents my sleeping at night.' Being decidedly eccentric herself, she went on to chronicle glorious 'English eccentricity' in all its forms.[5] The eighteenth-century artist and poet William Blake insisted on sitting with his wife, both naked in their garden, while he repeatedly read *Paradise Lost* to her. Squire Jack Mytton, famously reckless, tried to take a chaise and horse over a 5-bar gate to see if the horse could really jump and would set fire to his nightshirt as a cure for hiccups. The Scottish inventor of the telephone Alexander Graham Bell spent considerable time trying to teach his dog to talk. The twentieth-century composer Peter Warlock repaired to Eynsford in Kent to compose *The Curlew*, his idyllic song cycle, in between bouts of heavy drinking and roaring round the countryside naked on a motorbike. And Major General Orde Wingate, creator of the Chindits in Burma and a master of unconventional warfare, would wear an alarm clock on his wrist and hang an onion round his neck to nibble at. He regarded clothing as completely optional in hot climates, even at meetings. Examples are legion.[6]

Over the years Britain's anarchic persuaders have taken many forms that have flirted with the extremes of taste and toleration, and in the case of Orde Wingate, quite possibly certifiable madness. They have sometimes projected to the world an image of degeneracy. In the 1960s the emergence of the Beatles and the Rolling Stones, and the 'terrace pop' that emerged from the football stands at Liverpool, was thought to push at the boundaries of good taste – until they went onto a global stage. Punk music was created by British impresario Malcolm McLaren and his young designer girlfriend, Vivienne Westwood, during the latter half of the 1970s. 'Punk' thought of itself as a discernible movement and an ideology with its own signs and symbols. Punk became a phenomenon in Britain and then strutted defiantly across the wider world stage. Its beloved offspring, the Goths, went on to slouch their surly way across the same platform. To Vivienne Westwood, the anarchic symbols of Punk had been 'rips and dirt, safety pins, zips, slogans and hairstyles. These motifs were so iconic in themselves – motifs of rebellion.'[7] And in the post-Punk years, the Haçienda club in Manchester created a new music genre when it opened in 1982. House music, picked up in Chicago and brought to Britain, inspired individualistic freedom of dance and expression. It also inspired widespread drug use, and as police restrictions increased the movement disappeared underground to create an early rave scene – now so ubiquitous as to be an intrinsic part of Western youth culture. The 'Madchester years' of the 1980s and early 1990s catalysed an era as the 'second summer of love' and the fabled Haçienda is said to have inspired the forefathers of the US rave scene.[8] The illegal raves, or at least the unauthorized and unlicensed ones, have remained at once organized and anarchic, joyfully playing hide and seek with authority, making the most of social media's power to distribute the music outside the conventional industry and operate cannily in challenging the establishment to try to stop them.

The British establishment, with its extensive honours system, however, has always been shrewd enough to embrace sufficient elements of the anarchic to keep it effectively non-political – something that many other countries have not managed to do. Surviving members of the culture-busting Beatles and the observably degenerate Rolling Stones were honoured with awards for contributions to their industries and then with knighthoods. For her anti-establishment Punk fashion designs and contributions to all things contrarian, Vivienne Westwood was awarded a Damehood, recognition, too, of her standing and export value in the international fashion markets.

Official recognition of individualism is also designed to acknowledge its creative value. Challenging prevailing norms can lead to stunning creativity. Heston Blumenthal, for example, who specializes in molecular gastronomy, is one of the pioneers of multisensory cooking and now taken into the establishment with his appointment as fellow of the Royal Society of Chemistry. David Hockney's embrace of the I-Pad to create hi-tech modern art is, in its own terms, as anarchic as the work of Banksy, whose illicit urban artwork skirts the edges of pop and consumerism.

As we have pointed out in other chapters, Britain is now a largely digitized society operating within a highly globalized national economy. The technologies that create standardization and uniformity also facilitate anarchic individualism. Indeed, they give it a strong business case. Individualism can be big money, selling impressions, likes and endorsements. Tangible goods are not required as long as an individual is somehow authentic – believable and credible, worth imitating. In times past, well-known figures lent their names to endorse common products. The cricketer Denis Compton spent years advertising Brylcreem; the classic (non-smoking) footballer Stanley Matthews advertised Craven A – 'the cigarette for me' as he said on the posters. They endorsed products because they were famous.

But today's bloggers and vloggers have created their own demand precisely because they are not famous, at least not for anything other than being ordinary and 'authentic'. And those qualities can be offered to the international world without the need for studios, specialized equipment, distributors or agents. Zoella, born in 1990, with 9.7 million followers on Instagram, topped the list of female social media stars in 2019. She started her fashion and lifestyle blog a decade previously, and with sponsorships, brand deals, her own novels and beauty ranges, converted that into an estimated income of £4.7 million.[9] Her brother, Joe Sugg, has his own YouTube channel with over seven million followers. His social media celebrity status was given a massive boost when he joined the 2018 line-up for the BBC's *Strictly Come Dancing*. As a result, he represents one of the few social media sensations to make the move to more traditional on-screen and theatre performances. British food blogger and podcaster Ella Mills, with her Deliciously Ella brand, is worth an estimated £2.5 million. Tanya Burr made some £1.6 million from her blog and YouTube channel. The most successful British blogger is said to be PewDiePie, a Swedish 31-year-old called Felix Kjellberg who lives with his wife in Brighton and has well over 100 million subscribers to his 'Let's Play' series on YouTube. In 2016 *Time* named him as one of the 'world's 100 most influential people'. He describes himself as 'apolitical' and with his large fortune has become a noted philanthropist.[10]

It can work both ways, as well, for fashion entrepreneurs. The British online retailer ASOS (As Seen On Screen) saw in this new social phenomena a smart business opportunity. ASOS works on clothing first seen on Hollywood stars and other new celebrities from all parts of the social media, then quickly reproduces them for fashion-conscious buyers who want the same look straight away. The business grew so rapidly it went beyond just copying the clothes that stars and models were paparazzied in; it began its own-label garments too, worn by the likes of Michelle Obama, the Duchess of Cambridge and pop-star Rihanna.[11] David and Victoria Beckham, simply as individuals, became one of the world's first truly global brands – actually a series of multiple brands.[12] They represent celebrity at its most modern and far beyond that of sports people like Denis Compton and Stanley Matthews. With the exception of the astonishing cricketer and athlete, C. B. Fry – grandfather of the entertainer Stephen Fry – being offered the throne of Albania in the 1930s, the Beckhams have attained a unique position in the world of celebrity. In Bangkok, David Beckham's image appears alongside the Buddha at the Wat Pariwas temple.[13] And his career as an England international ended in 2009.

Perhaps the blogosphere will act as the springboard for new generations of anarchic individuals and entrepreneurs to leap, like Joe Sugg, into mainstream media and the more organized commercial and entertainment worlds. Thirty years ago, that would have been the logical, almost inevitable, conclusion. But in the new information order that we discuss further in Chapter 14, it is evident that the blogosphere can serve as its own reality and keep its stars and cultural anarchists bounded within their own, very profitable, boudoirs. The mainstream worlds of marketing and advertising brings its cash to them and agrees to play by the rules the bloggers and vloggers seem able to set for themselves. The nineteenth-century philosopher of anarchism William Godwin – husband of feminist writer Mary Wollstonecraft and father of Frankenstein creator, Mary Shelley – maintained that a community of individual anarchists was quite feasible. Perhaps in the modern blogosphere he would recognize one.

Individualism as a national characteristic

These individual vignettes of a new generation of soft power persuaders are not necessarily an accident that happens to pop up in British society only because of its high internet connectivity and English-language access to the rest of the world. And British eccentricity is not merely a social curiosity. There is good empirical evidence that British society is significantly more individualist than most others and is certainly the most individualist within Europe.

In 2017 Henri Santos led a study in global attitudes towards individualism, compared to collectivism. His team examined fifty-one years of data on individualist practices and values across seventy-eight different countries. They found that individualism had been steadily rising in most of the societies they analysed, including in Britain where socio-economic development was a key feature of society.[14] In the same year, a survey of political attitudes conducted by the European Commission showed Britain to be the most individualistic country in the European Union when it examined hopes and attitudes towards the EU in the decade to come.[15] Among the twenty-eight EU members at that time, British popular opinion indicated a country that scored the highest (along with Italy) for positive attitudes towards individualism, one of the lowest for natural sympathy towards 'solidarity' concepts – though in the EU case that was a heavily loaded question – and was one of the least sympathetic to any compromise between the two. The British tended to see the future, at least in EU terms, as an either/or choice between individualism and solidarity.

This could be further confirmed by one of the earliest frameworks for measuring cultural dimensions in a global perspective. In Geert Hofstede's work Britain scores consistently highly for its public attitude to individualism.[16] This does not imply any lack of commitment to national society, but it defines it in a particular way. The same was observed in the United States, Canada and Australia, where primacy is given to the rights of the individual, privacy, freedom of thought and expression. Asian countries like China, Thailand or Vietnam and African nations such as Burkina Faso, Ethiopia or Sierra Leone all score considerably higher in positive public attitudes towards collectivism.[17] The surveys also noted that Britain had a high score for what it conceived as national 'masculinity' which it equated with an emphasis on competition, achievement and success; the British, says social psychologist Hofstede, 'live to work and have a clear performance ambition'. They also score highly on his 'indulgence' scale, where the British 'act as they please, spend money as they wish'. This is in comparison to what his research characterizes as more 'feminine' societal attitudes – a greater value on quality of life and far less admiration 'for standing out from the crowd' – qualities his surveys perceive strongly in Scandinavian countries.

Some of the current British individualist attitude is driven by a long-term decline in deference and what has been defined as 'de-alignment' – a loosening of previously strong class and political ties alongside diminishing faith in national institutions.[18] Recent politics have exacerbated these trends. The Iraq Dossier of 2003 deeply wounded public confidence in the justification given for British military intervention in a war that became steadily more controversial. The global financial crisis of 2008 – a 'once-in-a-century credit tsunami' – showed systemically poor financial risk management by professionals and institutions across the whole Western banking sector. Within a year, the parliamentary expenses scandal broke out and in 2010 sex scandals began to engulf Oxfam and some other aid organizations and hit the reputation of the charitable sector very hard. Even in much-admired institutions, good governance and financial accountability seemed to have failed and came under acute scrutiny amid public disillusionment. The FIFA scandal in 2015 and the 2016 Panama Papers revelations appeared merely to reinforce a sense of cynical de-alignment among the public. Trust in erstwhile pillars of society was understandably shaken. Not surprising, then, that Britons also display a continuing soft spot for rascally, rebellious characters like Princess Diana and Prince Harry, at least until he moved with his wife permanently to the United States. Individuals like Jeremy Clarkson can sail close to the wind with the same confidence that an ultra-establishment figure like Member of Parliament Jacob Rees-Mogg can parade his studied eccentricities and eighteenth-century style and be curiously admired for it in wider society. Prime Minister Boris Johnson may emerge as the ultimate in rascally figures who excite wild admiration from some for his 'all too human' character flaws and his political insouciance. He even stimulates at least a sullen resignation for it from his opponents. 'He is, after all, a living tautology', says broadcaster Gavin Esler, ' "Boris being Boris" ideally suited for an age in which . . . "Brexit means Brexit".[19]

British individualism as a national characteristic, however, is not necessarily self-seeking or completely consumed by the phenomenon of celebrity. It feeds other impulses and endeavours that have international significance and open up a different window on British presence in the world. Much of it derives from individual, eccentric or frankly anarchistic behaviour that outflanks society's institutions and simply drives forward in its own ways. The world's wealthiest and most individualistic countries also happen to be some of the most altruistic. The Charities Aid Foundation publishes an annual index of 'global altruism', which analyses levels of volunteering, charitable giving and providing everyday help to strangers (even in relatively trivial ways).[20] Surveying international behaviour over the ten-year period to 2019, the CAF work ranked Britain as seventh overall in the world, close alongside other obviously wealthy and individualistic countries like the United States, Australia, New Zealand, Canada and Ireland.[21] Within the top ten, Britain was rated as the joint highest giver of charitable cash, though the least generous in offering charitable time to others.

Being an individually charitable country is also consistent with official aid policy, where for many years Britain set a standard in its financial support for overseas development. In 2017, British aid totalled £15 billion – the third largest sum from a donor country, after the United States and Germany – and at 0.7 per cent, the single highest proportion of GNI of any donor country.[22] This proportion, however, was reduced in 2020 to 0.5 per cent of GNI by the government caught in the economics of the Covid-19 crisis, taking the cash amount down to around £10 billion and halting aid to a number of countries and projects that really mattered to 'Global Britain'. It was regarded by many observers as a foolish soft power own goal at a time when British society was responding well to the public health crisis caused by Covid-19 and personal charitable giving, overall, was still high by any international standards.[23]

There are many telling individual examples of social media working in the opposite way to the anarchic bloggers and vloggers, where the same manipulation of technologies and use of some celebrity culture have served less self-interested purposes. The renowned war surgeon David Nott is a striking example of someone going it alone and thinking outside the normal channels. For decades he has been travelling to operate on civilians in war zones, often under siege and with little equipment. He pioneered the idea of creating specialized training tools for surgeons in war zones and began taking part via Skype video-link from London in delicate operations conducted by local surgeons in Aleppo.[24] He didn't try to work through the agencies that were overwhelmed or slow; indeed, he had a chequered relationship after working with some of them. He just fixed it up. He became something of a celebrity for a while, known as the 'Indiana Jones of surgery' – not a status he was comfortable with but one that helped serve the purposes of getting some momentum behind his projects. He and his wife, Elly, were able to utilize this fame to set up The David Nott Foundation in 2015 to organize training in emergency surgery for others within affected countries.[25]

Another example was James Le Mesurier, a British army officer who set up the MayDay Rescue Foundation in 2014 to support Syrian volunteers trying to carry out search and rescue operations of bombed buildings and medical evacuation during some of the worst bombings in the conflict. He co-founded the White Helmets – a volunteer civil defence organization operating in Syria and parts of Turkey, and therefore working in some of the most dangerous zones in the world. It required a huge amount of work to get specialist training done and the right equipment on hand. It was a very personal effort on his part using whatever communication and liaison tools were to hand. Once the White Helmets began operating, however, they were on the ground and in a position to confirm to the outside world the reality of civilian bombing, including deliberately targeted hospitals, by Syrian and Russian aircraft. The social media world exploded, too, and found its way into mainstream media in the West. Le Mesurier was subjected to unrelenting disinformation campaigns, accusing the White Helmets of many things, the least of which was of acting as useful idiots for jihadist groups in Syria. To its credit, in 2020 BBC radio did a long, multi-programme expose on the whole disinformation effort and the murky figures and organizations behind the attempts to discredit Le Mesurier.[26] And it made sure the programmes were broadcast around the world. But it was too late for Le Mesurier, who apparently committed suicide in November 2019. The White Helmets, however, are still working. Le Mesurier created a useful legacy.

In early April 2020, a 99-year-old ex-British army serviceman, Captain Tom Moore, set out to raise £1000 for the NHS by walking 100 laps of his garden during the first phase of the Covid-19 crisis. By the morning of his 100th birthday, 20 April 2020, he had raised £32,796,155, from over one and half million individual donations for his personal and eccentric marathon – the most ever raised on the JustGiving platform. He became a social media star immediately, was knighted by the Queen, went to Barbados and duetted with Michael Ball to produce a charity song. The most remarkable year of his long life was almost certainly the final one. He died peacefully in 2021, having set off the whole madcap thing merely because – in the words typical of his wartime generation – 'he wanted to do his bit', he said, during the Covid-19 crisis. For a man who lived all his life deep in the mainstream of British society, it might have seemed strange to be included in a group of stars and bloggers who tended to embrace the anarchic. But that is rather the point of British anarchism. It infuses persuaders who are rather surprised by it themselves as they are thrust onto an international stage.

Part Three

Soft power in practice

Britain's soft power realities

People in government don't have much time to think about abstractions. Officials have tight deadlines to produce briefings for their bosses, coordinate actions and 'deconflict' issues with other departments. They attend regular meetings endlessly while preparing for fresh meetings that are driven by someone else's timetable – often by the rigid schedules of international diplomacy. Ministers and political leaders lead even more fraught lives. They have a wider agenda to worry about, a domestic audience to please and usually the issue of getting re-elected hovering in the background. Many a government minister, from more than one Western country, has privately observed that 'we know exactly what we should do about this or that problem; we just don't know how to get re-elected when we've done it'. Everyone in government is seeking the 'policy levers' they can pull to make things happen and looking for definable evidence that something has. So, people in government don't think very often about something as abstract as the meaning of power, though they are very keen to exert it.

Policy-makers feel power much more than they think about it. When he worked in the US State Department and the Pentagon, Joseph Nye, the man who first investigated soft power ideas, decided that 'defining power in terms of resources was a shortcut that policymakers often use'. Anything else was too abstract to be immediately helpful.[1] In this analysis we start from the assumption that soft power is not much of a policy lever. Even if in some cases it can be discerned as a lever, it can be very hard to pull. And yet we also contend that soft power is an important part of the full spectrum of power that adheres to any state, in relation to whatever objectives it may be trying to achieve in the world.

If it were better understood in government, soft power would be seen as a very significant part of the whole context in which national power is exerted. Officials and ministers readily see a spectrum of British hard and soft power before them as they consider how to carry their chosen policies forward. They grasp the bare outlines of the concept easily enough, but thinking quickly gravitates towards the intuitive hard power end of the spectrum because that's where the policy levers with more neatly measurable outcomes seem to be. In this respect they tend to lack what might be called 'contextual intelligence'.

As analysts, neither of us are driven in the way policy-makers are, so let us try to cast the descriptive analysis of Part Two, looking at some key soft power behaviours in modern Britain, in terms of the conceptual assessment of power in Part One. How can a considered understanding of power, in other words, tell us more about what soft power really achieves? And how do we recognize its effects when we see them?

The ubiquity of the soft power arena

Power, as we said in Part One, is intrinsic to all political relationships. Indeed, much of what fundamentally defines politics is the process of managing power and the way it works as between one group of people and another. Power is intrinsic to all relationships and no one can opt out of it. One might try, but being passive is not an opt-out.

We take the view here, therefore, that wielding and reacting to power is an expression of the predicament of politics. The need to manage power is unavoidable, bequeathed to us by natural differences and the fact of human choice. Engaging in the politics of power is not something a state – or for that matter an individual – has much option about. The recognition that all power relationships are also multidimensional means that soft power relationships, as we defined them in Chapter 3, are equally unavoidable.

Soft power has not somehow been invented in the last thirty years. Attraction and preference, the urge to imitate, admiration or loathing, the perception of others' success are as intrinsic to any power relationships (or complex structures of different power relationships) as the crudest or most explicit use of compellence. But only in the last thirty years have analysts given these sorts of attributes the neat label of 'soft power' and tried to think about them in a more organized way. As Joseph Nye ruefully points out, he had no sooner coined the term 'soft power' than governments from Beijing to Washington were beating a path to his door to ask him to define more carefully this natural power source he seemed to have discovered that they had somehow overlooked all these years.[2]

Soft power is not, therefore, something that some countries possess and others do not. It is not a 'resource' in the way that natural gas deposits or military hardware might be viewed as national resources. Many politicians still think about soft power in these terms. It's a 'nice-to-have' attribute, they think, and in Britain we are certainly glad that we've got some when others evidently have little or none of it. It's a jolly helpful addition of power in navigating Britain through the choppy waters of international politics.

This is not our view. Instead, we see 'soft power' as a helpful term that illuminates some of the more subtle dimensions of all power relations and the political, economic, social, even psychological structures that emerge from them. Like every other dimension of power, soft power has to be recognized and managed. It's a natural part of the system, and indifference to it – or for that matter cynical and manipulative enthusiasm for it – won't change its systemic and ubiquitous existence. It is all part of the predicament of politics.

What, then, does 'managing' the soft power dimension of international politics really mean? We observed in Part One that governments, certainly in free societies, have very limited capacity to direct soft power assets towards a short or medium-term political goal. In Britain, the direct policy levers would reside only in a government's own official actions and in its broader strategic communications policy – 'strat comms' in the jargon – that flow from Whitehall ministries or No. 10. The government might encourage the BBC, the Arts Council, the British Council or even the institutions of the Monarchy to support this or that idea, but it could not compel them directly. Beyond that, British governments have many tools of influence to use but none that would imply an ability to somehow dragoon or 'manage' Britain's soft power in any direct way. They can pump-prime ideas with money and initiatives and create designated 'champions' for some national attribute they want to develop; they can wave a flag for a particular idea, but as we described in Part Two, most of those who figure prominently in soft power equations are not on the government's payroll. The institutions and behaviours that most matter lie outside the government's direct control and are only indirectly susceptible to its influence.

The essence of soft power, as we have tried to describe, lies fundamentally in British society, not in its government. And that is the key to understanding why the soft power dimensions of international politics work in the way they do and why governments have to take a different view of their own role in promoting and employing it. There are good and important things that organizations like the British Council can do in helping tell Britain's story, enthusiastically and honestly, to the world beyond. And they have been better at doing this over the years than most of their counterpart organizations in other countries. But the British Council can only tell the story of what is deeply and historically embedded in British society as a whole. *Society* is the real asset that soft power relationships revolve around. Societies, and the ways they are perceived, are the real currency of soft power, which is why democratic commentators tend to assume that autocracies and dictatorships will always underperform in soft power, because they are frightened to release the real human energy within their own societies or have them interact openly with others.[3]

Managing soft power relationships properly requires a different perspective to that conventionally taken by most who find themselves in government. To begin with, soft power relationships run on different timescales to conventional political relationships. They easily outstrip electoral cycles and the arts and secrets of managing soft power relationships need to be socialized into a civil service, or a political class, if they are to be maintained as strands of continuity that elected politicians can draw from. Next, it is necessary for government to understand better how its society interacts with others at many non-political levels. From this, it should have a sense of how its soft power assets fit into different global structures of soft power, many of them only implicit, and which patterns of behaviour provide some weight and influence in the relationships that matter most to it. Government should have some idea of how much skin it has in the soft power game.

If government understands the nature of soft power better and knows what its society has got to offer, what can it do about it? There are some measures any government can take to help mobilize its societal strengths in relation to others. In Britain's case it can promote its natural outreach arms, like the BBC, the City of London or the British Council. Or it can prop up key national brands during tough times if it judges them to be viable in the longer term. But for the rest, where government has no business operating directly itself in a free society, and certainly no business trying to command what private organizations should do, it can nevertheless work to structure the environments in which most soft power assets exist. Government can help create the conditions which nurture some aspect of society that has a high soft power value. British governments, for example, very successfully offered tax advantages for the film industry in Britain to help make it a significant player in the global media world. That was an efficient, and democratic, way to support the role of the industry in the international soft power entertainment arena it played in. It certainly beats several lumpen attempts by autocratic leaders to inflict their own films and biopics on the world of cinema.*

The relationship between government and society also goes deeper than this, however. We defined in Chapter 3 how the concept of 'smart power' was the

---

* Classic of the genre are the six biopics all made about President Nazarbayev of Kazakhstan between 2011 and 2019, the last of which, *Leader's Path: Astana*, was reputedly even worse than the five others.

art of using both hard and soft power assets in an integrated way to achieve the best outcome. The approach was 'smart' because it acknowledged that hard and soft power can be used simultaneously and could have the effect of reinforcing each other if used in a coordinated way. The smart power approach understands how multifaceted real power relationships tend to be and how most of them oscillate across the spectrum all the time. Governments, therefore, should be clear what they are trying to achieve, what effects they want to have on another state or within the international system and be very alive to the oscillations of power relationships and able to switch into the best combination of instruments available to them as situations evolve. This is all easy to say but we also observed how difficult it is to achieve in the real world. And at the soft power end of the spectrum there are very few convenient instrumentalities to use, no quick levers to pull. But great structural power nevertheless resides at that end of the spectrum because it derives from broader society and the myriad ways in which institutions and people interact with each other across borders.

So, a government that seeks to manage its power spectrum smartly should not only try to influence the environment in which its societal power assets operate. It should also be careful to act in ways that are truly consistent with the society it represents. Soft power relationships are based, as we said in Chapter 3, on some fundamental attributes of any society – whether it is prosperous, stable and offers opportunity; whether it is seen as a significant country in the world and 'on the right side of history'. The other virtues of soft power that are commonly discussed, such as arts and heritage assets, entertainment and sport, tourism, education, and so forth, are really subsets of these more fundamental perceptions the rest of the world will have about a country. It is certainly a wise investment for a government to help shape the environment in which arts, heritage and so on operate, to help them get on with their work to best international advantage. The deeper challenge, however, is for government to be fully aware, as it goes about its day-to-day, high pressure existence of the deeper societal attributes it represents and to make every effort to remain consistent with them. In an ideal world government actions would represent a daily demonstration of those societal values it thinks it should cherish and promote – in Britain's case, say, liberal freedom and honesty, peaceful values and respect for law, the pursuit of prosperity, professionalism and tactful understanding.

As we have seen, in responding to short-term pressures, governments will often act in ways that may seem to undermine the soft power societal values they want to showcase. They may not demonstrate enough respect for law or honest dealing; they may not be very professional in the way they handle international problems.

These are the normal failings of political life. Given that soft power relationships work on longer-term cycles and are societally based, such inconsistencies may not matter too much in the scheme of things. Nevertheless, if a government consistently undermines some of the most important attributes of its own society, that will eventually have an effect on its soft power relationships in the world.

This is one of the debilitating characteristics of autocracies, which generally fail to reflect the true nature of their own societies and ultimately undermines what they have to offer the wider world. The journalist Sumit Ganguly commented that Narendra Modi's democratic rule in India had been characterized by increasing authoritarianism, to the point that it cast doubt about whether India was still seriously committed to liberal democracy. Modi had, he said, squandered India's previous magnetism in soft power terms. 'Under these circumstances', he commented, 'few people, if any, around the world will look to India for inspiration, spiritual or otherwise.'[4] It raises a practical problem too. A government that habitually operates in ways that are inconsistent with its own deeper societal values and attributes is not able to mobilize the international influence of those societies to maximum effect. They are manifestly failing to achieve the best integration of the full spectrum of available hard and soft assets. They are not using power smartly.

The multidimensions of the soft power arena

If governments are prepared to take more than a passing interest in the soft power ends of the spectrum as they consider the relationships they must manage in world politics, they will be painfully aware of how multidimensional the soft power arenas really are. As we have tried to describe in Part Two, many institutions and professions – the business community, the researchers, the churches, city councils, the regulators and standard-setters, the architects and medics, the diasporas, the entertainers and sports people and many more – operate internationally in their own, largely functional structures that they understand pretty well. There are power relationships of one sort or another in all of these structures. They are multiple and overlapping.

Nevertheless, this is where soft power makes itself felt and takes some tangible form. It is where British institutions (like RICS referred to in Chapter 7), British individuals (like entertainers referred to in Chapter 11), specifically British expertise (like medical research referred to in Chapter 6) or British social values (conveyed by the diasporas referred to in Chapter 8) can be seen to have some shaping impact on the global power structures in which they participate. Making some assessment of that impact is a way of understanding what British soft power actually achieves and how it can influence and benefit the broader objectives of Britain in world politics. It takes the analysis conceptually further than the lists of favourable facts and vignettes the British Council or the FCDO produce – telling Britain's story, as they are required to do – while they address the issue of national soft power.

In most of the areas we have examined in Part Two, Britain's societal impact has some history on which to build. There are legacies from the nineteenth and twentieth centuries that gave Britons a shaping role, or else a prominent position, in most of them. This has clearly been to Britain's natural advantage, as we have described, though it can also lead to complacency.

More importantly, the forces of globalization are having rapid impacts on some of these functional structures which are changing as a result. The British economy is affected more than most by the globalization revolution, which has helped the City of London play a role in structuring international financial management since the 2008 crisis, but reduced to some very specific sectors (like biotech or aerospace) the influence that British industry can have internationally. So too with the rise of renewed 'hyper competition' between the big nations and particularly the influence of China's economy in shaping twenty-first-century functional structures towards Beijing's own interests. Britain still plays a significant political role at the UN, but China has now taken a prominent position in the more functional areas, like the UN Department of Economic and Social Affairs or the Food and Agriculture Organization.

The news on globalization is not all bad for British soft power, of course. The information revolution and the arrival of digital society have given new impetus to many of Britain's creative industries and increased their influence in their own international networks. It has underpinned new areas in research and innovation, created fresh opportunities to make the most of Britain's traditional reputation in world education and the lingua franca of English and opened up novel possibilities in global entertainment that Britain is well placed to exploit. The chance to exercise influence in the changing arenas of soft power will fall best to those who can be agile and flexible as globalization evolves further. British institutions should certainly not be frightened to play in these arenas or assume they are automatically at a disadvantage. But times are changing, and if they find themselves no longer the erstwhile institutional pillars of their functional worlds, they can still be significant players in them and help infuse those worlds with the deeper qualities and values of British society.

The global information revolution and the arrival of societies that are ever more digitalized in the ways they function obviously create immediate opportunities for many of the institutions of British soft power. But at the same time, these developments are also changing the arenas of soft power competition in ways that no one understands very well. There is a 'new information order' developing faster than politics can keep up with it – 'the very fabric of our democracy is threatened', said a Parliamentary Committee.[5] We described in Chapter 2 how power relationships – precisely because power can only exist in relationship to something – are also necessarily based on human perception. The 'post-truth world', as it is now characterized, is one in which perceptions can be shaped more than political analysts in the past would ever have believed possible. Governments and private institutions have always tried to shape the perceptual environment in their own favour; that is what public relations, political communication, strat comms, propaganda are all about. The difference now is in the extent and the personal depth with which this can be achieved – making a general point to an audience while simultaneously targeting individuals with versions of it geared to their particular concerns. Or planting material that goes instantly global but without attribution. For government this is strat comms, for private institutions this is effective advertising; but they are both taking advantage of the way the new information order works. Whether they do it truthfully or not is a question of their intentions and prevailing ethics. Mature technologies exist to suggest they can be remarkably effective either way. And all this goes on while the new information order is also teeming with wild conspiracy theorists, sinister disrupters, mischievous amateurs and the frankly bewildered.[6]

The different networks of soft power – the arenas in which soft power competitions take place – are now overlaid with a new information order that has the potential to alter human perceptions in dramatic fashion and thereby change the way soft power works. The new information order is an efficient vehicle for rewriting history; it is a good conduit for swamping unwelcome news with red herrings; an excellent place to nag away at a national or personal reputation until it's ripe for the killer information dump. It can allow malicious actors to work in what seem to be the most non-political and innocuous of ways by disguising campaigns in personalized social trivia.[7] We will return to the new information order in the next chapter. But here, we note it as a potentially vital agent of change in the equations of soft power within all the discernible arenas of competition. Whether the new information order is a force for good or bad depends on how political and private actors use it. It is a structural dimension of twenty-first-century power that no one deliberately invented or purposely brought to fruition. It is just part of the predicament of politics with which we all live.

The audit of soft power

Since soft power resides in society and its plethora of private institutions much more than in government, it is all the harder to assess accurately. To produce a full audit of British soft power and populate the net assessment approach we outlined in Chapter 1 would require a great deal more information about other societies, as well as more information than normally exists in the public domain about our own. We make no attempt to offer a proper net assessment here. But we do believe that it can be done; and that we have offered in this book some different behavioural categories for soft power assessment which can capture a greater range of the relevant interactions than categorization based mainly on government's actions and some key institutions. We do this because our understanding of the essentially dynamic concept of 'power' suggests that further analyses of 'soft power' should be similarly dynamic.

To that end, we offer below a summary of our essential judgements on the nine dynamic areas we identified in Part Two, with some indication of the strengths and weaknesses we discerned.

On the 'convening' activities we described in Chapter 4, it is evident that British institutions, governmental and private, remain well placed to offer something useful to world politics. The constitutional institutions, like the Monarchy and the Commonwealth, and governmental institutions, like those that flow from the FCDO and other parts of the official machinery, are all good convenors and likely to remain so. The churches, the City of London and the big metropolitan cities, the trade associations and the functional organizations that contribute to making the day-to-day, highly dynamic, global economy work as it does are generally well respected, vigorous and tend to be proactive. Successful convening is not merely about having lines of communication. If it were, then everyone in today's world would be a convenor. Successful convening means having a genuine stake in the game that other players recognize, even if the stake is only heavily reputational, and having the necessary skills and psychological mindset to do it properly when opportunity arises. Successful convenors are also patient and resilient in the face of setbacks. Not many governments, institutions or groups of individuals possess all these qualities.

For its size, Britain is well endowed with effective convenors. Institutional respect and competence are key components. Britain's central institutions of government and administration have long enjoyed a favourable international reputation.[8] In 2020 its economic institutions, too, were rated by the World Economic Forum as among the top of its scale in being trusted for competence and integrity, though it should be noted that this judgement was only averagely supported by others in their surveys.[9] Successful convening also depends on credibility and confidence. The sort of figure that Britain cuts in the world affects the credibility of all its institutions in the eyes of others. It may also have an impact on the confidence of Britain's natural convenors as they choose, or not, to engage. That will be a matter for the future and the success of the country in fulfilling the roles it set out for itself in the 2021 Integrated Review. The essential strength and depth of the institutional base, however, is clearly there.

British diplomacy, as conceived in Chapter 5, is something broader than the profession of the diplomat, though the FCDO and its Diplomatic Service is still an important core to the way Britain conducts its national diplomacy. Britain's enviable and long-standing reputation for conducting quiet but effective diplomacy has lived through a bad couple of decades. The end of the Cold War gave Britain and the Western world ten years of easy superiority in world affairs. But the turn of the millennium also marked the turning of some bigger geopolitical wheels that made life for all the European states more uncomfortable. For Britain, the global economic crisis of 2008 then ushered in a decade of austerity and introspection, characterized by assertive debates over the future of the United Kingdom itself, increasing political polarization within domestic politics, and finally the bitterness of the Brexit decision and the diplomatic hiatus and political crises that accompanied it.

Soft power is generally exercised over the long term. According to the theories of soft power, a bad couple of decades that left British diplomats trying to explain away repeated setbacks should not undermine the essential reputation that British diplomacy had established over many decades before that. All the benefits of quiet and effective diplomacy should be recoverable. The government reorganized its external relations machinery following the dysfunctional model it adopted during the Brexit hiatus, allowing more cash to go into external representation, and it made clear in the Integrated Review that it intended to be proactive again in world affairs, notwithstanding the economic setbacks of the Covid-19 crisis.

And yet, and yet? Since 2016 Britain has been slipping down the rankings recorded by the Lowy Institute (Appendix 2) for its diplomatic coverage around the world, assessed globally, within the OECD and also within the G20. In 2019 Britain was still just about in the top ten of well-represented nations, operating 208 foreign posts in total. That took no account of how thinly staffed many of them still are. There is a lot of ground to make up if Britain's reputation for 'punching above its weight' or being 'quietly effective' in its diplomacy is to be re-established. We also make the point that a persistent departure by government policy from deeper societal values must eventually have an impact on the exercise of real soft power and certainly inhibits using it 'smartly'. If British society is, by nature, globally orientated – and our study certainly suggests it is – the discontinuity of the last twenty years between 'Britain' and its 'foreign policy' may have done some damage to its soft power diplomatic reputation that might be difficult to make good. Years of introspection are not ideal for a society that is naturally global in its outlook.[10]

Britain makes a strong showing among the world's researchers and innovators. It always has, and our study in Chapter 6 identifies a more settled governmental attitude towards backing key research areas and a well-organized regime for helping Britain's world-class university research fit more easily into industry's development ambitions. Relative levels of government (and industrial) funding for research have been historically low for some years in comparison with OECD averages and will not catch up quickly in light of the long-term needs of Covid-19 economic recovery strategies. But government has targeted its funding in certain areas and is prepared to take the risks inherent in a 'backing winners' strategy to help key technologies develop quickly. Britain's Advanced Research and Invention Agency (ARIA), modelled on Washington's Defense Advanced Research Project Agency – DARPA – is designed to lead this strategy from 2022.[11] Thanks to the universities, the commercial sector and in part, government support, Britain has strong research and innovation momentum in some of the areas that represent the world's 'sunrise' technologies – biomedical and medical sciences, computing and quantum industries, aerospace, artificial intelligence and robotics. It also has a vibrant SME sector which is particularly flexible in taking pure research and applying it for the commercial world.

Translating these virtues into the soft power arena, it is significant that the research publication metrics are almost all favourable to Britain's researchers and innovators. Across the board, British research ranks comfortably alongside that of the United States and China in its influence and utility to the rest of the world. And in key innovation sectors like biomed, aerospace, defence technology or computing, it is apparent that British actors have real international influence as shapers of the global structures which support those industries. In the detailed metrics of the WEF in its thirty-seven-country comparison, Britain scores comfortably above the average in terms of its efforts to upgrade its information and technology infrastructure, to invest in long-term projects and education for new jobs, in its flexible taxation policy for growth.[12] This shows evidence of a drive to make Britain's research and innovation hot spots sustainable. There is much here that others might imitate.

Less worthy of imitation, however, is that these hot spots still don't transform the British economy in the way governments like to claim. As a whole, the economy does not rate anything more than average for its ability to embrace widespread technological transformation.[13] There is still a problematical skills gap in the economy – a glaring one in the matter of digital skills outside the hot spots – and the ever-present ball and chain of low productivity.[14] The fact is that the strength of research and innovation in Britain is not, in itself, the engine of growth for the British economy, as tended to be the case in times past. The hot spots speak for themselves, however, and as long as the British economy remains the sixth or seventh biggest in the world, its research and innovation will still be softly powerful.

One of the less obvious fields of British soft power, as we outline in Chapter 7, is in setting international standards and regulations that the rest of the world is prepared to observe. For historical reasons, Britain set lots of the technical and functional standards that applied to the rest of the world economy in the nineteenth and early twentieth centuries. Much of that earlier influence has persisted. It remains in the scope of the work the British Standards Institute does and its influence with the International Organization for Standardization. Because standards and regulations are primarily functional arrangements, best arrived at between fellow professionals, the international influence that British standards-setters have exerted has primarily flowed from the respect in which their institutions are held around the world. Acknowledged achievement in some fields gives any nation a community of experienced professionals and the moral right to suggest international standards that would be good for the whole business.

Britain still has a favourable measure of this sort of structural soft power. It exudes it in its financial industries. Its banking system is judged among the six most stable in the world.[15] The sheer size of the British financial sector means that its own regulatory framework cannot be ignored. Achievements in safety standards and architecture, in publishing or in the medical field, give Britain some demonstrable influence in the way those sectors regulate themselves and how they recognize good practice. British (and American) trails of logic, in fact, lie behind many of the world's regulatory frameworks.

A challenge to this favourable position has arisen in the increasing politicization of the functional organizations that oversee various international standards. This is hardly surprising. Britain and the United States had natural influence over so many standards because they were politically and economically dominant when they were being set. They enjoyed structural power which then allowed for many specific arrangements to be regarded as purely 'functional', precisely because their power was largely uncontested. But now their economic and social power is hotly contested, which includes the right to interpret standards differently. Britain may find its considerable soft power assets in the matter of regulations and standards being squeezed by the hard power politics that intrude into it.

In Chapter 8 we look at how the country's multiculturalism and its diaspora communities create many diverse persuaders for British society. Since it concerns real lived experience, this is one of the most potent, if largely intangible, arenas in which soft power is played out. Significant multiculturalism creates human transmission mechanisms and powerful images abroad of what any society is, for good and bad. More than ever in history, diasporas are able to maintain their heritage links, thanks to the communications revolution; people in diasporas talk to each other all the time. Diasporas become some of the most acute judges in assessing to the rest of the world the degree to which a society is *experienced* as prosperous, stable, law-abiding or providing opportunity. They reflect a certain undeniable reality to the world outside, whatever manufactured images might suggest to the contrary.

In Britain's case, its multicultural and multifaith make-up is not a matter of choice. As we describe, it is an intrinsic part of Britain's history, though it became a more sensitive political issue as demographic change speeded up after the 1970s. Multicultural Britain has had its successes in the last half century and the general attractions of British society have remained robustly high in the eyes of the world. But social mobility has been persistently poor in Britain during that time, which has stoked up more tension over the way Britain's multicultural nature should be expressed. And multiculturalism gets pulled into deeper economic and social arguments, including the Brexit decision, that have raised troubling structural issues for the country as a whole. Britain is struggling to affirm a national identity with which it is still comfortable. In this, the fate of the Union of the UK is at stake. Soft power, however, flows more strongly from a society than its politics, and multicultural, multifaith and cosmopolitan Britain in its different communities, and even its tourism, will continue to present powerful warts-and-all pictures – living pictures – of this society as it evolves.

Britain's educators remain persuasive in ways that go beyond the formal institutions, as we examine in Chapter 9. Education across the world is one of the very obvious arenas in which soft power operates and Britain has traditionally been good at it. In its attraction to foreign students and its higher education and research reputation, Britain still ranks within the top handful of countries, whatever metrics are applied. The organizations that produce overall soft power rankings always include 'education' among their calculations and with 515 'think tanks' now recognized in Britain, it remains within the top four countries in having such an extensive range of research institutions capping its formal education establishments (see Appendix 2).

Our interest in educational soft power persuaders in this study extends to what we also describe as the 'incidental' and the 'advocative'. Many organizations and key individuals have an important educative role with international appeal as part of the other work they do. They range from those in the entertainment or heritage industries to some of the most committed advocacy groups who have a point to make to the world at large. What gives such diverse groups of educational persuaders the soft power they wield – and the demonstrable influence of many of them in the wider world – is the perception that they are trying to behave truthfully and are committed to evidence-based arguments. Others may not agree with the incidental or the advocacy educators, but they do not normally regard them as dishonest. Britain's reputation for educational integrity and respect for truth still carries a lot of influence in the world. For the future, it will need to carry that influence into new realms of online and outsourced education as both the demand and the technologies of global education change.

In Chapter 10 we try to address 'creativity' as if it were a distinct human activity – a form of behaviour. Of course, it isn't; and it resides entirely in the eye of the beholder. But the world's beholders have paid a lot of attention to the creative things they see in British society. And in the soft power arenas inhabited by what we call the 'persuasive creators' and the 'story creators' it is clear that they demonstrate some shaping power – structural influence – in the different worlds they inhabit. The awareness of national creativity seems to wax and wane with the public mood, and that has been poor over most of the last decade. But the creatives are on an upswing, underpinned by the malleability of the British economy – for all its problems – and the flexibility of its workforce.

There are some remarkable crossovers. Operating from many small offices in provincial cities, British computer game designers are recognized as some of the best in the world. But in designing computer games, they have also spearheaded a change in the way Western military forces think they will fight future battles. Computer gamers can model a 'single synthetic environment'. An SSE can be created of more or less anything, including a physical model of a whole city or, in principle, of a complete society – economy, power supplies, utilities, homes, trains, traffic lights, petrol stations, food suppliers, rush-hour commuters, weather – everything. Single synthetic environments show in great detail how any element in the picture affects all others. Using breakthrough modelling techniques, artificial intelligence and data analytics, they have become computer games for real. And they can be modelled in a detail that would have been deemed impossible only a decade ago. No wonder Western military chiefs are both excited and appalled as this computer gaming niche moves into military planning centres.[16]

Creativity is infectious and it invites international imitation. The creative minds behind innovation frequently fail to reap the biggest benefits of it, and this is one of the stories of Britain's modern economic history. But at least in the arenas of soft power, the recognition of creativity is more important than the monetary rewards for it. British creativity ultimately arises from a societal commitment to intellectual freedom and openness, to an atmosphere that encourages experimentation and does not punish failure too harshly. In Britain's case it also benefits greatly from its ability to attract foreign talent into niche sectors, creating both tight hubs and loose networks where ideas bump up against each other.

The 'creatives' naturally overlap with the 'entertainers' that we outline in Chapter 11. Between them, creatives and entertainers employ around 3.2 million people in Britain, which makes us – at least statistically – a nation of myriad entertainers more than we are anything else. In our analysis we divide our entertainment sectors into the 'silver screens' and the 'bear pits', in which we also include sport. Entertainment and sport are two of the most impactful windows on any society, whether or not they are an accurate reflection of it. In the soft power equation Britain might well regard itself as a nation of entertainers; it is globally strong in many areas. Its strength lies not only in international recognition for British achievement in film and television, theatre, music, literature and across a surprising range of international sports. Just as significantly, Britain is a player – sometimes a very significant one – in the various industries and business structures that underpin the multiple worlds of entertainment and sports. It has enjoyed high levels of structural power in these realms.

But since entertainments and sports are big business, structural power follows the money, and that no longer flows so exclusively within the Western world. As with so many other arenas of soft power, where Britain has been successful, it has demonstrated its adaptability and willingness to move with the times. Its strong showing across the board in the entertainment fields might be interpreted as a final, glorious hurrah before the 'dismal science' of economics overtakes it. Or it may be seen as the next challenge to continue showcasing to the world the fundamentally entertaining nature of British society.

It will, in any case, draw from the ephemeral worlds that we characterize in Chapter 12 as the 'stars and bloggers' who move in and out of the realms of the socially anarchic. To assume that Britain's natural persuaders in these areas are offering another window on British society might also imply that it is a window of distorted or impure glass, a strange and untypical perspective on mainstream Britain. That is obviously true, but the window is accurate in a different sense in that it illuminates an interesting dimension on creativity in Britain. The lines between creatives, entertainers, stars, bloggers and the frankly anarchic are extremely blurred. And that is a sign of societal health for them all. It is easy to embrace the anarchic in such an environment – one that has always expressed social individualism and celebrated eccentricity. And British 'anarchy' has never been far from the creative surface but has also never been effectively politicized. What normally drives the anarchic instinct is the need to rebel and find symbols for it and there are many examples of that in popular British culture.

Our point is that a number of different forces can be seen at work in the way this ephemeral area develops. Britain presents itself to the world as a place where social non-conformity is not just tolerated but generally expected. It comes and goes with the national mood, and it normally creates outrage in some quarters and eventual acceptance everywhere. While the political atmosphere in Britain has become more tense in recent years, partly with the impact of 'culture wars' in national daily life, there is no sign of oppressive conformity dampening the areas we outline here. The British establishment, on the whole, shows itself to be relaxed when it is attacked from these quarters and has been adept at choosing the right moment to co-opt key figures of social rebellion with enough formal honours to convert them into national treasures. Then, too, with social media capabilities, the ability of the altruistic and the brave is just as great as the influencer entrepreneur to use their technical inventiveness and their anger to drive new ideas forward. The image these persuaders create in the world will vary according to what they do, but the more lasting impression they leave is of a society where they can function. In that respect, the world of the British individualist and social anarchist is manifestly in good shape.

In sum, therefore, and along with those who have ranked soft power attributes among different countries of the world, we judge Britain's position still to be generally favourable and, as Appendix 2 shows, Britain remains among the top handful of those who are well endowed with soft power assets. Our analysis in this study, however, has been less interested in the assets as much as the soft power relationships in which they engage. There are clearly bigger issues to be addressed if Britain is to get the best out of its soft power status. We turn to these in our final chapter.

Conditions for soft power success

There is a consistent theme running through all assessments of British soft power, whether they are made by the government or by independent analysts, in Britain or abroad. It is that Britain always was, and still is, a major force in the world of soft power. For many, Britain 'remains an undisputed "soft power superpower"', in that it ranks alongside the United States and China on many soft power scales and is never out of the top handful of states that dominate the cumulative assessment of soft power assets in a range of different metrics.[1]

Appendix 2 collates assessments from some of the main organizations that have been tracking and comparing soft power status over recent years. It tells a story of British soft power moving down the different international rankings but certainly not tumbling out of the leading group. Even a big *China Today* survey which, implausibly, rates the top three influencers in the world as United States, China and Russia nevertheless lists Britain as fourth.[2] The trend that Britain has recently ratcheted downwards in all rankings is generally regarded as cause for prudent concern, though alongside a sense of perspective over where Britain stands in relation to the rest on these lists. In particular, the *Monocle* analysis suggests a steeper decline in reputation. Nevertheless, global opinion surveys, particularly among the young, suggest grounds for measured confidence. In October 2020 a British Council survey indicated that Britain is 'generally viewed positively' by young people around the world, who see it as 'an influential international actor, especially in terms of diplomacy and foreign aid'. Most, it said, viewed China as their own country's 'best and closest international partner' followed by the United States and then Britain as the third-ranked partner of choice.[3] The Brexit process had not obviously damaged Britain's standing in the eyes of global public opinion, in either 2016 or 2020.[4] Brexit had a 'mixed impact on perception of the UK' among younger people, it said: 'by far the strongest response was a neutral one', and Britain's response to the Covid-19 crisis, overall, 'is viewed more positively than negatively'. Young people in particular, it appears from yet more surveys, are more interested in Britain's societal, cultural and popular attributes when making their judgements than its governmental institutions or its foreign policy.[5]

The bottom-line judgement for virtually everyone who has looked at British soft power is that the country is in an enviable position compared to most of its natural competitors in Europe and the wider world, and that on many dimensions it jostles with the biggest countries – the United States, China, India – since it has both history and popular culture working in its favour and a traditional reputation for being outward-facing.

But that judgement is always accompanied by the caveat that other prominent soft power players are catching up with the leaders and that the very nature of soft power competition has broadened in the era of globalization. What is at stake is more than merely national pride in sitting near the top of the rankings. The nature of soft power – like all power – being a relationship means that it is also naturally a competition. A country's ability to be persuasive, or to have a good image abroad, can affect thousands of marginal decisions in the world that tip matters its way rather than in another country's favour. Whether or not the rankings themselves are technically correct, the principles behind them are important; the ability of one country to enjoy the influence of soft power as opposed to another is an inescapable fact of politics.

For some, this chasing pack of competitors means that Britain should obviously guard against complacency as it considers its soft power status. They point, for example, to the fact that Britain's cultural institutes enjoy significantly greater total income than in many competitor countries, but that the British government contributes about 15 per cent to that total, whereas France puts 48 per cent into its comparable institutes; Germany and Japan well over 60 per cent. Or they point out that France maintains over 1,000 offices abroad to promote cultural activities, China over 600, the United States nearly 400 – and Britain, a defiant 214.[6] This looks like a symptom either of a quietly assured culture or of complacency. For others, the challenge is more urgent and Britain's current prominence as a soft power player is frankly 'precarious'. By this is meant that 'it would only take a few minor shifts in perceptions for the UK to fall' and that 'the UK may be first among equals for now, but that is no guarantee it will remain so in the days and years ahead'.[7] The response, at least from all those who examine soft power from a British perspective, is that the government 'should do more' to support its natural advantages. It should recognize more readily how cost-effective soft power is in creating political influence; it should be more willing to integrate soft power awareness into its working assumption; and it should certainly find more government money to support soft power activities and institutions.[8]

We would not demur from such persistent calls that government should do more of everything in bolstering British soft power. The underlying logic is true enough. Our analysis here, however, also suggests a somewhat different perspective on the issue. We have tried to situate our work in a more careful understanding of power relationships between countries. And that perspective suggests to us that the prospects for British soft power are both better *and* worse – that is, more 'precarious' – than the arguments outlined earlier really imply. It is not a matter of more money or more government interest, welcome though they both would be. As our analysis has tried to show, British soft power has been effective because it has some really deep roots. Our view is that some of the current challenges Britain is facing could shake them severely if not handled well. It is not a matter of government cash for soft power over the coming decade, so much as government policy for getting the country out of the multiple crises of the previous decade. The stakes are bigger than any cash involved.

We can be reassured about the strong roots of British soft power because of the natural strengths of British society. As our analysis in Part Two indicated, Britain's historical legacies in every area we examined contributed to an outward-facing society with global interests: commercially, in the cosmopolitanism that infuses its educational or media presence, in its own multiculturalism and in its many contributions to global science and arts. In the contemporary context, it is undeniable that the multiple political and economic crises of the last decade certainly stressed British society, but they did not push it to a breaking point. Underlying social tensions in Britain and the lopsided nature of its highly globalized economy have been well understood and consistently exposed for a long time.[9] There has been much discussion, too, about the consequent decline of public faith in the institutions of British society, characterized as 'the age of distrust'.[10] The 2020 edition of the Edelman Trust Barometer, polling annually in twenty-eight of the thirty-six OECD states, recorded British satisfaction levels with its public institutions as next to the bottom of the scale – twenty-seventh – just one place above the trust that Russians put in their own government and system.[11] It was a troubling revelation. Similarly, the Cambridge Centre for the Future of Democracy recorded that, whereas those expressing clear 'dissatisfaction' with British democracy had stayed below 50 per cent since the 1980s, it had shot up to almost 60 per cent in 2019.[12]

But the institutional structure did not buckle, even if many institutions struggled to command the sort of loyalty they had previously taken for granted. It was all very uncomfortable for the British public, who went through years of austerity, a Scottish independence debate, a more polarizing Brexit argument –

accompanied by a political nervous breakdown and a constitutional crisis – even before the Covid-19 pandemic swamped extant polito-economic troubles. If this was an unhappy decade, it nevertheless demonstrated an underlying resilience in British society. As we observed in Chapter 8, there were demonstrations but no riots; blood-curdling prophecies but (almost) no violence; public health fiascos but stoical faith in a vaccine programme.[13] Very little in British society seemed to improve during this troubled decade, but it didn't fracture either. And even while the Edelman Barometer recorded poor levels of public faith in Britain's governmental, media, business and even NGO institutions, it still noted in 2020 that most Britons 'think the country is on the right track'! Some 80 per cent even agreed on the main priorities for reform.[14] 'Situation desperate, everything normal', one might say.

If the real sources of soft power lie deep within a community, then the last decade has demonstrated, if not the robust health of British society in current circumstances, then at least its enduring resilience. It is perhaps for this reason that external views of Britain's standing in the world – not of its politics or global role – have remained largely unchanged. Elite opinion within the political classes in other countries has certainly responded to Britain's Brexit decision and all that followed. But popular opinion among publics around the world – save for in Western Europe – appears to have been remarkably unmoved in their long-standing views of Britain by its recent political traumas.[15] For these reasons the maintenance of British soft power – the attitude of the rest of the world towards Britain as a society – is still based on some surprisingly solid prospects.

The converse, however, is that the world's view of British society might be greatly changed by the way the country responds to some of the more immediate societal challenges it is facing. And if it loses traction in those spheres, there may be no way back for Britain's international reputation.

Maintaining soft power in a hard world

This is not the place to try to dissect the most pressing and serious challenges to British society, but their outlines are clear enough. The way these play out in the years to come, and the societal and government response to them, will have a major bearing on whether Britain will stay in the top rank of soft power countries or else slip rapidly down the scale and deprive itself of important sources of influence and opportunities to make the most of 'smart power' politics.

While Britain grapples with these challenges, the hard world abroad will move on apace. The great powers will likely shift into higher gears in the competition between themselves. They all intend to put more into their own soft power assets and play more vigorously in these arenas. The reinvigorated 'Quad' security arrangements between the United States, Japan, India and Australia, for example, are driven by their reactions to China's rising political power, but it is currently being expressed mainly in a bid to manipulate their collective soft power across the whole Asia-Pacific region.[16]

Others will follow as the number of serious global players in the soft power arenas of the world inevitably increases. And as relentless hard power realities seem destined to make life more uncomfortable for all European countries over the coming decade, the effects of being less consequential players on the global stage – if that is what happens – will inevitably diminish Britain's soft power status. As we established in Chapter 3, perceptions of soft and hard power do not exist in isolation to one another. An important foundation of any nation's soft power potential is the respect that others pay to its demonstrable hard power relationships.

In light of this – increasingly – hard world, what are the societal challenges that most matter to Britain, and therefore to the roots of its soft power, in the coming years?

The most immediate challenge is that Britain has got to be seen to make a success, or at least to cope competently, with the economic and political realities of Brexit. If the abstract and heated Brexit debates have had small effect on the country's soft power potential so far, the realities of such a strategic shift in Britain's role in the world will surely matter as their influence is felt on the sort of Britain that really emerges from the process. Whatever direction the economy and the political landscape takes in Britain over the coming years, the government needs to be seen to act with competence and vision, and British society to respond to the new challenges with a sense of confidence and optimism. The uncertainties that dogged the whole Brexit process from 2015 onwards will continue to raise constant questions in the minds of foreign observers as much as the British population itself.

The answers to such questions will become part of a more fundamental challenge over the national identity the country assumes into the coming decades – something that is, in any case, always evolving. We pointed out in Chapter 8 that social tensions around Britain's inherent multiculturalism, along with the emergence, in effect, of 'five kingdoms' – Scotland, Northern Ireland, Wales, London and 'England outside London' – had raised more troubling questions about how Britons express their national identity.[17] It really matters whether, and how, Britons in the future feel confidence in their existing national identity, or want to express it differently, or even fracture it into something else.

There is a paradox that in a society as regionally diverse as Britain, so much of the thinking, the policy and the funding around soft power should reside in a highly centralized governmental system based on London. In 2019 the incoming government led by Boris Johnson promised, again, that it would give high priority to 'levelling up' all the kingdoms and regions of Britain. In different words, the government was repeating a mantra of every government since the 1980s. In truth all policy in this area is pushing against the forces of globalization that naturally brings new investment and jobs to the areas where they already exist, and where the infrastructure already serves them. 'Levelling up' is a long and uphill task that will span a number of governments if it succeeds.

In the soft power realm, however, it seems strange that the country's natural assets are not recognized, or deployed, with more awareness of the country's regional diversity and consequent strengths. The Welsh government was unique in producing a five-year action plan for the promotion of its soft power on an international scale, partly after absorbing the conclusions of a Soft Power Barometer report in 2018.[18] In 2021, in frustration at London's reluctance to share its Integrated Review, the Scottish government proclaimed its own 'Good Global Citizen' statement that stressed some of Scotland's soft power attributes.[19] Nevertheless, Edinburgh and Belfast still relied on some further good work by Jonathan McClory for the British Council to reflect on the soft power status of Britain's 'small nations' in comparison with other small regions or nations. In a detailed comparison of many metrics across ten particular cases from Catalonia to Hokkaido, Puerto Rico or Corsica, McClory found that Quebec emerged with the strongest soft power identity in the eyes of others, Scotland was second, Wales sixth and Northern Ireland eighth in the list. It showed a patchy performance overall. Scotland's greatest asset was found to be its reputation for education; in Wales, education was its weakest element, sport one of its strongest. Northern Ireland was mid-table for 'entrepreneurship' but strongest on 'governmental' reputation (during years when the governing executive was suspended). Scotland's overall soft power scoring in this comparison, at 62 per cent (of a theoretically perfect score) was comparable with Quebec's top score of 66 per cent but well ahead of Wales at 49 per cent and Northern Ireland at 35 per cent.[20]

Meanwhile, cities in all the major countries have assumed greater global importance as image-creators in their own right.[21] As a result, there has been some tentative strategizing for an individual soft power presence in documents such as Manchester's 2020 International Strategy or in Birmingham's 'European and International Strategy'.[22] Newcastle upon Tyne made much of the fact that it was listed for the first time (at number 23 among 109) in the world's *Smart City Index* for 2020, putting it in company with high-tech cities like Bilbao, Hamburg, Los Angeles or San Francisco. London was ranked fifteenth and Manchester seventeenth in 'Smart City' terms.[23]

These are all bright spots of regional interest in a national picture that makes rather little of the rich and historic diversity within British society. As Stephen Gethins says in his analysis of Scotland's own global persona, British foreign policy has been poor at reflecting the realities of decentralization – unlike, say, Germany or Canada and has underplayed the soft power strengths this can create.[24]

This gets to the nub of a soft power problem in the hard world that Britain currently inhabits. National diversity across Britain's 'five kingdoms' and its great cities and sub-regions within them is not just an attractive patchwork that tourist authorities can promote or a certain quaintness that may appeal to foreign observers. *Successful* regional diversity is both a symptom and a driver of liberalism, tolerance, shared prosperity, rule of law and national cohesion. It can act as a *centripetal* force on society, binding the elements together as they move along their common trajectory. In contrast, if social and regional diversity acts as a *centrifugal* force, they weaken society as it confronts the future, moving further away from shared visions and core objectives.

As they emerged from the Covid-19 pandemic, leaders in both Scotland and Northern Ireland, for different reasons, challenged the national government in London; in Scotland over the demand for a second independence referendum; and in Northern Ireland in the claim that London had betrayed the province's future in the Brexit deal. These were both significant constitutional bones of contention. But they reflected a more underlying centrifugal tendency – a suspicion that Conservative governments since 2010 had effectively given up on the Union of the UK as a fundamental part of their traditional Conservative philosophy.[25] In 2021 the government announced that it would make preservation of 'the Union' a central part of its post-Covid-19 'build back better' campaign. The fact that the idea had to be so loudly trumpeted was revealing in itself, and for many critics of the government, an administration led by Boris Johnson would always struggle to escape from the English nationalist populism that had brought it to power in 2019.[26]

The future of the Union of the United Kingdom clearly bears massively on Britain's sense of itself, as well as its image abroad, as a naturally outward-facing, cosmopolitan society. Of course, proponents of breaking up the Union fiercely deny that doing so would diminish this or create a group of smaller, introspective nations in the British Isles. Supporters of Scottish independence point to their nation's long-standing cosmopolitanism – very evident in Edinburgh, Glasgow or Aberdeen – and their historic internationalism as the engineers and teachers of the British Empire. An independent Scotland, they argue, would be liberated to be even more cosmopolitan and outward-facing, and England would be challenged and stimulated to be more so. Similar arguments are heard among Nationalists across the island of Ireland, and Welsh social elites and leaders have been out and about for many years. This might turn out eventually to be true, but it would be a rocky ride in the meantime. Strong national identity and attractive cosmopolitanism require confidence: a society that enjoys its diversity and is not paranoid about it, that invests in itself and persuades others to invest, and which looks to its shared future with genuine optimism.

Some sort of constitutional reordering of Britain seems to be in the offing. Perhaps saving the Union by formally federalizing it and giving the English regions significantly more power, akin to their nineteenth-century status; perhaps 'levelling up' more dramatically to diminish the predominance of London and the South East over development and devolve greater accountability to the regions, to engender a renewed sense of British national identity.[27] There is already a quiet but growing debate on the feasibility of 'federating the UK to save it' which is at least a sign of greater engagement with the problem.[28] Nevertheless, to 'design' a United Kingdom, since that has never been done in the past, would be a challenge of historic proportions at the best of times, and in the economic circumstances of a post-Covid-19 global recovery may become an endless backdrop to a lot of other political and economic headaches. If the constitutional future of the UK is to be under the microscope during the 2020s, the image abroad of Britain as an essentially successful society will be affected in some important ways. The next few years could be dramatic for a number of reasons.

First, the idea that Britain's historically unique and politically successful Union has simply failed – for whatever reasons – would be debilitating to the reputation of Britain abroad. It would take some time for Britain itself, without Scotland or Northern Ireland, or both, to adjust psychologically to a new national status or convincingly plan a brighter future for Britain on the political ashes of the UK. National setbacks of this order are difficult for any nation to overcome. With the exception of the reasonably easy 'velvet divorce' between Slovakia and the Czech Republic in 1993 (and Czechoslovakia had only existed since 1918) modern examples of secessionism range from the deeply troubled (like Cyprus,

Kosovo, Sudan or Pakistan and Bangladesh) to the frankly disastrous (like almost everywhere in former Yugoslavia[29] or Ukraine and Crimea). There can be no escaping the fact that secessionism represents an immediate success for the secessionists but a massive failure for the status quo country and its leadership.

Even struggles over secessionism that do not then take place are noted for the lasting political bitterness they engender. Canada's Quebec Question of the 1960s was effectively ended with two pro-unity referenda results in 1980 and 1995. But the bitterness lingers still. Catalan separatism in Spain has proved politically debilitating and caused recurring constitutional crises. Great bitterness has long been engendered between Greece and its newly named 2019 neighbour, North Macedonia, which abuts directly onto the Macedonia province of northern Greece and threatens to excite corresponding separatism among those who assume kith and kin with Alexander the Great. There are no modern examples of serious secessionist arguments that ended happily and without a great deal of political falout.

Second, to embark on serious discussions about a secession has the effect of turning a society inwards. It represents painful soul-searching about its fundamental identity and what political values it should serve. Even where one might be sympathetic to secessionist pleas, the fact that they are being aired at all makes it impossible for a society to project confidence to the outside world – comfortable within itself. A government may try a degree of bravado, of course, and secessionists are characteristically confident about their own abilities to govern successfully. But no one outside is really fooled. Whether it is a good or bad idea in the centennial scheme of things, secessionism is a massive psychological blow to any society and a big leap in the dark for the secessionists. Honest politicians on both sides know it will hurt a lot and that any tangible benefits are likely to be a long time coming.

Third, and this is undoubtedly the most important point for Britain in the coming decade, the *way* in which such arguments are conducted, the *institutional structures* that are used, or adapted, the *atmosphere* in which they take place and the national *leadership* qualities of all those involved are key determinants of how the rest of the world will see the process unfolding. They will be fundamental to Britain's international persona as it goes through this debate, which in one way or another it now assuredly will.

It is possible to be optimistic and argue that the genius of Britain's muddle-through political culture might be able to defy the historical record and demonstrate that all its political and social institutions can cope with the pressure to dissolve the Union – even make a success of it, if that is the outcome. And that the arguments can be conducted in a manner which diffuses the underlying discontent that has created the problem. Optimists even point out that the manifest crises caused first by Brexit and then by the Covid-19 pandemic actually provide good opportunities for some major political change, on the 'never waste a good crisis' principle. As we observe, Britain's political institutions have ridden out the recent storms. The 2019 General Election campaign was bizarre in many ways but the outcome reverted to giving one major party a hefty majority. Perhaps Britain can get through the argument not to dissolve the Union, or else to reform it, with its customary and time-worn flexibility. And if the Union is doomed within the foreseeable future, then perhaps even that can be handled in a highly civilized, perhaps typically – even comically – British way that sets new standards for secessionism. The reality of whatever happens will undoubtedly be complex and will take time to work itself out.

But in soft power image terms, complex and important arguments about the fate of the Union will turn on more dramatic and simple assumptions for those observing from abroad. Few have much interest in probing beneath the headlines. The image of Britain in the outside world will tend to be binary: either it is successful in handling its new constitutional challenges and remains an open, outward-facing country; or it is failing and breaking up and hence 'not the Britain we knew'.

And while noisy arguments about the future of the Union will doubtless characterize British politics for some years to come, there is also a more subtle challenge for those aspects of British society that underpin much of its influence across different sectors in the soft power arenas where it engages. Whether considering diplomacy, the research world, the commercial or educational sectors or the creative and entertainment industries, the underlying story is the same; British influence to shape its environment and the respect in which it is held derives overwhelmingly from a reputation for professionalism, honesty and inventiveness. However many knocks Britain's reputation has taken in recent history, and however much the country now agonizes about the nature of its past, the erstwhile image of Britain in the rest of the world is still that of a country of practical people who get things done, who are essentially honest in their dealings and who display an inventiveness in the way they confront problems. In our examination of the various different fields of British soft power, we were led back to these attributes again and again. They appear to be fundamental to the resilience of British society during the sort of difficult decade we have just experienced, and they are still critical to Britain's international projection of itself.

The challenge, of course, is to maintain and reinforce these societal virtues. They could be labelled as a high level of 'societal integrity' which British people, both in the elites and across the rest of society, have repeatedly shown they care about and want to preserve. In the new information order of the twenty-first century this is not easy. British popular culture is pulled into the world of celebrities, conspiracists and fake news as much as any other and it has no natural immunity to the blandishments of 'post-truth society'. Indeed, there is an argument that it is a mistake to push back against this trend: that trying to ensure that truth and integrity emerge amid the babble of this new information order is not just a forlorn hope but a misplaced one. Some argue that when Western leaders like Presidents Macron and Biden press for the reinforcement of truthful and accurate reporting across the global media they are really only arguing for their own version of an ideology they prefer, because there are no objectively truthful discourses anyway. In the post-modern, post-truth world everything is relative.[30]

We do not agree with this thinking and align ourselves with those British philosophers – both radical and conservative – who defend the continuing relevance of enlightenment views: that truth and honesty in cleaving to it as much as humanly possible are virtues still universally shared by most people, most of the time.[31] Even if we concede the idea that all views are partial and every argument flows from some implicit ideology, the fact remains that Britain's soft power respect in the world was based on a very liberal democratic ideology that made a practical reality of enlightenment values. To work to uphold 'truth' and what we label as 'societal integrity', even if ideologically loaded, is a good investment in those things that originally gave Britain so much of its soft power.

A more practical question is what any British government, or the major economic and social institutions, can do to reinforce – or maybe in some cases restore – the societal integrity of Britain in the eyes of the world. Government attitudes and action are a good starting point. Policies tend to be judged by the rest of the world not just according to whether they succeed but also according to the way in which they are conducted. Amid the Brexit controversy, strong arguments have been put that the decision to leave the EU was a natural reflection of Britain's societal instincts, and that there were strong historical and social grounds for a sense of British exceptionalism in European politics. That view remains controversial. But there is little controversy that the way the Brexit decision was carried through was deeply inconsistent with prevailing societal values. The process was not pragmatic or handled smoothly or with evident competence, it was accompanied by shrill grandstanding on both sides of the negotiations, lots of brinkmanship and theatricality, and ultimately created in managers and leaders from every sector of British society a sense of deep uncertainty over where the process would leave them. It all seemed to be the antithesis of the way Britain normally did things in the world – professionally, practically, gradually and usually quietly. A clear line needs to be drawn under this aberration.

There is no shortage of official statements setting out the British government's acknowledgement of the essential values by which it aims to operate; it publishes them rather a lot as preliminary to all the major policy documents it produces. To make the most of Britain's soft power societal virtues, however, it also has to demonstrate them as a matter of course, on a daily basis, in all it does. That has not happened as naturally and automatically as ministers claim when they have been called to explain recent slippage from the government's stated principles. As we indicated in Chapter 5, there is some ground for British government to make up in restoring its previous image as a reflection of good British values.

Perhaps more importantly, British institutions have got to reinforce their credibility for truthful professionalism in the face of all the cynicism generated by the age of distrust. At present, the plethora of untruths and cynicism appears to be almost overwhelming and getting worse. Liberal democrats who believe in enlightenment values must hold on to the hope, and the belief, that at some point there will be a swing back towards a demand for real truthfulness and honesty in the new information order as individuals search for institutional reassurance in their lives.[32] As and when they do, Britain's most central institutions – governmental, in finance and business, law, in the media and in the civic sectors – need to ensure that they embody that inbred honesty that inspires confidence in others. In a highly globalized country and amid the new information order, that is not easy and suggests many moral and economic trade-offs. Pragmatism – like attracting foreign money into London, for example, may conflict with honesty – like saying where it has come from. Being successful and innovative in a new, Asia-orientated media environment might mean that British entertainment becomes more vanilla or politically timid in its outputs, and so on. But society only has its own national institutions to fall back on in times of uncertainty, and they are also the bedrock of those elements that make soft power relationships work in the ways they do. As Peter Hennessy says, 'A nation is more than simply its institutions, but they are an essential part of it.' And he quotes R. H. Tawney in 1917: 'Only those institutions are loved which touch the imagination.'[33] Britain's institutions might take on that challenge to express British values afresh as they confront the cynicism of a distrustful age.

Whitehall's challenge

We have outlined some of the mega-challenges that British society will face in the next few years and made consequently daunting demands on future British governments. If Britain's 'enviable position' in the world's soft power stakes is to be maintained or enhanced, these challenges will have to be met – or at least very carefully managed – over a long period. Government officials will nod sagely when this sort of thing is said and probably smile benignly, but they will still be asking themselves privately what they can do about it all – what policy levers are there to pull? As we have said, central government does not, and should not, have direct control over most of the institutions that constitute Britain's soft power assets, nor should it try to dragoon them into anything resembling 'coordination meetings'; and it should be careful how it uses the natural influence it will have with some of them. Government's most effective policies reside in helping to shape the domestic and international environments that nurture and assist the country's persuaders as they go about their business.

But there are some available policy levers that can be given serious consideration as we think about the future of British soft power. Many will say that, in light of the economic impact of the Covid-19 crisis, the most important policy lever in Whitehall is money to support the institutions and businesses that have fought for survival during the toughest years. This is almost certainly true and, notwithstanding the recent crisis, is a perennial concern.

Our purpose here, however, is to describe some of the less obvious questions that Whitehall might consider. The Integrated Review of 2021 claimed to be fully alive to the importance of British soft power and even included a separate essay on it, beginning with the assertion that Britain is 'a soft power superpower'.[34] It acknowledged the international prominence of the most obvious soft power assets and also the growing competition they were facing. But as in most other aspects of the 2021 Integrated Review, over a year of (Covid-19 interrupted) deliberation produced a shopping list of strategic aspirations rather than a well-worked strategy as such. It left a great deal to be decided in the future.

Meantime, the sense of strategic cohesion behind the Review was undermined by damaging announcements of swingeing cuts to parts of the foreign aid budget. Whether overall reductions in foreign aid were justified or not, the crude intention to cut expenditure in some of the conflict areas and to global campaigns Britain had particularly identified with hardly squared with the Review's self-image that Britain would be a 'reliable partner', a 'burden-sharer', a 'problem-solver' in the world.[35] The Review also quietly reversed long-standing policy on holding minimal nuclear warhead stocks – a decision that dented Britain's image for the postponed 2020 Non-Proliferation Review Conference – and it was frankly confusing about the mechanisms to implement its own conclusions. The immediate aftermath of the Review did not bode well for any new impetus in British soft power.

On the other hand, the government had already designated a senior ambassador as Head of a Soft Power Department within the FCDO's Communications Directorate, working to make British officials more sensitive to soft power needs (listening) and opportunities (coordinating) and generally playing the diplomatic long game. The department offered a 'tool kit' to try to keep soft power assets in play within Britain's broader diplomatic activities and to find new ways of promoting classic British values.[36] If these efforts seem to pale beside the resources that other countries, particularly China or Russia, or for that matter Germany or Australia, increasingly devote to soft power promotion, it is because Britain puts considerable faith in its general approach to soft power. Autocratic countries, in particular, put great resources into soft power but do not – in fact cannot – adopt the right approach to nurturing it. Britain believes it does have the right approach but doesn't back it up with extensive resources. But at least one part of the government is charged with strategizing soft power relationships on behalf of the others.

Thinking strategically, however, and being more aware of how soft power can be part of the equation in particular cases, is not just a matter for the centre of government. As Joseph Nye puts it, 'contextual intelligence' is an important attribute at all levels. In recent years, however, British government has become uniquely centralized – to an unprecedented peacetime degree. The problem this poses for strategically minded soft power policy is that so much of the natural connection between government and soft power assets naturally takes place at lower levels and in decentralized ways. Convening, entertaining, regulation-setting, informally educating – such activities work best when they operate with more local arms of government that have some discretion over the time and money they could put into supporting soft power presence or initiatives. Central government is the right place to consider policy levers such as tax policy changes, credit schemes, public expenditure shifts or regulation changes. But there are more opportunities to find smaller policy levers lower down in the system, and central government has not got a good reputation for doing such things efficiently or very strategically.

There is a good case for conducting an extensive review of British soft power separately to that of the Integrated Review and an even better one for doing a review regularly. It is in the nature of the societal elements which create soft power relationships that they are more naturally dynamic than government policy or central institutions. A regular review process that was based on a robust, essentially behavioural, methodology – as we have tried broadly to suggest in the structure of Part Two of this book – would help government develop and maintain the 'contextual intelligence' necessary to conceive of power more 'smartly' both up and down the machinery. In addition to keeping government in touch with the dynamic world of soft power relationships and more aware of the new territories and niches where it can be seen operating, a regular review process would also act as a focus to help soft power players be more aware of each other. As the Creative Industries Council put it, just setting up an organization to represent something as dynamic as 'creative industries' put many institutions and leaders into a network that helped them help each other.[37]

Then, too, government can give some priority to liaising between the private sector and some of the soft power institutions, particularly in the heritage, entertainment and cultural industries, not just to help facilitate funding links but also to nurture a greater sense of common commitment between public and private institutions – and key individuals – in facilitating British influence in the wider world. Politicians and ministers often do exactly this, particularly by putting willing funders together with worthy causes that have a soft power value. But these good works are mainly based on personal initiatives which fade or change as ministers and politicians move on. Much could be gained by building greater awareness across British society, public and private, of the conception and the ideas behind soft power, of being clear that it is not just about the BBC or the Commonwealth Games but something even more integral to Britain in the world that springs from across British society as a whole.

A long-term strategy to connect the private and the public sectors of soft power – the diaspora billionaires and the natural convenors or the formal educators and the outright entertainers, for example – might percolate people, money and ideas in an enriching mix that would command more influence in new niches around the world. As always in soft power, governments have to be prepared to play for the long term. The key is not really the amount of public funding that might go into such an approach – it would require very little public money. The issue would be the government's willingness not just to shunt such an initiative off into some corner of the DCMS – or even the more powerful BEIS – but to believe in it, and stick with it, for long enough to create sustained synergy between public and private activities in some of the more dynamic sectors that have a soft power benefit.

Not least, government could show how effectively it understands soft power by using it 'smartly' as a matter of course, not just occasionally when events make it appropriate. The British reaction to the Skripal poisoning in 2018 evolved into a model of 'smart power' policy – linking intelligence, diplomacy and forensic policing to British official credibility, its media and even then to its entertainers. The incident continues to harm Russia's image in the world and boosts that of Britain. The government did not dragoon the British media and comedy entertainment shows into the strategy (unlike the Russian media), but it set up the issue in ways that allowed them to follow their own noses in the matter and it facilitated a momentum where the truth emerged for the world at large, regardless of what Moscow said about it. The Covid-19 vaccine programme, too, evolved to become an exemplar of smart power. It began with excellent international research, conducted in Britain between the public and private sectors, and then applied and eventually extended through the COVAX scheme to other countries in the world.[38] It combined the hard power of Britain's demonstrated ability to produce an early vaccine, with the soft power messages that this could be done properly and honestly without recourse to clumsy propaganda. That was smart. These successes will continue to be occasional, however, as long as governmental understanding of soft power politics rates it only as a useful adjunct to British external policy, as opposed to an important end of a power spectrum that is there to be exploited.

We began our work for this book in the summer of 2019, before Brexit 'got done' and before the Covid-19 pandemic began. The first event created great national soul-searching and the second put effective policy-making for anything other than public health largely on hold for the duration of the pandemic. The years 2020 and 2021 may come to seem like the 'lost years' in modern British history – when so many consequences of policy were still awaited, so many necessary decisions still deferred. But this two-year break in political normality also served to emphasize the character of British society, for both good and bad. At least to us, it highlighted even more the underlying nature and dynamics of British society which is the very essence of soft power magnetism.

British politics in the 2020s may be highly volatile; that seems likely. International affairs in Europe look set to become more conflictual; the trends point that way. But even in the midst of difficult years British society appears resilient and keeps on generating that magnetism of being essentially prosperous and law-abiding, offering freedom and opportunity. It lacks success in many areas – like social mobility or constitutional contentment. But amid its failures, British society endures, it expects to endure, and it creates its own successes.

We also recognize that the values of essential honesty and basic integrity are key elements in creating and preserving those magnetic attractions in society; indeed, they are the bedrock of it. And they are under great pressure in the contemporary world – from globalization and social media, from autocratic adversaries and a decade of less than inspiring leadership across major Western countries. Our politicians and leaders so often let our society down. If they understood soft power better and respected its efficacy more, perhaps they would take greater care to align their political instincts with those deeper societal attributes that make Britain what it is.

Appendix 1

Table 1 Twinned cities

UK City	Twinned With									
London	Beijing	Berlin	Bogotá	Kuala Lumpur	Moscow	New York City	Santiago	Shanghai	Tehran	Tokyo
Birmingham	Chicago	Frankfurt am Main	Guangzhou	Johannesburg	Leipzig	Lyon	Milan			
Manchester	Chemnitz	Saint Petersburg	Wuhan							
Glasgow	Bethlehem	Dalian	Havana	Lahore	Marseille	Nuremberg	Pittsburgh	Rostov-on-Don	Turin	
Swansea	Cork	Ferrara	Mannheim	Pau	Sinop	Wuhan				
Belfast	Boston	Hefei	Nashville	Shenyang						
Leeds	Brno	Dortmund	Durban	Hangzhou	Lille	Siegen				
Nottingham	Beit Shemesh	Gent	Harare	Karlsruhe	Minsk	Ningbo	Timisoara	Września		
Bristol	Beira	Bordeaux	Guangzhou	Hannover	Porto	Puerto Morazán	Tbilisi			
Cambridge	Heidelberg	Szeged								

Source: ONS, Twinned towns and sister cities, Great Britain and Europe: September 2020.

Table 2 WEF Global Competitiveness Index, 2011–19

	2019		2018		2017–18		2016–17
Rank	Economy	Rank	Economy	Rank	Economy	Rank	Economy
1	Singapore	1	USA	1	Switzerland	1	Switzerland
2	USA	2	Singapore	2	USA	2	Singapore
3	Hong Kong SAR	3	Germany	3	Singapore	3	USA
4	Netherlands	4	Switzerland	4	Netherlands	4	Netherlands
5	Switzerland	5	Japan	5	Germany	5	Germany
6	Japan	6	Netherlands	6	Hong Kong SAR	6	Sweden
7	Germany	7	Hong Kong SAR	7	Sweden	7	UK
8	Sweden	8	UK	8	UK	8	Japan
9	UK	9	Sweden	9	Japan	9	Hong Kong SAR
10	Denmark	10	Denmark	10	Finland	10	Finland

	2015–16		2014–15		2013–14		2012–13		2011–12
Rank	Economy	Rank	Economy	Rank	Economy	Rank	Economy	Rank	Economy
1	Switzerland	1	Switzerland	1	Switzerland	1	Switzerland	1	Switzerland
2	Singapore	2	Singapore	2	Singapore	2	Singapore	2	Singapore
3	USA	3	USA	3	Finland	3	Finland	3	Sweden
4	Germany	4	Finland	4	Germany	4	Sweden	4	Finland
5	Netherlands	5	Germany	5	USA	5	Netherlands	5	USA
6	Japan	6	Japan	6	Sweden	6	Germany	6	Germany
7	Hong Kong SAR	7	Hong Kong SAR	7	Hong Kong SAR	7	USA	7	Netherlands
8	Finland	8	Netherlands	8	Netherlands	8	UK	8	Denmark
9	Sweden	9	UK	9	Japan	9	Hong Kong SAR	9	Japan
10	UK	10	Sweden	10	UK	10	Japan	10	UK

Source: See www.wef.org for annual Global Competitiveness Index reports. N.B. equivalent benchmarking data is not available for 2020. The WEF intends to resume the exercise for 2021. See https://www.weforum.org/reports/the-global-competitiveness-report-2020/digest_.

Table 3 Portland Soft Power Survey, 2015–19

2019		2018		2017		2016		2015	
Rank	Country	Rank	Country	Rank	Country	Rank	Country	Rank	Country
1	France	1	UK	1	France	1	USA	1	UK
2	UK	2	France	2	UK	2	UK	2	Germany
3	Germany	3	Germany	3	USA	3	Germany	3	USA
4	Sweden	4	USA	4	Germany	4	Canada	4	France
5	USA	5	Japan	5	Canada	5	France	5	Canada
6	Switzerland	6	Canada	6	Japan	6	Australia	6	Australia
7	Canada	7	Switzerland	7	Switzerland	7	Japan	7	Switzerland
8	Japan	8	Sweden	8	Australia	8	Switzerland	8	Japan
9	Australia	9	Netherlands	9	Sweden	9	Sweden	9	Sweden
10	Netherlands	10	Australia	10	Netherlands	10	Netherlands	10	Netherlands

Source: www.softpower30.com.

Table 4 Brand Finance Nation Brand Rankings, 2015–20

2020				2019			
Rank	Country	Value (USD)	Credit	Rank	Country	Value (USD)	Credit
1	USA	$23,738,342M	AAA-	1	USA	$27,751,172M	AAA
2	China	$18,764,298M	AA	2	China	$19,485,618M	AA
3	Japan	$4,261,272M	AA+	3	Germany	$4,854,854M	AAA
4	Germany	$3,812,942M	AAA	4	Japan	$4,532,854M	AAA
5	**UK**	**$3,314,556M**	**AAA-**	5	**UK**	**$3,850,553M**	**AAA**
6	France	$2,699,463M	AA+	6	France	$3,096,850M	AA+
7	India	$2,027,923M	A+	7	India	$2,561,985M	AA-
8	Canada	$1,900,396M	AAA-	8	Canada	$2,183,209M	AAA
9	Italy	$1,776,156M	AA-	9	South Korea	$2,135,485M	AA+
10	South Korea	$1,694,781M	AA	10	Italy	$2,110,225M	AA-

Nation Brands 2018				Nation Brands 2017			
Rank	Country	Value (USD)	Credit	Rank	Country	Value (USD)	Credit
1	USA	$25,899,231M	AAA	1	USA	$21,055,444M	AAA+
2	China	$13,868,822M	AA	2	China	$11,198,019M	AAA
3	Germany	$5,146,850M	AAA	3	Germany	$4,021,145M	AAA+
4	**UK**	**$3,750,286M**	**AAA**	4	Japan	$3,439,466M	AAA+
5	Japan	$3,597,548M	AAA-	5	**UK**	**$3,128,782M**	**AAA+**
6	France	$3,224,487M	AA+	6	France	$2,968,657M	AAA
7	Canada	$2,224,129M	AAA-	7	Canada	$2,056,245M	AAA+
8	Italy	$2,213,528M	AA-	8	India	$2,046,391M	AAA
9	India	$2,158,804M	AA	9	Italy	$2,034,358M	AAA-
10	South Korea	$2,001,235M	AA	10	South Korea	$1,844,730M	AAA

Nation Brands 2016				Nation Brands 2015			
Rank	Country	Value (USD)	Credit	Rank	Country	Value (USD)	Credit
1	USA	$20,574,439M	AAA	1	USA	$20,162,059M	AAA-
2	China	$7,880,823M	AA	2	China	$7,102,045M	AA-
3	Germany	$3,882,258M	AAA-	3	Germany	$4,426,637M	AAA-
4	Japan	$3,002,242M	AAA	4	Japan	$3,057,530M	AAA-
5	**UK**	**$2,942,178M**	**AAA**	5	**UK**	**$3,051,983M**	**AAA-**
6	France	$2,338,892M	AA+	6	France	$2,341,046M	AA
7	India	$2,065,781M	AA-	7	India	$2,267,878M	AA-
8	Canada	$1,809,994M	AAA-	8	Canada	$2,155,069M	AAA-
9	Italy	$1,521,410M	AA-	9	Italy	$1,557,012M	A
10	Australia	$1,304,852M	AAA-	10	Australia	$1,452,431M	AA+

Source: https://brandirectory.com/rankings/nation-brands.

Table 5 Countries with largest number of think tanks in 2020

1	United States	2203
2	China	1413
3	India	612
4	**UK**	**515**
5	South Korea	412
6	France	275
7	Germany	266
8	Argentina	262
9	Brazil	190
10	Vietnam	180

Source: 2020 Global Go To Think Tank Index Report.

Table 6 Lowy Global Diplomacy Index

2019							
Country	Population (Million)	GDP (Billion, USD)	Total Diplomatic Posts	G20 Rank	OECD Rank	Asia Rank	Overall Rank
China	1400.8	14026	276	1		1	1
USA	327.2	20494	273	2	1		2
France	67	2778	267	3	2		3
Japan	126.5	4971	247	4	3	2	4
Russia	144.5	1658	242	5			5
Turkey	82.3	767	235	6	4		6
Germany	82.9	3997	224	7	5		7
Brazil	209.5	1869	222	8			8
Spain	46.7	1426	215		6		9
Italy	60.4	2074	209	9	7		10
UK	**66.5**	**2825**	**208**	**10**	**8**		**11**
2017							
Country	Population (Million)	GDP (Billion, USD)	Total Posts	G20 Rank	OECD Rank	Asia Rank	Overall Rank
USA	323.2	18569	274	1	1		1
China	1378.7	11199	271	2		1	2
France	66.9	2465	266	3	2		3
Russia	144.3	1283	243	4			4
Japan	127	4939	240	5	3	2	5
Turkey	79.5	858	228	6	4		6
Germany	82.7	3467	225	7	5		7
Brazil	207.6	1796	221	8			8
Spain	46.4	1232	215		6		9
UK	**65.6**	**2619**	**207**	**9**	**7**		**10**
Italy	60.6	1850	207	10	8		11

(Continued)

Table 6 Lowy Global Diplomacy Index (*Continued*)

		2016				
Country	**Population (Million)**	**GDP (Billion, USD)**	**Total Posts**	**G20 Rank**	**OECD Rank**	**Combined Rank**
USA	318.9	17419	271	1	1	1
France	66.2	2829	267	2	2	2
China	1364.3	10355	263	3		3
Russia	143.8	1861	244	4		4
Turkey	75.9	798	225	5	3	5
Japan	127.1	4602	222	6	4	6
Brazil	206.1	2346	222	7		7
Germany	80.9	3868	219	8	5	8
UK	**64.5**	**2989**	**216**	**9**	**6**	**9**
Spain	46.4	1381	212		7	10
Italy	61.3	2141		10		11

Source: https://globaldiplomacyindex.lowyinstitute.org/

Table 7 Monocle Soft Power Rankings, 2012–20

2019–20		**2018–19**		**2017–18**		**2016–17**	
Rank	**Country**	**Rank**	**Country**	**Rank**	**Country**	**Rank**	**Country**
1	Germany	1	France	1	Canada	1	USA
2	South Korea	2	Germany	2	Germany	2	Germany
3	France	3	Japan	3	France	3	Japan
4	Japan	4	Canada	4	Japan	**4**	**UK**
5	Taiwan	5	Switzerland	**5**	**UK**	5	France
6	Switzerland	**6**	**UK**	6	Switzerland	6	Australia
7	New Zealand	7	Sweden	7	United States	7	Canada
8	Sweden	8	Australia	8	Sweden	8	Sweden
9	Greece	9	USA	9	Australia	9	Switzerland
10	Canada	10	Portugal	10	Italy	10	Denmark
2015–16		**2014–15**		**2013–14**		**2012–13**	
Rank	**Country**	**Rank**	**Country**	**Rank**	**Country**	**Rank**	**Country**
1	Germany	1	USA	1	Germany	**1**	**UK**
2	USA	2	Germany	**2**	**UK**	2	USA
3	**UK**	**3**	**UK**	3	USA	3	Germany
4	Japan	4	Japan	4	France	4	France
5	France	5	France	5	Japan	5	Sweden
6	Australia	6	Switzerland	6	Sweden	6	Japan
7	Sweden	7	Australia	7	Australia	7	Denmark
8	Switzerland	8	Sweden	8	Switzerland	8	Switzerland
9	Denmark	9	Denmark	9	Canada	9	Australia
10	Canada	10	Canada	10	Italy	10	Canada

Source: www.monocle.com.

Table 8 China National Image Global Survey of countries with biggest influence in global affairs

2019		2018	
Rank	**Country**	**Rank**	**Country**
1	US	1	US
2	China	2	China
3	**UK**	3	Russia
4	Russia	**4**	**UK**
5	Germany	5	France

Source: Academy of Contemporary China and World Studies. N.B. data for 2020 n/a.

Table 9 Brand Finance Soft Power Index

2021		2020	
Rank	**Country**	**Rank**	**Country**
1	Germany	1	US
2	Japan	2	Germany
3	**UK**	**3**	**UK**
4	Canada	4	Japan
5	Switzerland	5	China
6	US	6	France
7	France	7	Canada
8	China	8	Switzerland
9	Sweden	9	Sweden
10	Australia	10	Russia

Source: https://brandirectory.com/globalsoftpower/dashboard.

Notes

Chapter 1: Introduction

1 Andrew Roberts, *A History of the English-Speaking Peoples* (London: Weidenfeld & Nicolson, 2006), p. 423.

2 *The Voyager Interstellar Record: The Sounds of Earth* is available on YouTube. Greetings were recorded in fifty-five languages, with the secretary general's heavily accented greeting in English standing as *primus inter pares*.

3 Reprinted in *International Business Times*, 4 October 2016.

4 For an excellent overview of this perspective, see Robert Tombs, *This Sovereign Isle: Britain In and Out of Europe* (London: Allen Lane, 2021).

5 See, Michael Clarke and Helen Ramscar, *Tipping Point: Britain, Brexit and Security in the 2020s* (London: I.B. Tauris/Bloomsbury, 2019), pp. 232–3. Of the other four teams, two are based in Italy, one in Switzerland and one in the United States.

6 Brand Finance, *Monarchy 2017: The Annual Report on the Value of the British Monarchy* (London, Brand Finance, 2017), pp. 4–9.

7 Haroon Siddique, 'Marcus Rashford Forces Boris Johnson into Second U-turn on Child Food Poverty', *The Guardian*, 8 November 2020.

8 See Joseph S. Nye Jr., *Soft Power: The Means to Success in World Politics* (New York: Public Affairs, 2005); and Joseph S. Nye Jr., *The Powers to Lead* (Oxford: Oxford University Press, 2008); David Howell, *Old Links and New Ties: Power and Persuasion in an Age of Networks* (London: I.B. Tauris, 2013).

9 See, for example, James Pamment, *British Public Diplomacy and Soft Power* (London: Palgrave Macmillan, 2016), though this mainly deals with the governmental machinery for dealing with soft power assets.

10 Kieron Culligan, John Dubber and Mona Lotten, *As Others See Us: Culture, Attraction and Soft Power* (British Council, 2014); Bobby Duffy and Michael Clemence, *Global Influence in a Post-Brexit World: Who Is a Force for Good?* (London: Ipsos MORI, 2017); Christopher Hill and Sarah Beadle, *The Art of Attraction: Soft Power and the UK's Role in the World* (London: British Academy, 2014); and J. Holden, *Influence and Attraction: Culture and the Race for Soft Power in the 21st Century* (London: British Council/Demos, 2013).

11 Jonathan McClory, *The New Persuaders III: A 2012 Global Ranking of Soft Power* (London: Institute for Government, 2013); and Jonathan McClory, *The Soft Power*

30: A Global Ranking of Soft Power 2019 (California: Portland/University of Southern California, 2019); Brand Finance, *Global Soft Power Index 2020* (London: Brand Finance, November 2019).

12 Prime Minister's Office 'PM Outlines New Review to Define Britain's Place in the World', *Press Release*, Gov.UK, 26 February 2020.

13 See, for example, Robert Winder, *Soft Power: The New Great Game* (London: Little Brown, 2020).

14 British Council, *Sources of Soft Power: How Perceptions Determine the Success of Nations* (British Council, 2019), p. 3; Brand Finance, *Global Soft Power Index 2020*, pp. 4–5; Jonathan McClory, *The Soft Power 30: A Global Ranking of Soft Power 2017* (California: Portland, 2017).

15 British Council, *Sources of Soft Power*, pp. 37–43.

Chapter 2: Power in world politics

1 Thomas Hobbes, *Leviathan* (Oxford: Oxford University Press, 2008).

2 John Locke, *Two Treatises of Government and a Letter Concerning Toleration* (Yale: Yale University Press, 2003).

3 Harold D. Lasswell, *Politics: Who Gets What, When, How* (New York: Literary Licensing LLC, 2011).

4 William J. M. Mackenzie, *Power, Violence, Decision* (London: Penguin Books, 1975).

5 Herbert Butterfield, *The Whig Interpretation of History* (London: W. W. Norton & Company, 1965).

6 Martin Wight, *Power Politics* (Harmondsworth Middlesex: Penguin Books, 1979), p. 165.

7 Hedley Bull, *The Anarchical Society: A Study of Order in World Politics* (London: Macmillan, 1977).

8 See Lord Goldsmith, 'Advice on the Legality of Military Action against Iraq without a Further Resolution of the Security Council', 7 March 2003. In this statement he said that the United States had been arguing for 'a broad doctrine of a right to use force to pre-empt danger in the future. . . . If this means more than a right to respond proportionately to an imminent attack (and I understand that the doctrine is intended to carry that connotation) this is not a doctrine which, in my opinion, exists or is recognised in law.' Reported in *Irish Times*, 7 March 2003. Jeremy Wright QC MP, Speech at the International Institute for Strategic Studies on the modern law of self-defence, 11 January 2017, Office of the Attorney General.

9 Henry Kissinger, *Diplomacy* (Connecticut: Easton Press, 1994), p. 21.

10 See Christopher Hill, *The Future of British Foreign Policy: Security and Diplomacy in a World After Brexit* (Cambridge: Polity Press, 2019); Jeremy Greenstock, 'Reorienting Foreign Policy', *National Institute Economic Review* 250(1) (2019).

11 See, for example, Congressional Research Service, *Increased Great Power Competition: Implications for Defense – Issues for Congress*, 27 January 2021, pp. 1–2.

12 Bradley Peniston, 'Work: The Age of Everything Is the Era of Grand Strategy', *Defense One*, 2 November 2015.

13 Stephen E. Ambrose, *Rise to Globalism: American Foreign Policy since 1938* (London: Penguin Books, 2010).

14 Kenneth Waltz, *Man, the State and War* (Columbia: Columbia University Press, 1954).

15 Leo Tolstoy, *War and Peace* (Harmondsworth Middlesex: Penguin Books, 1957), p. 896, also pp. 1410–11.

16 Stephen Lukes, *Power: A Radical View*, 2nd ed. (London: Red Globe Books, 2005).

17 Lukes, Ibid., is very good in explaining this.

18 Tom Holland, *Dominion: The Making of the Western Mind* (London: Little Brown, 2019), p. xxiii.

19 See Rupert Smith, *The Utility of Military Force: The Art of War in the Modern World* (London: Vintage, 2008).

20 Serhii Plokhy, *Nuclear Folly: A New History of the Cuban Missile Crisis* (London: Allen Lane, 2021), pp. 192–4.

21 Eric Lorber and Julia M. MacDonald, 'Sensible Sanctions', *Foreign Affairs* 94(3) (2015): 1–4.

22 Max Hastings, *Vietnam: An Epic Tragedy 1945-1975* (London: William Collins, 2018), pp. 417–20.

23 Matthew D'Ancona, *Post Truth: The New War on Truth and How to Fight Back* (London: Ebury Press, 2017).

24 Zaki Laidi, 'The Hardening of Soft Power', *Project Syndicate*, 4 November 2019.

25 Rana Foroohar, *Don't Be Evil: The Case Against Big Tech* (London: Allen Lane, 2019).

26 Shoshana Zuboff, *The Age of Surveillance Capitalism: The Fight for a Human Future at the New Frontier of Power* (London: Profile Books, 2019).

27 Robert D. Kaplan, 'Coronavirus Ushers in the Globalization We Were Afraid of', *Bloomberg*, 20 March 2020.

28 See Ian Goldin and Robert Muggah, *Terra Incognita: 100 Maps to Survive the Next 100 Years* (London: Century, 2020), pp. 22–35.

29 Niall Ferguson, *The Square and the Tower: Networks, Hierarchies and the Struggle for Global Power* (London: Allen Lane, 2017).

30 Henry Kissinger, *World Order* (Connecticut: The Easton Press, 2014), pp. 367–70; Joseph S. Nye Jr., *The Future of Power* (New York: Public Affairs, 2011), pp. 113–39.

31 White House, *(US) Interim National Security Strategic Guidance*, March 2021, pp. 8–9.

32 Jan-Werner Muller, *What Is Populism?* (London: Penguin Books, 2017).

33 Francis Fukuyama, *Identity: Contemporary Politics and the Struggle for Recognition* (London: Profile Books, 2018).

Chapter 3: Persuasive power: Hard, soft and smart

1 See, for example, David Attenborough, *A Life on Our Planet: My Witness Statement and a Vision for the Future* (London: Ebury Press, 2020).

2 Steven Levitsky and Daniel Ziblatt, *How Democracies Die: What History Reveals About Our Future* (London: Penguin Books, 2019).

3 See, Joseph S. Nye Jr., *Soft Power: The Means to Success in World Politics* (New York: Public Affairs, 2005); Joseph S. Nye Jr., *The Powers to Lead* (Oxford: Oxford University Press, 2008); and Joseph S. Nye Jr., *The Future of Power* (New York: Public Affairs, 2011).

4 Rick Helfenbein, 'Facing Criticism in Xinjiang – China Moves on Pigs and Retail', *Forbes*, 20 April 2021; 'More Retail Brands Criticised on Chinese Social Media Over Xinjiang Statements', *Sharecast*, 23 April 2021.

5 Ministry of Defence, *Defence in a Competitive Age* (London: CP 411, March 2021), p. 15.

6 James M. Markham, 'TV Brings Western Culture to East Germany', *New York Times*, 13 February 1984.

7 Philip Zelikow and Condoleezza Rice, *To Build a Better World: Choices to End the Cold War and Create a Global Commonwealth* (New York: Twelve, 2020); Francis Fukuyama, *The End of History and the Last Man* (New York: Free Press, 2006).

8 Ian Goldin and Robert Muggah, *Terra Incognita: 100 Maps to Survive the Next 100 Years* (London: Century, 2020), pp. 223–4.

9 Anthony Blinken, US Secretary of State, 'A Foreign Policy for the American People', Speech in State Department, 3 March 2021.

10 Colin S. Gray, *Hard Power and Soft Power: The Utility of Military Force as an Instrument of Policy in the 21st Century* (Carlisle: Strategic Studies Institute, 2011), p. 30; see also, Edward N. Luttwak, *Strategy: The Logic of War and Peace* (Cambridge, MA: Harvard University Press, 2001).

11 Despite his scepticism, Colin Gray had almost, but not quite, accepted this point in an earlier publication. See Colin S. Gray, *The Strategy Bridge: Theory for Practice* (Oxford: Oxford University Press, 2010), p. 18.

12 See House of Lords, Select Committee on Soft Power and the UK's Influence, *Persuasion and Power in the Modern World* (HL 150, 28 March 2014), pp. 49–51.

13 Nye, *The Future of Power*, pp. 209–17.

14 See, for example, the annual surveys in 'Softly Does It – Global', *Monocle* 11(109), December 2017/January 2018.

15 Jonathan McClory, *The Soft Power 30: A Global Ranking of Soft Power 2017* (California: Portland/University of Southern California, 2017), pp. 30–1.

16 See Appendix 2.

17 Alistair MacDonald, *Sources of Soft Power: How Perceptions Determine the Success of Nations* (London: British Council, 2020).

18 'Boards Face Stiff Challenge to Win Trust Says IoD Report', *Sky News*, 7 September 2016. See also, *Ethical Boardroom*, Summer 2017, pp. 10–11; Institute of Directors, *Global Business Report*, 2019.

19 Ibid; Robert Winder, *Soft Power: The New Great Game* (Boston: Little Brown, 2020).

20 Brand Finance, *Global Soft Power Index 2020* (London: Brand Finance, November 2019), pp. 34–5.

21 See Ian Williams, *Every Breath You Take: China's New Tyranny* (London: Birlinn, 2021).

22 HM Government, *Global Britain in a Competitive Age: The Integrated Review of Security, Defence, Development and Foreign Policy* (CP 403, March 2021), p. 49.

23 HM Government, Press Release, *PM Outlines New Review to Define Britain's Place in the World*, 26 February 2020.

24 MacDonald, *Sources of Soft Power*, pp. 3, 37.

Chapter 4: The convenors: Bringing interests together

1 Foreign and Commonwealth Office, *Diplomatic Academy*, 2015.

2 For a good summary of ICANN's technocratic convening role, see https://www.icann.org/policy.

3 Tom Fletcher, *The Naked Diplomat: Understanding Power and Politics in the Digital Age* (London: William Collins, 2017), pp. 163–4.

4 Gordon Brown, *My Life, Our Times* (London: Bodley Head, 2017); Adam Tooze, *Crashed: How a Decade of Financial Crisis Changed the World* (London: Allen Lane, 2018).

5 Michael Clarke and Helen Ramscar, *Tipping Point: Britain, Brexit and Security in the 2020s* (London: I.B. Tauris/Bloomsbury, 2019).

6 The Preventing Sexual Violence in Conflict Initiative (PSVI) was founded in 2012 by former foreign secretary Lord Hague and United Nations Special Envoy of the High Commissioner for Refugees, Angelina Jolie; for example, see the works of the Modern Slavery and Human Rights Policy and Evidence Centre; the UK and Canadian government worked together on the 2019 Global Conference for Media Freedom, the first of its kind; in July 2018, the UK government hosted in London its first Global Disability Summit with the International Disability Alliance and the Government of Kenya; for example, see the work around the landmark Anti-Corruption Summit 2016 hosted in London and, with regard to aid agencies in particular, the UK Charity Commission published in June 2019 its inquiry findings that Oxfam GB failed to meet promises on safeguarding.

7   House of Commons, *The Sovereign Grant and Sovereign Grant Reserve Annual Report and Accounts 2019-20* (Controller of Her Majesty's Stationery Office, 24 September 2020).

8   John Koblin, 'Oprah, Meghan and Harry Draw 17.1 Million Viewers to CBS', *New York Times*, 8 March 2021; 'More Than 49 Million People Worldwide Watched Harry and Meghan Interview, CBS Says', *Reuters*, 10 March 2021.

9   'Prince Philip's Funeral: 13.6 Million Watch Ceremony in UK', *BBC News*, 18 April 2021.

10 @RoyalFamily, photograph by the Countess of Wessex, *Twitter*, 16 April 2021; @RoyalFamily, photograph by the Duchess of Cambridge, *Twitter*, 14 April 2021.

11 https://www.royal.uk/commonwealth

12 London Declaration, *22–27 April 1949*, https://thecommonwealth.org/london-decla ration

13 *A Connected Commonwealth*, 11 March 2019, https://library.commonwealth.int/Li brary/Catalogues/Controls/Download.aspx?id=6907.

14 Prime Minister The Hon Scott Morrison MP, Statement – His Royal Highness The Duke of Edinburgh, 10 April 2021.

15 David Howell, *The Mother of All Networks: Britain and the Commonwealth in the 21st Century* (London: Gilgamesh, 2018).

16 British Council, *Corporate Plan 2019-2020*, British Council 2019/J169, p. 42.

17 Arguments normally centre on the Council's choice of geographical priorities. See, for example, Helen Smith, 'Outcry as British Council Quits Europe to Woo Muslim World', *Guardian*, 5 August 2007; 'The British Council Is Wrong in Its Attitude to China', *The Observer*, 22 April 2012.

18 Robert Winder, *Soft Power: The New Great Game* (Boston: Little Brown, 2020) p. 78.

19 https://www.britishcouncil.org/organisation/press/british-council-announces-kate -ewart-biggs-obe-interim-chief-executive.

20 https://www.wiltonpark.org.uk/about-us/.

21 https://www.churchofengland.org/about/our-churches.

22 See Michael Nazir-Ali, 'Does the C of E Have a Future?', *Daily Telegraph*, 10 February 2021.

23 Emma Duncan, 'Cities of the Future Will Belong to the Young', *Financial Times*, 16 April 2021. See also Janan Ganesh, 'Why You Should Bet on London', *Financial Times*, 9 April 2021.

24 https://www.cityoflondon.gov.uk/about-us/about-the-city-of-london-corporation/ lord-mayor/role-of-lord-mayor.

25 'Coventry's Twin Towns and Cities', *Coventry City Council*, https://www.coventry .gov.uk/directory/25/coventrys_twin_towns_and_cities.

26 Ian Goldin and Robert Muggah, *Terra Incognita: 100 Maps to Survive the Next 100 Years* (London: Century, 2020), pp. 132–3.

27 Roger Cohen, 'The Age of Distrust', *New York Times*, 19 September 2016.

28 'Art of the Lie: Post Truth Politics in the Age of Social Media', *The Economist*,
    10 September 2016.

29 For more on Marshall McLuhan, who coined 'the global village' and 'the medium
    is the message' in his seminal work on the state of the then emerging phenomenon
    of mass media, see, for example, Marshall McLuhan, *Understanding Media: The
    Extensions of Man* (Cambridge, MA: MIT Press, 1994).

30 Matthew D'Ancona, *Post Truth: The New War on Truth and How to Fight Back*
    (London: Ebury Press, 2017).

Chapter 5: The officials: Speaking softly

1 *Documents on British Policy Overseas*, Gill Bennett and Keith A. Hamilton, eds., *The
   Conference on Security and Co-Operation in Europe, 1972-75,* Series III, Volume III,
   Docs 38 and 59 (London: The Stationery Office, 1998).

2 Institute of Contemporary British History, *The Helsinki Negotiations: The Accords
   and Their Impact* (ICBH Witness Seminar Programme, King's College London,
   2006); Henry Kissinger, *Diplomacy* (Connecticut: Easton Press, 1994), pp. 758–60.

3 Robin Renwick, *Not Quite a Diplomat: A Memoir* (London: Biteback Publishing,
   2019); Graham Ziegner, eds., *British Diplomacy: British Foreign Secretaries Reflect*
   (London: Politicos, 2007); Christopher Meyer, *Getting Our Way: 500 Years of
   Adventure and Intrigue* (London: Weidenfeld and Nicolson, 2010.)

4 Peter Ricketts, *Hard Choices: What Britain Does Next* (London: Atlantic Books,
   2021), pp. 142–66.

5 Geoffrey Moorhouse, *The Diplomats: The Foreign Office Today* (London:
   Humanities Press, 1977); John Dickie, *Inside the Foreign Office* (London: Chapmans
   Publishers, 1992).

6 House of Lords, International Relations Committee, *UK Foreign Policy in a Shifting
   World Order* (HL 250, 18 December 2018).

7 Following its incorporation of the Department for International Development,
   the FCDO now has a staff of over 17,000 people and operates a wide range of
   foreign embassies, high commissions, consular offices and missions to multilateral
   organizations. In India, for example, the FCDO is responsible for nine different
   offices; in the United States for fifteen, including new offices on behalf of the
   Department for International Trade.

8 See, for example, *Bloomberg News* or *The Economic Times*, 'Krueger – China
   Retaliation Is "11" on Scale of 1 to 10, Warn Wall Street Analysts', 5 August 2019.

9 Meyer, *Getting Our Way*, p. 10.

10 Conversation Between President Nixon and the President's Assistant for National Security Affairs (Kissinger), Foreign Relations of the United States, 1969-1976, Volume E-15, Part 2, Documents on Western Europe, 1973-1976, Second, Revised Edition. See https://history.state.gov/historicaldocuments/frus1969-76ve15p2Ed2/d6

11 See an excellent personal memoir by Peter Westmacott, *They Call It Diplomacy: Forty Years of Representing Britain Abroad* (London: Head of Zeus, 2021), especially Chapter 12.

12 John B. Ure, ed., *Diplomatic Bag: An Anthology of Diplomatic Incidents and Anecdotes from the Renaissance to the Gulf War* (London: John Murray, 1994); Tom Fletcher, *The Naked Diplomat* (London: William Collins, 2017), p. 174.

13 Bobby McDonagh, 'I Sat at the EU's Negotiating Table for Years – And Saw How Great Britain's Influence Was', *The Guardian*, 22 July 2019. He was Irish ambassador to the UK, 2009–13.

14 Joe White appointed HM Consul-General, San Francisco, and Technology Envoy to the USA, Press Release, FCDO, 4 December 2020.

15 UK Heads of Mission to the G7 countries: Canada (Susan Jane le Jeune d'Allegeershecque), France (Menna Rawlings), Germany (Jill Gallard), Italy (Jill Morris), Japan (Julia Longbottom) and the United States (Karen Pierce). Within 'Five Eyes': Australia (Victoria Treadell), Canada (Susan Jane le Jeune d'Allegeershecque), New Zealand (Laura Clarke) and the United States (now, Dame Karen Pierce). The UK Permanent Representative to the UK's Delegation to NATO was Dame Sarah MacIntosh. Caroline Wilson was the British ambassador in Beijing; Deborah Bronnet was in Moscow; and the UK envoy to the UN was Dame Barbara Woodward. The British representative in Nigeria was Catriona Laing and in Kenya, Jane Marriott.

16 Michael Clarke and Helen Ramscar, *Tipping Point: Britain, Brexit and Security in the 2020s* (London: I.B. Tauris/Bloomsbury, 2019), p. 198.

17 HM Government, *Global Britain in a Competitive Age: The Integrated Review of Security, Defence, Development and Foreign Policy* (CP 403, March 2021), pp. 97–9.

18 Personal Interviews.

19 Westmacott, *They Call It Diplomacy*, pp. 282–3.

20 Erik Brattberg, *The E3, The EU, and the Post-Brexit Diplomatic Landscape* (Carnegie Endowment for International Peace, 18 June 2020), p. 5. See also an excellent summary of Franco, German, British policy nuances and differences in Paul Lever, *Berlin Rules: Europe and the German Way* (London: I. B. Tauris, 2017), pp. 129–42.

21 House of Commons Foreign Affairs Committee, *Global Britain*, HC 780, 12 March 2018.

22 HM Government, *National Security Strategy and the Strategic Defence and Security Review 2015* (Cm 9161, November 2015). Also the prime minister's 'Foreword' and

'Vision' in the Integrated Review, HM Government, *Global Britain in a Competitive Age*, pp. 4–7.

23 HM Government, *Global Britain in a Competitive Age*, p. 11. See a counterview in Philip Stephens, *Britain Alone: The Path from Suez to Brexit* (London: Faber and Faber, 2021).

24 See Tyler Rogoway, 'Look Inside Putin's Massive New Military Command and Control Center', *Jalopnik,* 19 November 2015. It remains an open question, of course, whether the sheer scale of this coordinating centre will have the effect of reproducing the diversity of the external world inside its own copious facilities.

25 Michael McFaul, 'How to Contain Putin's Russia: A Strategy for Countering a Rising Revisionist Power', *Foreign Affairs*, 19 January 2021.

26 Clarke and Ramscar, *Tipping Point,* pp. 179–82.

27 Ibid., pp. 198–9.

28 Anand Menon, 'Little England, The United Kingdom's Retreat from Global Leadership', *Foreign Affairs*, 94(6), November/December 2015.

29 Lawrence D. Freedman, 'Britain Adrift: The United Kingdom's Search for a Post-Brexit Role', *Foreign Affairs*, 99(3), May/June 2020.

30 United Kingdom Internal Market Bill; Overseas Operations (Service Personnel and Veterans) Bill; the targeting of British nationals overseas; and the UK's defiance of UN resolutions over the Chagos Islands.

31 HM Government, *Global Britain in a Competitive Age*, p. 6.

32 See a good analysis in Robin Niblett, *Global Britain, Global Broker: A Blueprint for the UK's Future International Role* (Europe Programme Research Paper, Chatham House, 11 January 2021).

Chapter 6: Researchers and innovators: Shaping the global stage

1 The first industrial revolution was based on steam and water power in the late eighteenth century; the second on electrical power just a century later; the third on communications and internet power another century later again; and the fourth, less than half a century on, is (thought to be) based on the power of information and artificial intelligence that fuses the physical, digital and biological worlds.

2 https://interestingengineering.com/michael-faraday-a-true-scientific-hero-behind-electromagnetism.

3 https://www.britannica.com/biography/Robert-Whitehead-British-engineer; https://www.britannica.com/biography/Frank-Whittle.

4 Donald G. McNeil Jr., 'This $40 Crank-Up Radio Lets Rural Africa Tune In', *The New York Times*, 16 February 1996.

5 Paul Nurse, *Ensuring a Successful UK Research Endeavour: A Review of the UK Research Councils* (BIS/15/625, 2015).

6 Peter Hennessy, *The Prime Minister: The Office and Its Holders Since 1945* (London: Penguin, 2001), p. 287.

7 David King and Les Levidow, 'Introduction: Contesting Science and Technology, from the 1970s to the Present', *Science as Culture* 25(3) (24 August 2016), pp. 367–72.

8 Peter Hennessey, *Winds of Change: Britain in the Early Sixties* (London: Allen Lane, 2019), p. 467.

9 Campaign for Science and Education, 'History of CaSE', https://www.sciencecampaign.org.uk/about-us/history-of-case.html.

10 See, for example, HMG, *Realising Our Potential: A Strategy for Science, Engineering and Technology* (CM 2250, May 1993), p. 3.; House of Lords Select Committee on Science and Technology, *Science and Society Report*; DTI, *Excellence and Opportunity: A Science and Innovation Strategy for the 21st Century*; HMG, *Investing in Innovation: A Strategy for Science, Engineering and Technology*, 2002; Council for Science and Technology, *Policy through Dialogue: Informing Policies Based on Science and Technology* (2005).

11 Lord Sainsbury of Turville, *The Race to the Top – A Review of Government's Science and Innovation Policies* (London: Her Majesty's Stationery Office, 2007).

12 Paul Nurse, *Ensuring a Successful UK Research Endeavour: A Review of the UK Research Councils* (BIS/15/625, 2015).

13 In 2018 the Higher Education Funding Council for England (which also covered Wales) was abolished and replaced by two new agencies: the Office for Students and Research England. The other devolved administrations had separate arrangements.

14 https://www.ukri.org/.

15 https://www.gov.uk/government/publications/industrial-strategy-the-grand-challenges/missions.

16 UK Research and Innovation (UKRI), *Annual Report and Accounts 2018–2019* (HC 2087, 2019). The 'Haldane Report' can be found at: Ministry of Reconstruction, *Report of the Machinery of Government Committee* (London: Her Majesty's Stationery Office, 1918).

17 'Science and Society, Twenty Years On', UKRI, 22 September 2020.

18 *International Comparative Performance of the UK Research Base 2016*, Elsevier BEIS, 2017, p. 11. UK levels: 3.0 per cent GDP 2011/3.2 per cent 2013/2.7 per cent 2016.

19 Quoted in Peter Hennessy, *Winds of Change*, p. 421.

20 HMG, *UK Research and Development Roadmap*, Department for Business, Energy & Industrial Strategy, July 2020, p. 4.

21 HM Government, *Global Britain in a Competitive Age: The Integrated Review of Security, Defence, Development and Foreign Policy* (CP 403, March 2021), p. 4. It is indicative of the 'language inflation' involved in government S&T policy that a commitment to 'redoubling' implies the government will make 4X its original commitment to British R&D. It is very doubtful this is really what the prime minister intends – welcome as that might be.

22 Office for National Statistics, *Business Enterprise Research and Development, UK, 2019*; and *Research and Development Expenditure by the UK Government*, 2019.

23 See the figures presented in British Academy, *Lessons from the History of UK Science Policy* (Department for Business, Energy and Industrial Strategy, August 2019), pp. 56–7.

24 Ibid., p. 55.

25 The seven existing research councils are Medical Research Council (1913), Economic and Social Research Council (1965), National Environmental Research Council (1965), Biotech and Biological Sciences Research Council (1994), Engineering and Physical Sciences Research Council (1994), Arts and Humanities Research Council (2005), Science and Technology Facilities Council (2007).

26 HM Government, *Research and Innovation Organisations in the UK: Innovation Functions and Policy Issues* (Department for Business, Innovation and Skills, DBIS Research Paper 226, July 2015), pp. 41–51. Some thirty-one are medical organizations, twenty-one are cultural and thirty-one cover other various applied technologies.

27 Ibid., p. 7; The British Academy, *Lessons from the History of UK Science Policy* (DBEIS, August 2019).

28 Claire Craig, 'Policy Towards Science and Science in Policy: Questions and Answers?', in British Academy, *Lessons from the History of UK Science Policy* (DBEIS, August 2019), pp. 45–7.

29 *International Comparison of the UK Research Base, 2019: Accompanying Note* (DBEIS, 2019), p. 7. See also Octopus Ventures, *Research to Riches Entrepreneurial Impact Ranking 2019: Measuring the Success of UK Universities in Converting Research into Successful Companies*, 2019.

30 The 'field-weighted citation impact' score measures the number of citations for a work over and above the average number of citations for all works in that field. The global average is therefore measured as 1.0. In 2018 the British figure averaged 1.56. Ibid., p. 5.

31 https://www.gov.uk/government/publications/international-comparison-of-the-uk-research-base-2019, Accompanying Note, p. 10.

32 *International Comparative Performance of the UK Research Base 2016* (Elsevier BEIS, 2017), p. 35.

33 Ibid., pp. 50–1.

34 Ibid., pp. 100, 108–11.

35 Work of Keith Campbell and his team (and PPL Therapeutics).

36 James O'Malley, 'The Multinational Make-Up of the Oxford University Vaccine Team', *The New European*, 11 September 2020.

37 'The Top 10 Pharma Companies by 2019 Revenue', www.fiercepharma.com, 20 April 2020.

38 https://royalsociety.org/about-us/history/.

39 Ben Goldacre, *Bad Pharma* (London: Fourth Estate, 2012), p. 15.

40 Association of Medical Research Charities, Open Letter to the Prime Minister, 1 September 2020.

41 See Robin Shattock, 'In the Vaccine War, UK Must be Able to Make Its Own Ammunition', *Daily Telegraph*, 14 February 2021.

42 'BAE Systems, Third Biggest Global Military Contractor, Approaches Major Leadership Change', Forbes.com, 27 March 2017.

43 'Facts & Figures 2020', www.adsgroup.org.uk, 19 June 2020.

44 Airbus Industries is a major consortium, concentrated on civilian aerospace products with annual pre-Covid-19 revenues of around 70 billion euros.

45 PWC, *Harnessing Innovation in Aerospace and Defence* (PWC/ADS, London, November 2020), p. 2.

46 Ibid., pp. 5–7.

47 Michael Clarke, *The Challenge of Defending Britain* (Manchester: Manchester University Press, 2019), pp. 23–7.

48 'A Business Is Born Every Two Hours at UK Universities', Universities UK, 28 August 2020; to calculate the number of graduate start-ups per hour, the average number of graduate start-ups in the last five years (20,039) was divided by the number of hours in a year (8760).

49 Daphne Leprince-Ringuet, 'Start-ups: Why Can't UK Universities Be More Like MIT?', *Zdnet.com*, 12 November 2019.

50 Jonathan Moules, 'UK Universities Intensify Efforts to Develop Start-Ups', *Financial Times*, 8 November 2019.

51 Peggy Hollinger and Sarah Neville, 'Drug Wars: How AstraZeneca Overtook GSK in UK Pharma', *Financial Times*, 27 May 2020.

52 See government tender call during 2019 in https://re.ukri.org/knowledge-exchange/university-enterprise-zones/.

53 As one among many examples see, even as early as 2010, 'Nobel Prize Winners Warn Against Immigration Caps', *BBC News* 7 October 2010.

54 HM Government, *Global Britain in a Competitive Age*, p. 35.

55 For example, David Nield, 'Ingenious "Wrinkled" Graphene Could Be the Most Promising Water Filter Yet', *Science Alert*, 25 January 2021.

56 Reported in *The Guardian*, 3 December 2013. See also Jennifer Carpenter, 'UK Invests in Graphene Technology', *BBC News*, 3 October 2011.

Chapter 7: Leaders and regulators: Setting the standards

1   International Organization for Standardization (ISO), the International Electrotechnical Commission (IEC) and the European Standards Organizations (CEN, CENELEC and ETSI), see https://www.bsigroup.com/en-GB/about-bsi/uk-n ational-standards-body/.

2   S. Muthesius, *The English Terraced House*, 1982, cited in Nicholas Boys Smith, *More Good Homes: Making Planning More Proportionate, Predictable and Equitable* (Legatum Institute/Create Streets, 2018), p. 61.

3   https://www.fema.gov/media-library-data/20130726-1903-25045-6866/building_ codes_toolkit_fact_sheet.pdf.

4   www.imo.org.

5   'Obituaries – Jim Davis', *Daily Telegraph*, 19 April 2021.

6   See 'The History of the ISO 9000 Series', *CABEM Technologies*, 24 February 2017.

7   Gary Strong, *International Fire Safety Standards* (RICS), International Fire Safety Standards (rics.org)

8   James Landale, 'How the UK Lost International Court of Justice Place to India', *BBC News*, 21 November 2017.

9   They are the Food and Agriculture Organization, the International Telecommunication Union, the International Civil Aviation Organization, the UN Industrial Development Organization and, within the core organization, the UN Department of Economic and Social Affairs.

10 Tung Cheng-Chia and Alan H. Yang, 'How China Is Remaking the UN in Its Own Image', *The Diplomat*, 9 April 2020.

11 National Audit Office, *A Short Guide to Regulation* (London: NAO, 2017.)

12 For Trade Associations and Regulatory Bodies UK, see www.britishservices.co.uk.

13 On individual benefits to companies, see British Standards Institute, *ISO 9000 Case Studies,* https://www.bsigroup.com/en-GB/iso-9001-quality-management/case-s tudies/.

14 That is, 37.4 per cent of annual labour productivity growth translated into 28.4 per cent annual GDP growth. Centre for Economic and Business Research, *The Economic Contribution of Standards to the UK Economy*, June 2015, p. 9.

15 Ibid., p. 10.

16 Though even some big enterprises complain about the costs of compliance. One ex-Chairman of a major retail bank complained in a private interview that around

a third of his entire workforce was involved, in one way or another, in meeting compliance standards.

17 See, for example, the GOV.UK statements at https://www.gov.uk/guidance/the-uks -national-quality-infrastructure.

18 www.icann.org/policy for an outline of its role in convening relevant professional expertise.

19 'The Future of the Four Kingdoms of the Internet', *Financial Times*, 30 December 2018.

20 OECD, *Regulatory Policy Outlook 2018* (Paris: OECD Publishing, 2018), p. 238. It is also notable that more of Britain's oversight functions in the regulatory sphere are run by non-ministerial bodies (six out of ten key regulatory functions being performed by non-governmental bodies) in contrast to its major competitors, where regulation is handled mainly, or completely, within central government.

21 Ibid., pp. 190, 188, 202.

22 Ibid., p. 240.

23 'UK Government Must Improve Image to Lift Business Confidence, Report Warns', *Financial Times*, 22 January 2021.

24 *London: The Global Powerhouse*, February 2016. See also GLA Economics, *London's Central Business District: Its Global Importance*, 2008.

25 'UK Government Must Improve Image to Lift Business Confidence, Report Warns', *Financial Times*, 22 January 2021.

26 https://www.fca.org.uk/about/international-standards-regulations.

27 Huw Jones, et al., 'Brexit Britain's Financial Sector Faces "slow puncture"', *Reuters*, 11 December 2018.

28 Philip Stafford, 'Amsterdam Ousts London as Europe's Top Share Trading Hub', *Financial Times*, 10 February 2021.

29 Siobhan Riding, 'What Does the Post-Brexit Future Hold for City on London Fund Managers?', *Financial Times*, 1 August 2020.

30 Mehreen Khan and Michael Peel, 'Brussels Pushes to Create the World's First Green Gold Standard', *Financial Times*, 11 November 2019.

31 https://www.adjaye.com/work/moscow-school-of-management-skolkovo/.

32 https://www.architecture.com/awards-and-competitions-landing-page/awards/riba -international-awards.

33 See, for example, Ben Quinn, et al., 'England's Planning Changes Will Create "Generation of Slums"', *The Guardian*, 5 August 2020; Simon Jenkins, 'Boris Johnson's "Mutant" Planning Algorithm Could Scar England for Ever', *The Guardian*, 27 November 2020.

34 https://www.cambridge.org/about-us/who-we-are/history/brief-history-press.

35 https://global.oup.com/academic/aboutus/?cc=ch&lang=en&.

36 Allison Ford, 'UK Publishes More Books Per Capita Than Any Other Country, Report Shows', *The Guardian*, 11 October 2014.

37 'India Has the Greatest Potential for a Thriving "Reading" Nation', *International Publishers Association*, 29 June 2018; 'Net Revenue of the Book Publishing Industry in the United States from 2008 to 2019', *Statistic Research Department*, 9 October 2020.

38 https://www.cogconsortium.uk/.

39 'Genomic Sequencing in Pandemics', *The Lancet*, 397(10273) (6 February 2021), p. 445.

40 Department of Health and Social Care, Press Release, 'UK to Support Rest of the World to Find COVID-19 Virus Variants', 26 January 2021.

41 European Medicines Agency, *Annual Report 2016*, European Medicines Agency, 2017, p. 69.

42 Lucy Warwick-Ching, 'Grenfell Fire Leads to Global Safety Standards', *Financial Times*, 5 November 2020.

43 Nelson Yap, 'UN Adopts Fire Safety Standards', *Australian Property Journal*, 19 November 2020.

Chapter 8: Cosmopolitans and diasporas: Reflecting global cultures

1 See, for example, Visit Britain, *Inbound Consumer Sentiment Research* (Visit Britain/ICM Unlimited, October 2020).

2 Andrew Marr, *Elizabethans: How Modern Britain Was Forged* (London: William Collins, 2020), p. 320.

3 See David Goodhart, *The Road to Somewhere: The New Tribes Shaping British Politics* (London: Penguin Books, 2017), pp. 122–3; Douglas Murray, *The Strange Death of Europe: Immigration, Identity, Islam* (London: Bloomsbury, 2018), pp. 11–13.

4 John Kampfner, *Why the Germans Do It Better* (London: Atlantic Books, 2020).

5 See, for example, Lord Hodgson, *Overcrowded Islands?* (London: Civitas, 2020).

6 HM Government, *Commission on Race and Ethnic Disparities: The Report*, March 2021, p. 8.

7 The 2021 census, conducted in March of that year, is not due to be published until 2022 and not fully analysed until 2023.

8 See Robert Winder, *Bloody Foreigners: The Story of Immigration to Britain* (London: Abacus, 2010): Phil Wood, Charles Landry and Jude Bloomfield, *Cultural Diversity in Britain: A Toolkit for Cross-Cultural Co-operation* (York: Joseph Rowntree Foundation, 2006).

9 Kampfner, *Why the Germans Do It Better*, p. 124.

10 It is certainly possible to find racism on both the right and left-wing extremes of British politics, but they have never penetrated to the centre with any force. The

United Kingdom Independence Party was accused by many of an underlying racism in its anti-EU stance, but nevertheless kept its focus, successfully, on pressing for Britain to leave the EU.

11 Wood et al., *Cultural Diversity in Britain.*

12 Winder, *Bloody Foreigners*, p. 5.

13 Sathnam Sanghera, *Empireland: How Imperialism Has Shaped Modern Britain* (London: Penguin/Viking Press, 2021), pp. 208–9.

14 It is important to note that the census asks people to 'describe' an ethnicity that they feel best fits them – it is a personal choice.

15 Social Mobility Commission, *Social Mobility in Great Britain: State of the Nation 2018 to 2019*, 30 April 2019, pp. 12–13.

16 Patrick Butler, 'Social Mobility in Decline in Britain, Official Survey Finds', *The Guardian*, 21 January 2020.

17 Kampfner, *Why the Germans Do It Better*, pp. 280–1.

18 Quoted in Kampfner, *Why the Germans Do It Better*, pp. 278–9; *Die Zeit*, 31 January 2020.

19 Bear, Paddington. *Paddington*. Film. Directed by Paul King (London: Studio Canal, 2014).

20 Wood et al., *Cultural Diversity in Britain*, p. 1.

21 Clarke and Ramscar, *Tipping Point*, pp. 53–4.

22 Ibid., Chapters 8 and 13.

23 See Christopher Thornton, 'The Iran We Don't See: A Tour of the Country Where People Love Americans', *The Atlantic*, 6 June 2012; Richard Wike et al., 'Global Attitudes and Trends', *Pew Research Center*, 8 January 2020; Tom Rosentiel, 'The Problem of American Exceptionalism', *Pew Research Center*, 5 June 2006; Ivan Kratsev and Mark Leonard, *The Crisis of American Power*, European Council on Foreign Relations, Policy Brief, 19 January 2021.

24 Grant Thornton, *India in the UK: The Diaspora Effect* (London: Grant Thornton UK LLP, February 2020), p. 4.

25 Ben Chapman, 'Richest Six People in UK Own as Much as Bottom 13 Million, Report Finds', *The Independent*, 3 December 2019.

26 'Leicester Hosts Biggest Diwali Celebrations Outside of India', *Enable Inclusive Support*, 14 October 2019.

27 Winder, *Bloody Foreigners,* p. 79.

28 In 2021, the Henley Passport Index ranked the UK passport joint seventh in the world. See https://www.henleyglobal.com/passport-index.

29 Speech by Irish ambassador Daniel Mulhall, 'Irish Diplomacy in a Globalised World', *University of Kent*, 2 February 2015.

30 www.diaspora.iom.int.

31 See 'Diasporas and Contested Sovereignty', *ERC/Frontline Club*, 26 September 2017.

32 Ciarán Devane in British Council, *Sources of Soft Power: How Perceptions Determine the Success of Nations* (British Council: 2019), p. 2.

33 British Council, *Sources of Soft Power*, p. 10, Table 1.

34 'Britain's Visitor Economy Facts', www.visitbritain.org, 2020.

35 Rebecca Smithers, 'English Wines Win Record Number of Awards in Global Tasting Competition', *The Guardian*, 22 September 2020.

36 *How the World Views the UK – 2020: Foresight Issue 178*, Visit Britain, November 2020.

37 *Daily Telegraph*, 27 March 2017. Visit Britain, *Visitor Attraction Trends in England 2019 Full Report*, October 2020.

38 Kathy McArdle, 'UK City of Culture Reflects the Global Identity of UK Cities', *British Council*, December 2017; Professor Jo Beall and David Adam, 'Cities, Prosperity and Influence', *British Council*, March 2017.

Chapter 9: Educators: Pursuing truthful minds – and truth

1 British Council evidence to House of Lords, *UK Foreign Policy in a Shifting World Order* (HL 250, December 2018), p. 90.

2 HM Government, *Global Britain in a Competitive Age: The Integrated Review of Security, Defence, Development and Foreign Policy* (CP 403, March 2021), p. 49.

3 Quacquarelli Symonds, *QS World University Rankings 2021*. It should be noted that the other big ranking exercise for 2021, by *Times Higher Education*, rates Britain at 2 out of the top 10 and only 11 of the top 100, assessing rather more US universities highly. On both ratings China has between 9 and 11 of the top 100 (up to 5 of which are in Hong Kong), France 3 and Germany between 3 and 7. Russia features just once in the top 100 in only one of the rankings. See 'QS World University Rankings 2021', topuniversities.com and 'World University Rankings 2021', timeshighereducation.com

4 In 2017 it constituted 11 per cent of the total as against 24 per cent for the United States, according to Project Atlas at the International Institute of Education. See www.iie.org/projectatlas.

5 British Council APPG, *Influence and the Integrated Review: Opportunities for Britain's Global Vision*, October 2020, p. 8.

6 Matt Mathers, 'Nearly Three Quarters of British Universities Fall in Global Rankings', *The Independent*, 19 June 2020.

7 See 'The UK's International Education Ranking', *Full Fact*, 24 February 2017 at The UK's international education ranking – Full Fact.

8 Ilker Koksal, 'The Rise of Online Learning', *Forbes*, 2 May 2020; HTF Market Intelligence Consulting, Press Release, 'Online Education Market to Witness Massive Growth by 2021-2026', 18 January 2021.

9 '10 Top UK Universities Ideal for Distance Learning', *Distance Learning Portal*, 5 January 2021. This source combines rankings from *QS World University Rankings 2020* and *Times Higher Education Rankings 2020*, setting them against the scope of online courses offered at British universities. The other universities on the list were Warwick, Glasgow, Sheffield, Birmingham, Leeds and Nottingham.

10 Giles Smith, 'What Comes Naturally', *Daily Telegraph*, 2 April 2019.

11 *Daily Telegraph*, 30 January 2013.

12 See https://www.britishmuseum.org/our-work/departments/egypt-and-sudan/circulating-artefacts.

13 https://www.edenproject.com/eden-story/about-us.

14 https://www.kew.org/science/our-science/where-we-work.

15 https://www.kew.org/wakehurst/whats-at-wakehurst/millennium-seed-bank.

16 See www.bellingcat.com.

17 See Matthew Campbell, 'Unmasking the Salisbury Poisoners', *Sunday Times Magazine*, 24 January 2021.

18 Eliot Higgins, *We Are Bellingcat: An Intelligence Agency for the People* (London: Bloomsbury, 2021).

19 Muhammad Idrees Ahmad, 'Bellingcat and How Open Source Reinvented Investigative Journalism', *New York Review of Books*, 10 June 2019.

20 *The Heritage Alliance: International Report 2018*, Scottish Confucius Institute for Business & Communication/Heriot Watt University.

21 It should be noted that this is not mostly direct revenue generated by the sector but rather its contribution in adding value to the revenues of other sectors, though of course the heritage industry also generates its own independent revenue streams.

22 Winder, *Bloody Foreigners*, p. 66.

23 https://www.englishpen.org/about/history/.

24 https://www.savethechildren.org/us/about-us/why-save-the-children/history.

25 Hannah Bock, '60 Years of Amnesty International: How the World's Biggest Human Rights Campaign Was Founded through One Newspaper Article', *mediummagazine .nl*, 16 January 2021.

26 www.stopecocide.earth.

27 'Facts about Our Ecological Crisis Are Incontrovertible. We Must Take Action', *The Guardian*, 26 October 2018.

28 Vikram Dodd and Jamie Grierson, 'Terrorism Police List Extinction Rebellion as Extremist Ideology', *The Guardian*, 10 January 2020.

29 Mark Townsend, 'Tube Protest Was a Mistake, Admit Leading Extinction Rebellion Members', *The Guardian*, 20 October 2019.

30 Henry Foy, 'Echoes of the Cold War as Russia Boosts Number of Foreign Students', *Financial Times*, 19 December 2019.

Chapter 10: Creatives: Opening new ideas

1 https://ukiepedia.ukie.org.uk/index.php/Notable_Dates_in_UK_Games_Industry_ History.
 2 Andrew Marr, *Elizabethans, How Modern Britain Was Forged* (London: William Collins, 2020), pp. 168–70.
 3 Ibid., p. 166.
 4 Kenneth O. Morgan, ed., *The Oxford History of Britain* (Oxford: Oxford University Press, 2010), p. 668.
 5 It should be recorded, however, that the conversion was handled by Swiss architects.
 6 Jessica Chou, 'A Brief History of Olympic Sponsorships', *thedailymeal.com*, 18 July 2012.
 7 www.hatads.org.uk/about/.
 8 See Winston Fletcher, *Powers of Persuasion: The Inside Story of British Advertising* (Oxford: Oxford University Press, 2008).
 9 Ellen Hammett, 'UK Pitches Itself as "Next Port of Call" for Asian Brands Looking to Export', *marketingweek.com*, 19 March 2019.
10 *UK Advertising Association Report 2020*, Advertising Association/UK Advertising Export Group, London, p. 4.
11 John Tylee, 'Celebrating 100 Years of Iconic British Advertising', *Campaign*, 6 March 2017.
12 Adam Smith used the phrase as a positive comment on the British economy. It was then more famously quoted by Napoleon as an expression of contempt.
13 Katie Jones, 'Ranked: The Most Valuable Brands in the World', *visualcapitalist.com*, 30 January 2020.
14 Tylee, 'Celebrating 100 Years of Iconic British Advertising'.
15 'Marketing vs. Advertising', www.ama.org.
16 www.dandad.org.
17 https://en.wikipedia.org/wiki/Campaign_(magazine).
18 https://www.consultancy.uk/consulting-industry/best-uk-firms.
19 'The Quintessentially Scottish Studio behind Grand Theft Auto', *inews.co.uk*, 5 October 2016.
20 'LOADED Minecraft Gaming Masterminds from Dundee Propelled into The Times' 2020 Rich List', *The Scottish Sun*, 15 May 2002.
21 https://ukiepedia.ukie.org.uk/index.php/Notable_Dates_in_UK_Games_Industry_ History.

22 Dr Mark Taylor, *UK Games Industry Census: Understanding Diversity in the UK Games Industry Workforce* (UKIE/University of Sheffield/UKRI/Arts and Humanities Research Council, February 2020).

23 'UKIE UK Consumer Games Market Valuation', *ukie.org.uk*, 19 March 2021.

24 www.publishers.org.uk/about-publishing/.

25 'Number of Employees in the Music, Performance and Visual Arts Economy of United Kingdom (UK) from 2011 to 2019*', *Statista Research Department*, 8 January 2021.

26 'Art Market in the United Kingdom – Statistics & Facts', *Statista Research Department*, 24 March 2021.

27 See Arts Economics, *The British Art Market 2017* (London: BAMF, 2018), and the reports of the British Art Market Federation. In 2017 Britain imported about 16 per cent by value from EU countries but exported only 3 per cent to the EU area.

28 'Leading British Contemporary Artists 2020, by Auction Revenue', Statista Research Department, 17 March 2021.

Chapter 11: Entertainers: Feeding a human need

1 See Creative Industries Council annual assessments. The September 2020 assessment is at: Design (thecreativeindustries.co.uk). 'Gross value added' calculations are accepted by government statisticians as a meaningful metric to assess the monetary value of a service even though it may show up in another service or sector. It does not necessarily represent total turnover or profit to the supplier.

2 See Creative Industries Council, *UK to the World 2019;* also, Michael Clarke and Helen Ramscar, *Tipping Point: Britain, Brexit and Security in the 2020s* (London: I.B. Tauris/Bloomsbury, 2019), pp. 231–2.

3 Creative Industries Council, *UK to the World 2019.*

4 Ben Fritz, *Big Picture: The Fight for the Future of Movies* (New York: Mariner Books, 2019), pp. 236–8.

5 Geoffrey Macnab, *Stairways to Heaven: Rebuilding the British Film Industry* (London: I.B. Tauris, 2018), pp. 220–1.

6 See *The Economic Value of Post-production in the UK* | UK Screen Alliance.

7 'International Film and HETV Production Spend in the UK Tops £2.34bn in 2020 Despite Initial Impact of COVID-19' – British Film Commission.

8 http://arts.leeds.ac.uk/screeningeuropeanheritage/files/2013/11/Centre-for-World -Cinemas-and-BFilm-submission.pdf.

9 Clarke and Ramscar, *Tipping Point,* p. 233.

10 Macnab, *Stairways to Heaven*, pp. 221–4.

11 Fritz, *Big Picture*, pp. 211–2.

12 Tom Fish, 'The Highest Grossing Movies of the Century So Far', *Newsweek*, 26 April 2021.

13 'The British TV Shows That Are Watched All over the World', *CNN*, 15 November 2017.

14 Jeremy Egner, 'A Bit of Britain Where the Sun Never Sets', *New York Times*, 3 January 2013.

15 'Strictly Come Dancing: The Worldwide Phenomenon', *Daily Telegraph*, 9 December 2011.

16 House of Lords, *Persuasion and Power in the Modern World*, Select Committee on Soft Power and the UK's Influence, HL 159, 28 March 2014, p. 19.

17 'BBC World Service to Receive Continued Additional Funding from the FCDO', *BBC Media Centre*, 1 May 2021.

18 National Audit Office, *The BBC's Strategic Financial Management* (HC 1128, 20 January 2021), p. 6.

19 Ofcom, *Public Service Broadcasting in the Digital Age*, 8 March 2018, p. 14.

20 See, for example, Patricia Nilsson, 'Can the BBC Funding Model Survive?', *Financial Times*, 8 November 2019; 'The BBC Is a Beacon for Other Broadcasters', Letters, *Guardian*, 20 September 2015.

21 'Fun International Facts about Shakespeare', *British Council*, 19 March 2015. The accepted Shakespearean canon of thirty-seven plays was augmented by the Royal Shakespeare Company with the addition of *The Two Nobel Kinsman* as a final, collaborative work.

22 'How Many Theatres Are There in the UK?', www.theatretrust.org.uk.

23 'Theatre and the West End in the United Kingdom (UK) – Statistics & Facts', *Statista Research Department*, 3 December 2020.

24 Kenneth O. Morgan, ed., *The Oxford History of Britain* (Oxford: Oxford University Press, 2010), pp. 692–3.

25 '5 Statistics That Highlight How Amazing Adele's "25" Really Is', *Forbes*, 3 December 2015.

26 'One in 10 Songs Streamed Globally Are by British Artists', *NME*, 4 January 2021.

27 Michael Haan, '"We're Not Being Given a Viable Future", How Brexit Will Hurt British Music', *The Guardian*, 3 April 2019.

28 Anton Spice, 'Beyond Borders: How Immigration Shaped British Jazz', *The Vinyl Factory*, 8 September 2015.

29 In fact, the Corinthian ideals of Baron de Coubertin in founding the modern Olympics in 1896 were a romantic misunderstanding of the cynical patriotism that had always underlain the ancient games.

30 Melvin Bragg, *12 Books That Changed the World* (London: Hodder and Stoughton, 2006), pp. 89–118.

31 The English Premier League earns more every year than the combined incomes of the Bundesliga, La Liga, Ligue 1 and Serie A, and almost three times the combined totals of all North American sports. See Mark Gregory, *Premier League: Economic and Social Impact* (London: Ernst and Young, 2019), pp. 2–3.

32 See Mark Gregory, *Premier League*, pp. 9, 11–12; Jonathan McClory, 'Soft Power and the World's Game: The Premier League in Asia', *University of Southern California, Center on Public Diplomacy*, 30 September 2019.

33 Janan Ganesh, 'Football: Britain's Premier Soft Power Asset', *Financial Times*, 9 August 2019.

34 'Golf – Statistics & Facts', *Statista.com*, 21 March 2021.

35 'The Untold Story of the Daring Cave Divers Who Saved the Thai Soccer Team', *National Geographic*, 4 March 2019.

Chapter 12: Stars and bloggers: Embracing the anarchic

1 https://edition.cnn.com/2005/SHOWBIZ/Music/07/01/liveaid.memories/index.html.

2 Susanne Franks, 'Ethiopian Famine: How Landmark BBC Report Influenced Modern Coverage', *BBC News*, 22 October 2014.

3 https://www.theguardian.com/arts/pictures/0,,1328579,00.html.

4 George Santayana, *Soliloquies in England and Later Soliloquies* (London: Read Books Classic Reprints, 2013), p. 29.

5 See Edith Sitwell and Richard Ingrams, *English Eccentrics* (London: Pallas Athene, 2006).

6 See also David McKie, *Bright Particular Stars: A Gallery of Glorious British Eccentrics* (London: Atlantic Books, 2011).

7 'Anarchy in the UK', www.theculturecrush.com.

8 'History of the Rave Scene: How DJs Built Modern Dance Music', www.djtechtools.com, 19 December 2013.

9 'Zoella Tops Influencer Rich List', *BBC Newsround*, 29 October 2019.

10 'The Highest Earning Social Media Influencers in the UK', *Influencer Matchmaker*, 17 February 2021.

11 'Asos Shares Plummet after Profits Warning', *The Guardian*, 5 June 2014; 'Asos and Boohoo Rip up Centuries of British Retail Heritage', *Financial Times*, 7 February 2021.

12 'How David Beckham Became Football's First Truly Global Brand', *vice.com*, 8 July 2017.

13 'How David Beckham's "brand" Was Made', *GQ Magazine*, 4 February 2017.

14 Henri C. Santos et al., 'Global Increases in Individualism', *Psychological Science*, 13 July 2017.

15 'Britain Is the Most Individualistic Country in the EU, Europe-Wide Survey Finds', *The Independent*, 19 December 2017.

16 www.hofstede-insights.com/country-comparison/the-uk/.

17 'Understanding the 6 Dimensions of UK Culture', *translatemedia.com*, 1 September 2017.

18 See Roger Eatwell and Matthew Goodwin, *National Populism: The Revolt Against Liberal Democracy* (London: Pelican Books, 2018), Chapter 6.

19 Gavin Esler, *How Britain Ends: English Nationalism and the Rebirth of Four Nations* (London: Head of Zeus, 2021), p. 288.

20 'Could a More Individualistic World Also Be a More Altruistic One?', *npr.org*, 5 February 2018.

21 *CAF World Giving Index 2019: Ten Years of Giving Trends*, Charities Aid Foundation, October 2019.

22 'Which Countries Provide and Receive the Most Foreign Aid?', Wristband Resources.

23 Patrick Wintour, 'UK Aid Cut Seen an Unforced Error in "Year of British Leadership"', *The Guardian*, 23 April 2021.

24 David Nott, *War Doctor: Surgery on the Front Line* (London; Picador, 2019), pp. 167–9, 312, 316–7.

25 Eleanor Jupp and David Nott, 'Surgery's Indiana Jones Finally Gets the Girl', *The Times*, 28 March 2015. See also Eleanor Nott's 'Afterword', in *War Doctor*, pp. 349–60.

26 Chloe Hadjimatheau, 'Mayday: How the White Helmets and James Le Mesurier Got Pulled into a Deadly Battle for Truth', *BBC News*, 27 February 2021.

Chapter 13: Britain's soft power realities

1 Joseph S. Nye Jr., 'Soft Power: The Evolution of a Concept', *Journal of Political Power*, February 2021.

2 Ibid.

3 See, for example, Robert Winder, *Soft Power: The New Great Game* (London: Little Brown, 2020), pp. 334–9.

4 Sumit Ganguly, 'Modi Spent India's Soft Power – and Got Little in Return', *Foreign Policy*, 14 February 2021.

5 House of Commons, Digital, Culture, Media and Sport Committee, *Disinformation and 'Fake News'* (HC 1791, 14 February 2019), p. 5.

6 See, for example, Eliot Higgins, *We Are Bellingcat* (London: Bloomsbury, 2021), pp. 37–41.

7 See Richard Stengel, *Information Wars* (London: Grove Press, 2019).

8 Peter Hennessy, *Whitehall* (London: Secker & Warburg, 1989), pp. 3–9; Peter Ricketts, *Hard Choices: What Britain Does Next* (London: Atlantic Books, 2021), pp. 143–9.

9 Klaus Schwab and Saadia Zahidi, *The Global Competitiveness Report: Special Edition 2020, How Countries Are Performing on the Road to Recovery* (Geneva: World Economic Forum, 2020), Figure 1.4, p. 15.

10 See Robert Tombs, *This Sovereign Isle: Britain In and Out of Europe* (London: Allen Lane, 2021), pp. 160–2.

11 See *The Times*, 17 February 2021.

12 Klaus Schwab and Saadia Zahidi, *The Global Competitiveness Report*, Tables 2.1, 2.3, 5.1, pp. 22, 24, 45.

13 Ibid., Table 5.2, p. 51.

14 In the WEF metrics, Britain is one of the least improved performers in developing both general job skills and particularly digital skills. Ibid., Tables 2.1, 2.3, pp. 22, 24.

15 Ibid., Table 3.1, p. 30.

16 See Alex Lynn, 'Single Synthetic Environment Technology Demonstrator Developed', *Electronic Specifier*, 23 November 2020; also 'Improbable's Single Synthetic Environment', *Global Defence Technology*, Vol 116, October 2020.

Chapter 14: Conditions for soft power success

1 British Council/APPG, *Influence and the Integrated Review: Opportunities for Britain's Global Vision*, October 2020, p. 5.

2 This particular survey records 11,000 respondents in 22 countries. If they were evenly distributed, that would equate to 500 respondents per country – well below the 1,000+ regarded as the baseline for accurate opinion polling.

3 British Council Research and Policy Insight Team, *International Affairs Unit Survey, Final Report*, 12 October 2020.

4 See British Council, 'British Council Releases New G20 Post-Brexit Survey', *Press Release*, 15 December 2016.

5 Kieron Culligan, John Dubber and Mona Lotten, *As Others See Us: Culture, Attraction and Soft Power* (British Council, 2014).

6 British Council/APPG, *Influence and the Integrated Review*, p. 6.

7 British Council, *Sources of Soft Power: How Perceptions Determine the Success of Nations* (British Council, 2019), p. 37.

8 British Council/APPG, *Influence and the Integrated Review*, p. 13.

9   A summary of these issues can be found in Michael Clarke and Helen Ramscar, *Tipping Point: Britain, Brexit and Security in the 2020s* (London: I.B. Tauris/Bloomsbury, 2019), pp. 33–59.

10 Pierre Rosanvallon and Arthur Goldhammer, *Counter-Democracy: Politics in an Age of Distrust* (Cambridge: Cambridge University Press, 2008).

11 Edelman, *2020 Trust Barometer: UK Results*, 21 January 2020.

12 Cambridge Centre for the Future of Democracy, *Global Satisfaction with Democracy 2020*, p. 21.

13 The violence that most affected prevailing images in this respect was the murder of Jo Cox MP in the week of the Brexit referendum.

14 Edelman, 'Disenchanted with Democracy – But Divided Brits Unite Around What We Need to Fix', *Press Release*, 20 January 2020. It should be noted that *Private Eye*, 18 February 2021, p. 19, disputed the way Edelman interpreted its data.

15 See Clarke and Ramscar *Tipping Point*, p. 225.

16 John McCarthy, 'The Quad's Waging a Soft-Power Battle for Asian Hearts and Minds', *Financial Review*, 16 March 2021.

17 See, for example, '"Get Brexit Done" Will Be Won or Lost in the UK's "Fifth Kingdom"', www.tippingpoint2020s.com, 2 January 2020.

18 See *Wales Soft Power Barometer 2018: Measuring Soft Power Beyond the Nation State*, British Council/Portland, 2018; Welsh Government, *Action Plan: International Relations Through Public Diplomacy and Soft Power 2020-2025* (Welsh Government, 2020).

19 The Scottish Government, *Scotland: A Good Global Citizen* (Edinburgh, March 2021).

20 *Gauging International Perceptions: Scotland and Soft Power*, British Council/Portland, 2019, pp. 14–16.

21 See Jian Wang, 'Localising Public Diplomacy: The Role of Sub-National Actors in Global Branding', *Place Branding* 2, 2006.

22 Greater Manchester Combined Authority, *Greater Manchester: One Year International Strategy*, October 2020; Also www.distinctlybirmingham.com/home/.

23 IMD-SUTD, *Smart City Index: Report 2020*; 'Newcastle Joins More Than 100 Leading Cities in Global Smart City Index', www.newcastle.gov.uk/citylife-news, 29 September 2020.

24 Stephen Gethins, *Nation to Nation: Scotland's Place in the World* (Edinburgh: Luath Press, 2021).

25 See, for example, Philip Stephens, 'Boris Johnson's Tories Have Given Up on Saving the UK Union', *Financial Times*, 29 April 2021. Even the magazine the prime minister once edited ran an earlier piece, Stephen Daisley, 'Boris Doesn't Understand the Union', *The Spectator*, 1 July 2020.

26 Bagehot, 'The Disruptive Rise of English Nationalism', *The Economist*, 20 March 2021.

27 See, for example, Vernon Bogdanor, *Beyond Brexit: Towards a British Constitution* (London: I.B. Tauris, 2019); Constitutional Reform Group, Towards a New Act of Union, DP01, September 2015.

28 See, for example, the options as set out in Gavin Esler, *How Britain Ends: English Nationalism and the Rebirth of Four Nations* (London: Head of Zeus, 2021), pp. 334–9.

29 Slovenia might be regarded as a minor success among the successor states of former Yugoslavia.

30 See, for example, Johan Farkas and Jannick Schou, *Post-Truth, Fake News and Democracy* (London: Routledge, 2020).

31 See, for example, A. C. Grayling, *Liberty in the Age of Terror: A Defence of Civil Liberties and Enlightenment Values* (London: Bloomsbury, 2009), pp. 157–9; or Roger Scruton, *Conservatism: Invitation to the Great Tradition* (London: Profile Books, 2018), pp. 148–55.

32 Ian Leslie, *Conflicted: How Arguments Are Tearing Us Apart and How They Can Bring Us Together* (London: Faber, 2021).

33 Peter Hennessy, *Winds of Change: Britain in the Early Sixties* (London: Allen Lane, 2019), p. 501.

34 HM Government, *Global Britain in a Competitive Age: The Integrated Review of Security, Defence, Development and Foreign Policy* (CP 403, March 2021), pp. 49–50.

35 See Patrick Wintour, 'UK Aid Cut Seen as an Unforced Error in "Year of British Leadership"', *The Guardian*, 23 April 2021; Mihir Sharma, 'The UK Only Hurts Itself by Slashing Aid Budget', *Bloomberg Opinion*, 29 November 2020.

36 Personal interviews.

37 Personal interview.

38 The COVAX scheme is an amalgam of CEPI, the GAVI Alliance, UNICEF and the WHO. From the outset of the pandemic, Britain played a genuinely leading role in convening, promoting and financing this attempt to create a mechanism for fair and equitable access to Covid-19 vaccines.

Select Bibliography

Ambrose, Stephen E. *Rise to Globalism: American Foreign Policy since 1938*. London: Penguin Books, 2010.

Arts Economics. *The British Art Market 2017*. London: BAMF, 2018.

Attenborough, David. *A Life on Our Planet: My Witness Statement and a Vision for the Future*. London: Ebury Press, 2020.

Bennett, Gill, and Hamilton, Keith A., eds. *The Conference on Security and Co-Operation in Europe, 1972–1975, Series III, Volume III, Docs 38 and 59*. London: The Stationery Office, 1998.

Blinken, Anthony, US Secretary of State. 'A Foreign Policy for the American People', Speech in State Department, 3 March 2021.

Bragg, Melvin. *12 Books That Changed the World*. London: Hodder and Stoughton, 2006.

Brand Finance. *Global Soft Power Index 2020*. London: Brand Finance, November 2019.

Brand Finance. *Global Soft Power Index 2021*. London: Brand Finance, February 2021.

Brand Finance. *Monarchy 2017: The Annual Report on the Value of the British Monarchy*. London: Brand Finance, 2017.

Brattberg, Erik. *The E3, The EU, and the Post-Brexit Diplomatic Landscape*. Washington, DC: Carnegie Endowment for International Peace, 18 June 2020.

British Academy. *Lessons from the History of UK Science Policy*. London: DBEIS, August 2019.

British Council. *Corporate Plan 2019–2020*. London: British Council, 2019/J169.

British Council. *Sources of Soft Power: How Perceptions Determine the Success of Nations*. London: British Council, 2019.

British Council/APPG. *Influence and the Integrated Review: Opportunities for Britain's Global Vision*. British Council APPG, October 2020.

British Council Research and Policy Insight Team. *International Affairs Unit Survey*, Final Report. British Council, 12 October 2020.

Brown, Gordon. *My Life, Our Times*. London: Bodley Head, 2017.

Bull, Hedley. *The Anarchical Society: A Study of Order in World Politics*. London: Macmillan, 1977.

Butterfield, Herbert. *The Whig Interpretation of History*. London: Norton Books, 1965.

Cambridge Centre for the Future of Democracy. *Global Satisfaction with Democracy 2020*. Cambridge, 2020.

Centre for Economic and Business Research. *The Economic Contribution of Standards to the UK Economy*. London, June 2015.

Clarke, Michael. *The Challenge of Defending Britain*. Manchester: Manchester University Press, 2019.

Clarke, Michael, and Ramscar, Helen. *Tipping Point: Britain, Brexit and Security in the 2020s*. London: I.B. Tauris/Bloomsbury, 2019.

Congressional Research Service. *Increased Great Power Competition: Implications for Defense – Issues for Congress*. Washington, DC: Congressional Research Service, 27 January 2021.

Culligan, Kieron, Dubber, John, and Lotten, Mona. *As Others See Us: Culture, Attraction and Soft Power*. London: British Council, 2014.

D'Ancona, Matthew. *Post Truth: The New War on Truth and How to Fight Back*. London: Ebury Press, 2017.

Dickie, John. *Inside the Foreign Office*. London: Chapmans Publishers, 1992.

Duffy, Bobby, and Clemence, Michael. *Global Influence in a Post-Brexit World: Who Is a Force for Good?* London: Ipsos MORI, 2017.

Eatwell, Roger, and Goodwin, Matthew. *National Populism: The Revolt Against Liberal Democracy*. London: Pelican Books, 2018.

Esler, Gavin. *How Britain Ends: English Nationalism and the Rebirth of Four Nations*. London: Head of Zeus, 2021.

Farkas, Johan, and Schou, Jannick. *Post-Truth, Fake News and Democracy*. London: Routledge, 2020.

Ferguson, Niall. *The Square and the Tower: Networks, Hierarchies and the Struggle for Global Power*. London: Allen Lane, 2017.

Fletcher, Tom. *The Naked Diplomat*. London: William Collins, 2017.

Foroohar, Rana. *Don't Be Evil: The Case Against Big Tech*. London: Allen Lane, 2019.

Freedman, Lawrence D. 'Britain Adrift: The United Kingdom's Search for a Post-Brexit Role', *Foreign Affairs*, 99(3), May/June 2020.

Fritz, Ben. *The Big Picture: The Fight for the Future of Movies*. New York: Mariner Books, 2019.

Fukuyama, Francis. *The End of History and the Last Man*. New York: Free Press, 2006.

Fukuyama, Francis. *Identity: Contemporary Politics and the Struggle for Recognition*. London: Profile Books, 2018.

Ganguly, Sumit. 'Modi Spent India's Soft Power – and Got Little in Return'. *Foreign Policy*, 14 February 2021.

Goldacre, Ben. *Bad Pharma*. London: Fourth Estate, 2012.

Goldin, Ian, and Muggah, Robert. *Terra Incognita: 100 Maps to Survive the Next 100 Years*. London: Century, 2020.

Goodhart, David. *Head, Hand, Heart: The Struggle for Dignity in the 21st Century*. London: Allen Lane, 2020.

Goodhart, David. *The Road to Somewhere: The New Tribes Shaping British Politics*. London: Penguin Books, 2017.

Grant, Thornton. *India in the UK: The Diaspora Effect*. London: Grant Thornton UK LLP, February 2020.

Gray, Colin S. *Hard Power and Soft Power: The Utility of Military Force as an Instrument of Policy in the 21st Century*. Carlisle: Strategic Studies Institute, 2011.

Gray, Colin S. *The Strategy Bridge: Theory for Practice*. Oxford: Oxford University Press, 2010.

Grayling, A. C. *Liberty in the Age of Terror: A Defence of Civil Liberties and Enlightenment Values*. London: Bloomsbury, 2009.

Gregory, Mark. *Premier League: Economic and Social Impact*. London: Ernst and Young, 2019.

Greenstock, Jeremy. 'Reorienting Foreign Policy'. *National Institute Economic Review*, 250(1), 2019.

Hastings, Max. *Vietnam: An Epic Tragedy 1945–1975*. London: William Collins, 2018.

Hennessy, Peter. *Whitehall*. London: Secker & Warburg, 1989.

Hennessy, Peter. *Winds of Change: Britain in the Early Sixties*. London: Allen Lane, 2019.

Hennessy, Peter. *The Prime Minister: The Office and Its Holders since 1945*. London: Penguin, 2001.

Higgins, Eliot. *We Are Bellingcat: An Intelligence Agency for the People*. London: Bloomsbury, 2021.

Hill, Christopher. *The Future of British Foreign Policy: Security and Diplomacy in a World After Brexit*. Cambridge: Polity Press, 2019.

Hill, Christopher, and Beadle, Sarah. *The Art of Attraction: Soft Power and the UK's Role in the World*. London: British Academy, 2014.

HM Government. *Global Britain in a Competitive Age: The Integrated Review of Security, Defence, Development and Foreign Policy*. CP 403, March 2021.

HM Government. *National Security Strategy and the Strategic Defence and Security Review 2015*. Cm 9161, November 2015.

HM Government. *PM Outlines New Review to Define Britain's Place in the World*. Press Release, 26 February 2020.

HM Government. *Realising Our Potential: A Strategy for Science, Engineering and Technology*. CM 2250, May 1993.

HM Government. *Research and Innovation Organisations in the UK: Innovation Functions and Policy Issues, Department for Business, Innovation and Skills*. DBIS Research Paper 226, July 2015.

HM Government. *UK Research and Development Roadmap*. Department for Business, Energy & Industrial Strategy, London, July 2020.

Hobbes, Thomas. *Leviathan*. Oxford: Oxford University Press, 2008.

Hodgson, Lord. *Overcrowded Islands?* London: Civitas, 2020.

Holden, J. *Influence and Attraction: Culture and the Race for Soft Power in the 21st Century*. London: British Council/Demos, 2013.

Holland, Tom. *Dominion: The Making of the Western Mind*. London: Little Brown, 2019.

House of Commons. *The Sovereign Grant and Sovereign Grant Reserve Annual Report and Accounts 2019–2020*. Controller of Her Majesty's Stationery Office, 24 September 2020.

House of Commons Digital, Culture, Media and Sport Committee, *Disinformation and 'Fake News'*. HC 1791, 14 February 2019.

House of Commons Foreign Affairs Committee. *Global Britain*. HC 780, 12 March 2018.

House of Lords, International Relations Committee. *UK Foreign Policy in a Shifting World Order*. HL 250, 18 December 2018.

House of Lords, Select Committee on Soft Power and the UK's Influence. *Persuasion and Power in the Modern World*. HL 150, 28 March 2014.

Howell, David. *Old Links and New Ties: Power and Persuasion in an Age of Networks*. London: I.B. Tauris, 2013.

Howell, David. *The Mother of All Networks: Britain and the Commonwealth in the 21st Century*. London: Gilgamesh, 2018.

Institute of Contemporary British History. *The Helsinki Negotiations: The Accords and Their Impact*. ICBH Witness Seminar Programme, King's College London, 2006.

Institute of Directors. *Global Business Report*. 2019.

Kampfner, John. *Why the Germans Do It Better*. London: Atlantic Books, 2020.

Kissinger, Henry. *Diplomacy*. Connecticut: Easton Press, 1994.

Kissinger, Henry. *World Order*. Connecticut: Easton Press, 2014.

Lasswell, Harold D. *Politics: Who Gets What, When, How*. New York: Literary Licensing LLC, 2011.

Leslie, Ian. *Conflicted: How Arguments Are Tearing Us Apart and How They Can Bring Us Together*. London: Faber, 2021.

Lever, Paul. *Berlin Rules: Europe and the German Way*. London: I.B. Tauris, 2017.

Levitsky, Steven, and Ziblatt, Daniel. *How Democracies Die: What History Reveals About Our Future*. London: Penguin Books, 2019.

Locke, John. *Two Treatises of Government and a Letter Concerning Toleration*. Yale: Yale University Press, 2003.

Lukes, Stephen. *Power: A Radical View*, 2nd ed. London: Red Globe Books, 2005.

Luttwak, Edward. *Strategy: The Logic of War and Peace*. Cambridge, MA: Harvard University Press, 2001.

MacDonald, Alistair. *Sources of Soft Power: How Perceptions Determine the Success of Nations*. London: British Council, 2020.

Mackenzie, William J. M. *Power, Violence, Decision*. London: Penguin Books, 1975.

Macnab, Geoffrey. *Stairways to Heaven: Rebuilding the British Film Industry*. London: I.B. Tauris, 2018.

Marr, Andrew. *Elizabethans: How Modern Britain Was Forged*. London: William Collins, 2020.

McClory, Jonathan. *The New Persuaders III: A 2012 Global Ranking of Soft Power*. London: Institute for Government, 2013.

McClory, Jonathan. *The Soft Power 30: A Global Ranking of Soft Power 2017*. California: Portland, 2017.

McClory, Jonathan. *The Soft Power 30: A Global Ranking of Soft Power 2019*. California: Portland/University of Southern California, 2019.

McKie, David. *Bright Particular Stars: A Gallery of Glorious British Eccentrics*. London: Atlantic Books, 2011.

McLuhan, Marshall. *Understanding Media: The Extensions of Man*. Cambridge, MA: MIT Press, 1994.

Menon, Anand. 'Little England, The United Kingdom's Retreat from Global Leadership'. *Foreign Affairs*, 94(6) (November/December 2015): 93–100.

Meyer, Christopher. *Getting Our Way: 500 Years of Adventure and Intrigue: The Inside Story of British Diplomacy*. London: Weidenfeld and Nicolson, 2009.

Ministry of Defence. *Defence in a Competitive Age*. CP 411, London, March 2021.

Ministry of Reconstruction. *Report of the Machinery of Government Committee*. London: Her Majesty's Stationery Office, 1918.

Moorhouse, Geoffrey. *The Diplomats: The Foreign Office Today*. London: Humanities Press, 1977.

Morgan, Kenneth O., ed. *The Oxford History of Britain*. Oxford: Oxford University Press, 2010.

Muller, Jan-Werner. *What Is Populism?* London: Penguin Books, 2017.

Murray, Douglas. *The Strange Death of Europe: Immigration, Identity, Islam*. London: Bloomsbury, 2018.

National Audit Office. *A Short Guide to Regulation*. NAO, 2017.

National Audit Office. *The BBC's Strategic Financial Management*. HC 1128, 20 January 2021.

Niblett, Robin. *Global Britain, Global Broker: A Blueprint for the UK's Future International Role*. Europe Programme Research Paper, Chatham House, 11 January 2021.

Nott, David. *War Doctor: Surgery on the Front Line*. London: Picador, 2019.

Nurse, Paul. *Ensuring a Successful UK Research Endeavour: A Review of the UK Research Councils*. BIS/15/625, 2015.

Nye, Jr., Joseph S. 'Soft Power: The Evolution of a Concept'. *Journal of Political Power*, 14(1) (February 2021).

Nye, Jr., Joseph S. *Soft Power: The Means to Success in World Politics*. New York: Public Affairs, 2005.

Nye, Jr., Joseph S. *The Future of Power*. New York: Public Affairs, 2011.

Nye, Jr., Joseph S. *The Powers to Lead*. Oxford: Oxford University Press, 2008.

Octopus Ventures. *Research to Riches Entrepreneurial Impact Ranking 2019: Measuring the Success of UK Universities in Converting Research into Successful Companies*. London: Octopus Group, 2019.

OECD. *Regulatory Policy Outlook 2018*. Paris: OECD Publishing, 2018.

Ofcom. *Public Service Broadcasting in the Digital Age*. London: Ofcom, 8 March 2018.

Pamment, James. *British Public Diplomacy and Soft Power*. London: Palgrave Macmillan, 2016.

Plokhy, Serhii. *Nuclear Folly: A New History of the Cuban Missile Crisis*. London: Allen Lane, 2021.

PWC. *Harnessing Innovation in Aerospace and Defence*. London: PWC/ADS, November 2020.

Renwick, Robin. *Not Quite a Diplomat: A Memoir*. London: Biteback Publishing, 2019.

Ricketts, Peter. *Hard Choices: What Britain Does Next*. London: Atlantic Books, 2021.

Roberts, Andrew. *A History of the English-Speaking Peoples*. London: Weidenfeld & Nicolson, 2006.

Rosanvallon, Pierre, and Goldhammer, Arthur. *Counter-Democracy: Politics in an Age of Distrust*. Cambridge: Cambridge University Press, 2008.

Sainsbury of Turville, Lord. *The Race to the Top – A Review of Government's Science and Innovation Policies*. London: Her Majesty's Stationery Office, 2007.

Sanghera, Sathnam. *Empireland: How Imperialism Has Shaped Modern Britain*. London: Penguin/Viking Press, 2021.

Santayana, George. *Soliloquies in England and Later Soliloquies*. London: Read Books Classic Reprints, 2013.

Schwab, Klaus, and Zahidi, Saadia. *The Global Competitiveness Report: Special Edition 2020, How Countries Are Performing on the Road to Recovery*. Geneva: World Economic Forum, 2020.

Scottish Government, *Scotland: A Good Global Citizen* (Edinburgh, March 2021).

Scruton, Roger. *Conservatism: Invitation to the Great Tradition*. London: Faber, 2018.

Sitwell, Edith, and Ingrams, Richard. *English Eccentrics*. London: Pallas Athene, 2006.

Smith, Rupert. *The Utility of Military Force: The Art of War in the Modern World*. London: Vintage, 2008.

Social Mobility Commission. *Social Mobility in Great Britain: State of the Nation 2018 to 2019*. London: Social Mobility Commission, 30 April 2019.

Stengel, Richard. *Information Wars*. London: Grove Press, 2019.

Stephens, Philip. *Britain Alone: The Path from Suez to Brexit*. London: Faber and Faber, 2021.

Tolstoy, Leo. *War and Peace*. Harmondsworth Middlesex: Penguin Books, 1957.

Tombs, Robert. *This Sovereign Isle: Britain in and Out of Europe*. London: Allen Lane, 2021.

Tooze, Adam. *Crashed: How a Decade of Financial Crisis Changed the World*. London: Allen Lane, 2018.

UK Research and Innovation (UKRI). *Annual Report and Accounts 2018–2019*. HC 2087, 2019.

Ure, John B., ed. *Diplomatic Bag: An Anthology of Diplomatic Incidents and Anecdotes from the Renaissance to the Gulf War*. London: John Murray, 1994.

Waltz, Kenneth. *Man, the State and War*. Columbia: Columbia University Press, 1954.

Welsh Government. *Action Plan: International Relations Through Public Diplomacy and Soft Power 2020–2025*. Cardiff: Welsh Government, 2020.

Westmacott, Peter. *They Call It Diplomacy: Forty Years of Representing Britain Abroad*. London: Head of Zeus, 2021.

White House. *(US) Interim National Security Strategic Guidance*. March 2021.

Wight, Martin. *Power Politics*. Harmondsworth Middlesex: Penguin Books, 1979.

Williams, Ian. *Every Breath You Take: China's New Tyranny*. London: Birlinn, 2021.

Winder, Robert. *Bloody Foreigners: The Story of Immigration to Britain*. London: Abacus, 2010.

Winder, Robert. *Soft Power: The New Great Game*. Boston: Little Brown, 2020.

Wood, Phil, Landry, Charles and Bloomfield, Jude. *Cultural Diversity in Britain: A Toolkit for Cross-cultural Co-Operation*. York: Joseph Rowntree Foundation, 2006.

Zelikow, Philip, and Rice, Condoleezza. *To Build a Better World: Choices to End the Cold War and Create a Global Commonwealth*. New York: Twelve, 2020.

Ziegner, Graham, eds. *British Diplomacy: British Foreign Secretaries Reflect*. London: Politicos, 2007.

Zuboff, Shoshana. *The Age of Surveillance Capitalism: The Fight for a Human Future at the New Frontier of Power*. London: Profile Books, 2019.

Index

1917   142
100,000 Genome Project   98
20th Century Fox   141

Aardman Animations   140
Abbco Tower (2020 fire)   100
Active Pharmaceutical Ingredients
        (APIs)   81
Adele   146
Adidas   130
Adjaye, David   97
ADS   53
Advanced Manufacturing Research Centre
        (AMRC)   83
Advanced Research and Project Agency
        (US)   173
Advertising Association (AA)   129
advertising industry   127–30
Afghanistan   17, 60, 118
Airbus   81–2
Alexander the Great   187
Ali, Monica   134
Alliss, Peter   149
Amazon   130, 141
Amnesty International   120, 122–3
Amsterdam   96, 99
Anderson, Elizabeth Garrett   118
Anholt-Ipsos   111
Annan, Kofi   113
Antarctic Heritage Trust   121
Apple   86, 130
Archers, The   129
Argentina   118
Armenia   22
Armstrong, Neil   117
Arts Council   29, 150, 164
Assad, Bashir   43
Association of British Travel Agents
        (ABTA)   91
Aston Martin   130
Aston University   83

Astor, Nancy   49
AstraZeneca   74, 78–9, 84
astronomy   117
Astronomy Society of the Pacific   117
Atlanta   140
Atomic Weapons Establishment
        (AWE)   75
Attenborough, David   117, 143
Audi   129
Austen, Jane   134
Australia   6, 34
    China relations   25
    in Quad grouping   183
    soft power status   192
    TV imports   143
Autocar   131
autocracy and dictatorship. *See also*
        geopolitics
    convening power of   43, 54
    and entertainment   139
    growth of   26, 27
    misperceptions of power   19, 20
    soft power manipulation   34–5, 65,
        168
Avatar   142
Avengers Endgame   142
Avengers Infinity War   142

Bad Boys for Life   142
BAE Systems   81–2
BAME   103–7, 110
Bangalore   149
Bangladesh   81, 94, 184
Bank for International Settlements
        (BIS)   90
Bank of England   96
Banksy   135
Barker, Pat   134
Bath, City of   112
Bayliss, Trevor   70
BBC World Service   4, 143–4

Beamish Museum (County Durham)   69
Belarus   65, 93
Belfast   107, 140
Bellingcat   119–20
Benenson, Peter   122
Berkeley Human Rights Investigation
        Lab   120
Beveridge, William   49
Biden, Joseph   189
Big Bang Theory, The   118
Bilbao   185
BioNTech   78, 80–1
Bird's Eye   128
Birmingham   184–5
Birmingham Science Park   83
Birmingham University   83
Black Lives Matter (BLM)   16, 22, 102–4
Blinken, Anthony   27
Blink Studios   129
Bloomsbury   98
Boeing   81–3
Bond, James   60, 134, 140
Bonhams   135
Bournmouth Symphony Orchestra   147
Boyle, Danny   141, 143
BP   86
Bradbrook, Gail   123
Bragg, Melvin   148
Branagh, Kenneth   141
Brazil   6, 128
Brick Lane   134
Brief History of Time, A   118
Bristol   108, 140
Britain
    advertising and marketing in   127–31
    arts and heritage sector   167
    attributes of government   63–4
    Brexit implications   2–2, 29, 31, 66–7,
            96, 175, 179, 182, 183
    broadcasting in   128–9, 143–4, 160
    charity sector in   121–3, 158–60
    China relations   58
    consultancy industry in   131–2
    and Covid-19 crisis   35–6, 67, 73,
            79–80, 106, 108, 179
    Covid-19 vaccine   78–81, 194, 229
    diaspora communities in   109–10
    diplomatic structure of   57–9, 62
    disaster responses   99–100

dissolution prospects   108–9, 183–8
education exports of   114–16
empire of   18, 47, 103–5
entertainment sector   167
fashion and design   131–2
film industry in   134, 142–4, 166
fine arts in   127, 134–5
five kingdoms of   107–9, 183–4
foreign aid policy of   159, 191
Global Britain   2–3, 35–6, 68, 169,
        172, 183, 190
governmental convening
        strengths   44–5
governmental policy-making   164–7,
        191–4
government departments/agencies
    Attorney General's Office   57
    Border Force   57, 62
    Business, Energy and Industrial
            Strategy   57, 72, 91, 95, 193
    Cabinet Office   57
    Department of Culture, Media and
            Sport (DCMS)   193
    Foreign, Commonwealth
            and Development Office
            (FCDO)   42, 57–62, 144, 169,
            171–2, 192
    HM Revenue and Customs   57, 62
    Home Office   57
    intelligence services   57, 64
    International Crime Coordination
            Centre   62
    MI6   60, 62
    Ministry of Defence   57, 62
    Ministry of Justice   57
    National Crime Agency   57
    National Cyber Security Centre   57
    National Security Council   57
    No 10   57, 62
    police   57
    Serious Fraud Office   100
    Treasury   57, 96
heritage industries of   118–21
higher education in   114–21
individualism in   156–9
influencers in   155–6, 159–60
innovation within   75–6, 79–85
institutions of soft power   4–5, 29–30,
        34–5, 168–9, 190

Integrated Review (2021)   6, 25, 35,
    62, 64, 67–8, 73, 85, 172, 191–3
intelligence services of   60–1
international organizations
    and   89–90
laissez-faire approach to science   71–3
levelling up   108
literature in   132–4
London's position in   106–8
migration in and out of   103–5
Monarchy   4, 29, 45–8
    death of The Duke of
        Edinburgh   46, 48
    Diamond Jubilee   60
    London Olympics 2012   101–2
    Oprah Winfrey interview   46
    Platinum Jubilee   37
    Prince Harry   149
    Prince's Trust, The   47
multicultural nature of   102–7
musical heritage of   126–7, 146–7,
    152, 154
net assessment approach   5–6, 29–30,
    171
non-governmental
    organizations   122–4
nuclear policy of   191–2
Olympics in   101–2, 149
pluralist nature of   124–5, 136, 145,
    150, 154–5, 177–8
regional diversity within   184–5, 192
research publications   77
roots of soft power in   180–9
social media in   155–6
social mobility in   105–6, 175
social stability in   181–2
soft power rankings of   35–6, 179–80,
    198–203
and sports   147–9, 151, 156
sports sector   167
standards setting   86–91, 94–9
tourism and hospitality   111–12,
    120–1
twentieth century history of   62–3, 70
twenty-first century history of   65–8
United States and   65–6
university sector of   83–4
values of   64, 68, 189–90, 195
video games industry   126, 133–4

British Academy of Film and Television
    Arts (BAFTA)   133, 141
British Accreditation Council   116
British Antarctic Survey (BAS)   75
British Broadcasting Corporation
    (BBC)   29, 37, 86, 164, 166, 193
    famine reports of   152
    and ITV launch   128–9
    and radio history   128
    TV industry and   143
    and White Helmets   160
British Council   4, 6, 29, 48–9, 111, 150,
    165, 166, 169, 184
British Geological Survey   75
British Medical Journal, The   79
British Motor Corporation
    Mini car   136
British Museum   75, 112, 118
British Skydiving   149
British Standards Institute (BSI)   86–7,
    91, 174
British Sub-Aqua Club (BSAC)   149
Bronte sisters   134
Brown, Cecily   135
Brown, Sam   146
Burberry   130
Burns, Paddy   133
Business, Energy and Industrial Strategy,
    Department of (BEIS)   57, 72,
    91, 95, 193

Cambridge   108
Cambridge Centre for the Future of
    Democracy   181
Cambridge University   74, 83, 115, 118
Cambridge University Press   98
Cameron, David   104
Campaign   131
Campaign for Nuclear Disarmament   123
Canada   128, 140
    regional nature of   184, 185, 187
Cancer Research UK   74
Cannes Film Festival   141
Canterbury, Archbishop of   50
Captain America   140
Cardiff   107, 127
Catalonia   184
Catalyst (Belfast)   83
Cats   5

CEN (European standards' agency)   86
Centre for Economic and Business
        Research (CEBR)   91
Centre Pompidou (Paris)   97
CERN (Geneva)   117
Chamber of Shipping   91
Channel 4   129
Chariots of Fire   141
Chartered Institute for Archeologists   92
Chartered Institutes   91
Chartered Society of Designers   53
Chester Zoo   112
China   2, 6, 121. *See also* geopolitics
    advertising market in   129
    Australia relations   25
    Beijing Daxing International
        Airport   97
    Belt and Road Initiative (BRI)   90
    construction collapses   100
    Covid-19 vaccine   31, 80
    cultural promotion   180
    economic power of   169
    education policy   115
    film industry   141
    and fine arts market   135
    Guangzhou Opera House   97
    individualism in   157
    and international law   13
    and Joseph Nye   164
    manufacturing   93
    and Quad grouping   183
    research publications   77
    research ranking   173
    soft power status   179, 192
    technology   71
    TV imports   143
    and the UN   90
    Wuhan   21
    Xinjiang   25, 90
China Today   179
Chow, Yun-fat   142
Christie, Agatha   134
Christies   135
CircArt platform   119
Cities
    comparisons   184–5
    London   51–2, 105–8
    twinning   197
    and urbanisation   52–3

City of Culture 2021   112
City of London   51, 95–6, 166, 169, 171
Civil Aviation Authority (CAA)   91
Clarke, Arthur C   117
Coca Cola   130
Cochrane, Archie   79
Cochrane Centre (Oxford)   79
Coldplay   146
Cold War. *See also* geopolitics
    aftermath   172
    diplomacy   56
    education   124–5
    soft power in   26, 28
Commedia dell'arte   145
Committee for Medicinal Products for
        Human Use (CHMP)   99
Commonwealth   4, 45, 47–8, 63, 104, 171
    Association of Commonwealth
        Universities (ACU)   48
    CHOGM   47
    Commonwealth Day   47
    Commonwealth Games   37, 47,
        52, 193
    Commonwealth Parliamentary
        Association (CPA)   48
    Commonwealth Scholarship
        Commission   48
Competition and Markets Authority
        (CMA)   91
Conan Doyle, Arthur   142
Concorde   70
Confederation of Business Industry
        (CBI)   88, 91
Conference on Security and Cooperation
        in Europe (CSCE)   56
convening. *See also* Soft power
    assessment of   171–2
    and cities   51–3, 184–5
    conditions for success   54–5
    formal institutions of   45–51
    nature of   42–4
    and NGOs   43–4
COP26   41, 45
Copyright Act 1842   87
Core Design (software company)   126
Corsica   184
cosmopolitanism. *See also* soft power
    assessment of   175
    based on multiculturalism   101–5

and diaspora communities   109–11
London as exemplar of   105–8
and tourism   111–12
COVAX   80, 194
Covaxin   80
Coventry   112
Covid-19   20, 21, 36, 67–8, 72–3, 78–81,
    106, 185, 194
Covid-19 Genomics UK Consortium
    (COG-UK)   98
Cox, Brian   117–18
Creative Circle   128
Creative Industries Council   193
Crick Centre   74
Crimea   44, 187
Crimean War   118
Croft, Lara   126
Cuba   65, 93
culture
    and national character   35
    and power perceptions   23
    wars   16, 144
Cyprus   186
Czechoslovakia   28
Czech Republic   186

Daily Mail   129
Dalai Lama, the   43
Davis, Jim   4, 88
Dawkins, Richard   117–18
Dayton Ohio   43
de Bretton-Gordon, Hamish   4
Decanter World Wine Awards   111
Defense Advanced Research Project
    Agency (DAPRPA)   173
Deller, Jeremy   135
Deloitte   105, 132
    William Welch Deloitte   132
democracy. *See also* Britain
    and convening   55
    health of   23–4, 32–3
    and urbanisation   52–3
Denmark   6
Department of Culture, Media and Sport
    (DCMS)   193
Design and Art Direction (D&AD)   131
Design Museum   70
Dickens, Charles   132, 134
Dinner for One   138

diplomacy. *See also* Britain
    assessment of   41–2
    British reputation for   172–3
    broader profession of   54–7,
        59–61
    and social media   57–9
Disasters Emergency Committee
        (DEC)   122
Disney   94, 141, 142
Disraeli, Benjamin   107
Diwali   110
DNA   70, 78
Doctor Who   143
Doig, Peter   135
Dolly the Sheep   78
Dominican Republic   140
Downton Abbey   140, 142–3
Drake, Maurice   129
Dubai Marina (2018 fire)   100
Dubai Torch Tower (2015 and
        2017 fires)   100
Dundee   132, 133
Dunlop   130
Durham, University of   83

Ealing Studios   140
East Germany   28. *See also* Cold War
Edelman Trust Barometer   181, 182
Eden Project   112, 119
Edinburgh   107, 127
Edinburgh, University of   116
Edinburgh Castle   112
Edinburgh Festival   107, 127
education. *See also* Soft power
    assessment of   176
    British institutions of   114–16
    British performance in   114, 174
    and creativity   136–7
    importance of   113
    incidental educators   116–21
    nature of   113–14
    outsourcing of   116
    and research   75
Eidos Interactive   126
Einstein, Albert   113
Elsevier   77
Emerson, Ralph Waldo   27, 30
Emin, Tracy   135
Ennis-Hill, Jessica   101

entertainment. *See also* soft power
  assessment of   176–8
  and education   116–18
  film industry   134, 139–42
  music   146–7, 152, 154
  political significance of   139, 149–51
  size of sector   138–9
  sport   147–9, 151, 156
  theatre   144–6
  TV industry   142–4
  video games   126, 133–4, 176–7
environmental issues   14–15
  and advocacy groups   123–4
  and climate change   23
  COP26 conference   41, 45
  and education   117, 119
  Leaders' Summit on Climate   41
Epidemiology Research Centre   75
Equatorial Guinea   99
Ethiopia   120
Eton School   115
European Common Market   60
European Medicines Agency (EMA)   99
European Securities and Markets
     Authority (ESMA)   96
European Union (EU). *See also*
     Geopolitics
  fine arts market   135
  Frontex   120
  migration crisis   44, 102
Extinction Rebellion (XR)   123–4
EY   132

Facebook   93
Faldo, Nick   149
Faraday, Michael   69, 85
Farah, Mo   101
Faros (charity)   119
Faulks, Sebastian   134
Festival UK 2022   37, 112
Figgis, Mike   141
Financial Conduct Authority (FCA)   53,
    94–6
Financial Stability Board (FSB)   96
FitzAilwin, Henry   52
Fletcher, Tom   59
Flixborough explosion (1974)   100
Floyd, George   22
Foden, Giles   134

Foreign, Commonwealth and
    Development Office
    (FCDO)   42, 57–62, 169,
    171–2, 192
  and BBC World Service   144
  diversity   61
  Technology Envoy to the US   61
  on Twitter   61
former Yugoslavia   187
Formula 1   4, 147
FourFourTwo   131
France   77, 94, 99, 118
  cultural promotion   180
  fine arts market   135
  TV imports of   143
Frankfurt   94
Freelon, Philip   97
Freud, Lucian   135
Frinton, Freddie   138

G20   44, 172
Gagarin, Yuri   117
Gallagher, Bernard   149
Gambia   99
Game of Thrones   140
Ganguly, Sumit   168
GAP   94
Gard, Toby   126, 136
Geim, Andre   85
Genomics England   98
geopolitics
  convening power of states   43
  historic shifts in   2, 13, 65–6, 172, 183
  major players in   13–14
  Russia and Europe   18
  social media in   152–3
Georgia   22
Germany   6, 52, 77, 94, 104, 106, 140
  advertising in   128, 130
  cultural promotion   180
  fine arts market   135
  regional nature of   185
  soft power efforts   192
Gethins, Stephen   185
Gilbert   130
Gilbert and George   135
Gin and Vodka Association   91
GKN Aerospace   81
Glastonbury Festival   127

GlaxoSmithKline (GSK)   74, 79
globalization   2. *See also* Cold War
   British crisis of   67–8
   development of   20, 21
   and effects on soft power   169–70
   foreign policy requirements of   64
God Delusion, The   118
Goldache, Ben   79
Goldcrest Films   140
Golden Globe Awards   141
Good Friday Agreement (Belfast
       Agreement 1998)   37
Google   86, 130
Gormley, Anthony   135
Grand Theft Auto   133
Graphene   85
Great British Bake Off   143
Greece   127, 187
Grenfell Tower (2017 fire)   89, 99–100
Guinness   129
Guttman, Ludwig   149

Hadid, Zaha   97
Hague, the   61, 89
Haldane Principle   72
Hallé Orchestra   147
Hamburg   185
H&M   94
Hardy, Thomas   134
Harriott, Joe   146
Harrow School   115
*Harry Potter and the Deathly
       Hallows*   134
Hawking, Stephen   118
Haymarket Media Group   131
Health and Safety Laboratory   75
Hennessy, Peter   190
Heritage Alliance   120
Heseltine, Michael   131
Heysel Stadium disaster (1985)   100
Higgins, Eliot   119
Higgins, Polly   123
Highclere Castle   140
Hillsborough stadium disaster (1989)   99
Hirst, Damian   135
Historic England   51
Hobbes, Thomas   12
Hokkaido   184
Holland, Jools   146

Holland, Tom   15
Home Office (HO)   116
Hong Kong (Hong Kong SAR)   94. *See
    also* Britain, China relations
Huawei   58, 93, 130. *See also* Britain,
    China relations
Huguenots   103
Human Rights Watch (HRW)   120
Hungary   81
Hutton Report (2004)   145

ICANN   43, 93
Imperial College London   74, 83
   White City Innovation Campus   83
India   6, 131. *See also* Globalization
   Covid-19 vaccine   80–1
   film industry in   141
   relationship with China   13
   rise of influence   13
   and soft power   168, 180
   technology   71
Indonesia   6
Innovate UK   72
innovation. *See also* soft power
   aerospace sector   81–2
   assessment of   76–7, 173–4
   biomed sector   78–81
   British approach in history   71–2
   British historical lead in   69–70
   charity sector   74
   commercial sector   74
   current R&D and   72–3, 75–6, 85
   defence sector   82–3
   R&D component of   70–1
   and SMEs   83–5
Institute of Directors (IoD)   88
International Astronomical Union   117
International Civil Aviation Organization
    (ICAO)   88, 216
International economy   14
   2008 crisis of   44, 169
   stresses on   26, 27
International Fire Safety Standards
    Common Principles
    (IFSS-CP)   89
International Labour Organization
    (ILO)   90
International law   13, 68
International Maritime Court (IMC)   88

International Maritime Industries Forum
(IMIF)   88
International Maritime Organization
(IMO)   87, 90
International Monetary Fund (IMF)   90
International Organization for
Standardization (IOS)   86,
88, 174
International Organization of Securities
Commissions (IOSCO)   96
International organizations   88–90
International Seabed Authority (ISA)   90
International Telecommunications Union
(ITU)   90
Invictus Games   149
Iran
and BBC World Service   144
Iraq   17, 60, 118
Iraq war 2003   145
Ireland   6, 34
Israel   80
Issigonis, Alec   136
Italian Job, The   136
Italy   94, 99
MAXXI Museum   97

Japan   6
advertising market of   129
cultural promotion   180
in Quad grouping   183
Jebb, Eglantyne   122
Jenner, Edward   78
Jenner Institute (Oxford)   78
Johnson, Boris   3, 73, 184, 185
John Wiley Company   79
Jorvik celebration (York)   112
Jumanji   142
Jurassic World   143

Kapoor, Anish   135
Kazakhstan   65, 166
Kelly, David   145
Kelvingrove Art Gallery   112
Kenya   104
Kew Gardens   119
Khan, Kishon   146
King James II of Scotland   148
King Lear   147
King's College London (KCL)   116, 118

King's Cross fire (1987)   100
Kissinger, Henry   13, 56, 59
Kitchener, Lord   128
Kitemark   86
Kjellberg, Felix (aka Pew Die Pie)   155
Kosovo   187
KPMG   132
Kuyl, Chris van der   133

Laboratory of Molecular Biology
(Cambridge University)   78
Laker, Freddie   4
Lambeth Conference   37, 51
Lancet, The   79–80, 98
language   1, 44, 60, 113, 156, 169
La Senza   94
Lawrence, D. H.   133
Lawrence, Stephen   145
League of Nations   121
Leavesden Studios   140
Le Carre, John   134
Leete, Alfred   128
Leicester   110, 148
Les Miserables   5
Lewis, Martha D.   146
Leyser, Ottoline   72
LIBOR   100
Libya   44, 66
Lie, Trygve   56
Littleton, Humphrey   146
Liverpool   148, 154
Locke, John
Lockheed Martin   81–2
Lombe, John   69
London   107–8. *See also* Britain
and centralisation   184
fashion week   131
financial attraction of   190
fine arts market centre   135–6
pop music capital   126–7
and smart city index   185
London Broadcasting Company
(LBC)   128
London Metropolitan Police   4
London School of Economics (LSE)   115
London Symphony Orchestra (LSO)   147
Lord Mayor of London, The   52
Lord of the Rings   134
Los Angeles   185

Lowy Institute   172
Lukes, Steven   15

McClory, Jonathan   29, 184
McDonald's   130
McIlroy, Rory   149
McKinsey   132
McLaren   83
McLuhan, Marshall   54
McQueen, Steve   141
Macron, Emmanuel   189
Malaysia   120, 140
Manchester   148, 184
Manchester, University of   85, 116, 117
Manchester bombing (2017)   99
Marks & Spencer   94
Marr, Andrew   102–3, 127
MasterChef   143
Medical Research Council (MRC)   75
medicine   118
Medicines and Healthcare products
      Regulatory Agency
      (MHRA)   99
Mehta, Jojo   123
Mendes, Sam   141, 142
Mercedes   130
Met Office   75
Meyer, Christopher   59
Microsoft   86, 130
Middle East   17, 131. *See also* geopolitics
   Arab Uprising   17, 22
Milan   131
Millennium Seed Bank Partnership   119
Minecraft   133
MinTech   71, 75
Mitre   130
Moderna   78
Modi, Narendra   29, 110, 168
Monarchy   4, 29, 45–8, 164, 171. *See also*
      Britain
   death of The Duke of Edinburgh   46,
      48
   Diamond Jubilee   60
   London Olympics 2012   101–2
   Oprah Winfrey interview   46
   Platinum Jubilee   37
   Prince Harry   149
   Prince's Trust, The   47
Moore, Patrick   117

Museum of Science and Industry
      (Manchester)   69

National Advertising Benefits
      Society   128
National Gallery   112
National Health Service (NHS)   67, 79,
      101, 106
National Lottery   150
National Museum of African American
      History and Culture
      (NMAAHC)   97
National Museum of Scotland   112
National Physical Laboratory
      (NPL)   75
National Railway Museum (York)   69
National Theatre (NT)   143
Natural History Museum   112
Navalny, Alexei   120
Nazarbayev, Nursultan   166
Netflix   140, 141
Netherlands   132
Newcastle Evening Chronicle   129
Newcastle upon Tyne   185
New Information Order   19, 170,
      189–90
New Variant Assessment Platform   99
New York   94, 131, 149
New York Review of Books   120
New York Times   120
New Zealand   34
Nigeria
   film industry in   141
Nightingale, Florence   118
Nike   94, 129, 130
Nikken Europe   83
Nixon, Richard   59
Nobel Peace Prize   123
Nobel Prize   85
Nolan, Christopher   141
Non-Proliferation Conference
      (Nuclear)   192
North Atlantic Treaty Organization
      (NATO)   89
North East Technology Park   83
Northern Ireland   99. *See also* Britain
   and golf   149
   Good Friday Agreement (Belfast
      Agreement 1998)   37

Northern Ireland Assembly
        (Stormont)   184–6
    in theatre   145
North Macedonia   187
Norway   43
Notting Hill Carnival   107
Novartis   84
Novoselov, Konstantin   85
Nunn, Trevor   5
Nurse, Paul   71–2
Nye Jr., Joseph S.   163–4, 192

Obama, Barack   129
Obama, Michelle   118
Observer, The   122
Office of Communications, the
        (OFCOM)   91
Office of Gas and Electricity Markets, the
        (Ofgem)   91
Office of Rail and Road, the (ORR)   91
Offshore Safety Act (1992)   100
Ofili, Chris   135
Olympics   60, 129, 147
    1908 London Games   128
    1960 Rome Games   147
    2012 London Aquatics Centre   97
    2012 'super Saturday'   101–2
    lottery cash for   150
One Direction   146
on-line education   115–16
Oosterhuis, Peter   149
Open Source Intelligence (OSINT)   119–
        20
Open University   115
Organization for Economic Cooperation
        and Development (OECD)   94,
        172–3, 181
Oxfam   45, 122
Oxford   108, 112
Oxford University   74, 83, 115
Oxford University Press   98
Oxo   128

PA Consulting   132
Paddington Bear   107
Pakistan   22, 187
    Taliban   22
Pantomime   145
Paracel and Spratly Islands   13

Paramount (distributors)   141
Paris   131
Pearson   98
PEN International   121
Peniston, Bradley   14
People's Friendship University
        (Moscow)   125
Perry, Grayson   135
Perth   148–9
Pfizer   78, 80–1
Philippines   81
Piano, Renzo   97
Pine, Courtney   146
Pinewood studios   140
PingAn   130
Pink Floyd   118
Piper Alpha explosion (1988)   100
Pirates of the Carribbean   142
PlayStation   133
Plymouth, University of   83
Plymouth Science Park   83
Poland   28
Ponte Morandi collapse (2018)   100
Pope, the   43
Pop Idol   143
Popular Television Association   129
Portugal   122
Potter, Beatrix   134
Potter, Harry   140
power. *See also* geopolitics; soft power
    collapse of   16–17
    concept of   2, 11–12, 23, 163–4
    dispersed nature of   3, 20–2, 54
    hard and soft distinctions   2–4, 8,
        24–6, 62–3, 163–4
    new instruments of   22
    perception and   18–19, 23–4
    and political philosophy   13, 14
    and populism   22
    relationship nature of   17–18, 23–4,
        164–6
    social media in   19, 22, 25, 130–1,
        152–3
    systemic expressions of   14–15
Pratchett, Terry   134
Premier League (English Premier
        League)   4, 148, 151
Price Waterhouse Cooper (PWC)   132
Professions   53, 87–9, 92, 174, 190

Prudential Regulation Authority (PRA)   94
PRWeek   131
Public Sector Research Establishments (PSRE)   75
Publisher's Association (PA)   134
Puerto Rico   184
Pullman, Philip   134

Qatar   34, 43
  Al Wakrah Stadium   97
QUBIS (Queen's University Belfast)   83
Quebec   184, 187. *See also* Canada
Queen's University Belfast   83

RAND Europe   132
Rashford, Marcus   5
Ray, Mabel   146
Rees, Dai   149
Rees, Martin   117, 118
Reform Club   136
Regent Club   128
regulations and standards   53, 87–9
  and architecture   96–7
  assessment of   174–5
  and biotech   98–9
  disasters and   99–100
  and financial sector   94–6
  history of   86–7
  international nature of   88–9, 93
  organizations for   91
  and publishing   98
  requirements for   92–4
religion   15–16, 103, 107, 110, 168, 175.
    See also Soft power
  Anglican Church   50–1
  Anglican Communion   44, 50
  christianity and   15, 44
RELX Group   98
Research and Innovation Organizations (RIOs)   75
Research England   72
Ridgeway (OSINT Company)   119
Rockstar Games   133
Rogers, Richard   97
Rolex   86
Rolls-Royce   81, 83
Romney, Mitt   129
Roslin Institute (Edinburgh)   78

Routemaster bus   70
Rowling, J. K.   132, 134
Royal Academy of Music   147
Royal Albert Hall   147
  The Proms   147
Royal Charter   86
Royal Dutch Shell   130
Royal Institute of British Architects (RIBA)   97
Royal Institution of Chartered Surveyors (RICS)   89, 168
Royal Liverpool Philharmonic Orchestra   147
Royal Shakespeare Company (RSC)   145
Royal Society   69, 79
Rule Book of the Football Association   148
Rushdie, Salman   134
Russell, Bertrand   49
Russia   6, 13, 18, 34, 56, 65. *See also* Geopolitics
  advertising in   128
  hacking   61
  manufacturing   93
  military capabilities   2
  National Defence Management Centre   65
  and Sergei Skripal   194
  Skolkovo Moscow School of Management   97
  soft power efforts   192
  soft power rankings   179, 181
  and university education   124–5
Rutherford, Greg   101

Saatchi, Maurice   131
Saatchi & Saatchi   129
Sagan, Carl   117
Sahel   44
Sainsbury, David   71
St Andrews   148–9
St Paul's Cathedral   97, 112
St Paul's International School   115
Salford   127
Samsung   130
San Francisco   185
Sanghera, Sathnam   105
Save the Children   122
Saville, Jenny   135
Schmidt, Eric   130–1

Schultz, Bettina   106
Scotland. *See also* Britain
   challenges to UK government   185,
     186
   devolution   37
   Government of   184
   Independence Referendum 2014   66–
     7
Scott, Ridley   141
Scott, Ronnie   146
Sears   94
Sephardic Jews   103
Serbia   93
Shakespeare, William   132–4, 145
Shaw, Percy   70
Sheeran, Ed   146
Sheffield, University of   83
Shepperton studios   140
Sherlock   142
Sierra Leone   99
Simpsons, The   118
Singapore   94
Sino-British Joint Declaration on Hong
     Kong   58
Sinovac   80
Skolkovo Moscow School of
     Management   97
Skripal, Sergei   60–1, 120, 186, 194
Skyfall   60
Skytrain   4
Sky TV   143
Slovakia   186
Slumdog Millionaire   143
Small and Medium Enterprises
     (SMEs)   83–4, 112–14, 126,
     155–6, 176–7
Smart Cities Index   185
Smith, Adam   129
Smith, Giles   117
Smith, Sam   146
Smith, Zadie   134
Social Mobility Commission   105–6
Society for the Protection of Ancient
     Buildings   121
Society of Master Saddlers   91
soft power. *See also* Cold War; geopolitics;
     power
   concept of   5–6, 164–5
   and imitation   25, 26

   magnetism of   27
   management of   165–6
   multi-dimensional nature of   168–9
   and national character   31–3, 188
   patterns of behaviour   7–8, 37
   and prosperity   34
   rankings of   5, 198–203
   smart power expression of   28–30,
     166–8, 194
   societal basis of   27, 30–2, 49, 165,
     181–9, 194
   special characteristics of   30–4
   strategy and   27–8, 165
SOLAS Convention   87
Solus Club   128
Sonic the Hedgehog   142
Sony   126, 141
Sotheby's   135
South China Sea   13, 58
Spain
   and Catalan separatism   187
Spice, Anton   146
Spice Girls   127
Spitfire, the   70
Sputnik V   80, 98
Star Trek   118
Star Wars   142
Stoke Mandeville Hospital   149
Stonehenge   112
Stop Ecocide Campaign   123
Stratford on Avon   112
Strictly Come Dancing   143
Stuff   131
Sudan   187
Suez Crisis   60
Surman, John   146
Sweden   43
Switzerland   43
Syria   65, 93, 120, 122
Syrian Civil War   43, 44, 66

Take Two Interactive   133
Tandan Loveleen   143
Tate Modern   112, 127
Tawney, R. H.   190
Thailand   149
Thames Valley   108
Tham Luang Caves   149
Thirty Club   128

Thompson, Robert   59
Thunberg, Greta   22, 123
Tiktok   93
Times Rich List   133
Titanic, the   87, 100
Titanic Quarter (Belfast)   83, 107
Titanic studios   140
Tolstoy, Leo   15
Tomb Raider   126, 133, 136
Top Gear   143
Tower of London   112
Tracey, Stan   146
Treaty of Glasgow (1502)   148
Trinity College Cambridge   83
Trump, Donald   26
Turkey   65, 131
Twitter   93

Uganda   104
UK Atomic Energy Authority
        (UKAEA)   83
UK Music   146
Ukraine   22, 44, 120, 187
UK Research and Innovation
        (UKRI)   72, 75
United Arab Emirates (UAE)   6, 100, 120
United Nations (UN)   90
    Department of Economic and Social
        Affairs (DESA)   90, 169
    Food and Agriculture
        Organization   169
    Institute of Migration   110
    International Court of Justice   89
    Security Council   90
    Sustainable Development Goals   90
United Nations Organisation (UNO)   55
United States of America (USA). *See also*
        Cold War; Geopolitics; Power;
        Soft power
    advertising in   129, 131
    Broad Art Museum   97
    charities in   158–9
    consultancy in Britain   131–2
    consumerism in   128
    and education   116
    film industry   141
    fine arts market   135
    genome sequencing   99
    golf in   149

    individualism in   157
    and Julian Assange   153
    Library of Congress   120
    manufacturing   93
    military capabilities   2, 17
    National Museum of African
        American History and Culture
        (NMAAHC)   97
    National Security Strategy   21
    Pentagon   163–4, 173
    policy community   63
    pop music and   146
    Quad grouping member   183
    research in   173
    research publications   77
    riots in   120
    soft power effects   192
    soft power rankings   179
    and standards   174–5
    and terrorism   13
    Trump Administration   31, 66
    TV imports   143
    and Vietnam   17–19
Universal (distributors)   141
    NBC Universal   142
Universities UK   79
University College London (UCL)   116
University Enterprise Zones   84
University global rankings   114
Unknown Soldier   118
Urquhart, Brian   56

Venezuela   65, 93
Venice Film Festival   141
Venice in Peril campaign   121
Vettriano, Jack   135
Victoria and Albert Museum
        (V&A)   75
Victoria's Secret   94
Vietnam   17–18
Voyager I   1

Wales. *See also* Britain
    devolution   37
    government   184
Wallace and Gromit   140
Walmart   94
Walsall   127
Warden, Mary   138

warfare
    new wars   13–14
    twentieth century wars   18–19
Warner Brothers   140, 141
Warwick University's European Research
        Council   111
Water Services Regulation Authority, the
        (Ofwat)   91
Waugh, Evelyn   134
Welland, Colin   141
Wellcome Trust   74
Westminster Abbey   112, 118
WhatCar?   131
White, Joe   61
White City Innovation Campus   83
Whiteread, Rachel   135
White Teeth   134
Whittington, Dick   52
Who Wants to be a Millionaire?   143
Wight, Martin   12
Williamson, Steve   146
Wilson, Harold   71, 73
Wilton Park   48–50

Winder, Robert   105
Windrush   104
Women in Advertising and
        Communications (WACL)   128
World Anti-Doping Agency (WADA)   61
World Economic Forum (WEF)   171,
        173
World Health Organization (WHO)   90
World Monuments Fund (WMF)   121
World Trade Organization (WTO)   88
World War One   127, 128
World War Two   122, 129, 146
World Wide Web (www)   21, 93
Wren, Christopher   97
Wright, Orville   117

X Factor   143

Yemen   118, 122
Yousafzai, Malala   22

Zimbabwe   118
ZTE   93